ROADSIDE GEOLOGY of WISCONSIN

ROADSIDE GEOLOGY
of WISCONSIN

Robert H. Dott, Jr., and John W. Attig

2004
Mountain Press Publishing Company
Missoula, Montana

ROADSIDE GEOLOGY IS A REGISTERED TRADEMARK
OF MOUNTAIN PRESS PUBLISHING COMPANY

Cover art and illustrations by Susan L. Hunt,
Wisconsin Geological and Natural History Survey

The authors' proceeds from the sale of this book go to the University of
Wisconsin–Madison Department of Geology and Geophysics to help
support the Geology Museum, the Geology and Geophysics Library,
research, and field trips.

Library of Congress Cataloging-in-Publication Data

Dott, Robert H., 1929–
  Roadside geology of Wisconsin / Robert H. Dott, Jr. and John W. Attig.
    p. cm. — (Roadside geology series)
Includes bibliographical references and index.
  ISBN 978-0-87842-492-4 (pbk. : alk. paper)
  1. Geology—Wisconsin—Guidebooks. 2. Wisconsin—Guidebooks.
I. Attig, John W. II. Title. III. Series.
  QE179.D67 2004
  557.75—dc22

                                                           2003024029

PRINTED IN THE UNITED STATES

Mountain Press Publishing Company
P.O. Box 2399 • Missoula, Montana 59806
(406) 728-1900

We dedicate this volume to all geologists who have contributed to our knowledge of Wisconsin geology, especially to Rachel and Richard Paull, who published the first comprehensive guide to Wisconsin geology.

Roads and sections of Roadside Geology of Wisconsin.

CONTENTS

Large crossbedding in sandstone, which was deposited by wind dunes in Cambrian time, at the Wisconsin Dells. The Dells are a network of steep-walled channels cut by an enormous flood when Glacial Lake Wisconsin drained suddenly about 14,000 years ago. —R. H. Dott, Jr., photo

PREFACE

The first-time visitor to Wisconsin will find much diversity—diversity of landscapes and geology, of vegetation, of economy, of people, and especially of names. Take the name of the state—what does it mean and how did it come about? There is little agreement about either. Claims have been made for its origin in five different Native American languages plus French, and we know of at least fifteen different spellings. Several translations link the name with the Wisconsin River, varying from "gathering of waters" to "muskrat house," but "red earth place" is also a contender. Names of towns like Chippewa Falls, Manitowoc, Menomonie, Oshkosh, and Waupaca reflect a pre-European history. La Crosse, Eau Claire, Prairie du Sac, and Fond du Lac record early French exploration and trading. And you can imagine that you are touring Europe as you go from Athens to Berlin and New Berlin, or Germantown to Rhinelander, Denmark to Friesland, Brussels to Belgium and Luxemburg, or to Lake Geneva and New Glarus, New Lisbon, and New London, or from Genoa to Cazenovia. As for Embarrass and Endeavor, Friendship, Loyal, and Plain, as well as Spooner and Bloomer, well, they invite puns or limericks.

Although Wisconsin has no lofty Rocky Mountains today, it surely did in the past, in fact several times. Although today it has no white ocean beaches like Florida's, it did have a tropical past with coral reefs and hurricanes. Although you cannot visit a blue ice glacier in Wisconsin today, you could have a mere 15,000 years ago. And, while Wisconsin's only dinosaurs are in its museums, there is a state fossil, a trilobite; a state mineral, galena; and a state rock, red granite. There are some other mighty strange and wondrous phenomena in this Land of Hiawatha, Paul Bunyan, and Holstein cows. Quite possibly, Wisconsin is the only state having a state soil and a song about it. Then there is the world's Fishing Hall of Fame at Hayward, where there is also the headquarters for the annual American Birkebeiner Ski Race (our country's largest cross-country event), a Dairy Shrine at Fort Atkinson, the Mustard Museum at Mt. Horeb, the Wisconsin Concrete Park at Phillips, the House on the Rock near Dodgeville, the Lake Superior Big Top Chautauqua at Bayfield, several grottoes, and the Coney Island of the Midwest at the Wisconsin Dells. Moreover, as we shall see, many of these wonders have some geological component.

We wrote this book for you who are not geologists, but who are curious about the landscapes, the underlying rocks, and the geological histories of your surroundings. We wanted to help you envision mastodons roaming in front of great glaciers 12,000 years ago, feel storm waves pounding sea cliffs 500 million years ago, and hear volcanoes exploding 1,900 million years ago. We did not write the book for professional geologists, but we hope even they may find it useful. We have drawn heavily upon the work of the countless geologists who have worked here for more than 150 years, but we can present only the highlights of their work as well as our own. It is inappropriate to present specific citations of published material in a book such as this, but the professional will recognize most of the sources.

It will be easier to use this book if certain conventions are understood. The introductory chapter, as its name implies, introduces some general basics of geology and summarizes broadly the geology of Wisconsin. Because the landscape makes the first impression upon any traveler, we have organized our more detailed discussions around three distinct topographic regions and two especially popular tourist regions. Following an introduction for each region, we then discuss geologic highlights along highway routes arranged with Interstates first, U.S. highways next, and Wisconsin state highways last. State parks, state forests, and state recreation areas as well as county parks with geological highlights are given special attention. Answers to important geological questions like, How can we reconstruct ancient environments? or, How do different glacial landforms develop? are developed primarily within the discussion of whatever region best exemplifies a particular topic. Inevitably, however, some of the same questions will come up while reading about another region. Therefore, we urge you to scan the introduction to each chapter in order to discover where the answers to certain questions may lie.

Interstate highways and regular U.S. highways are numbered in Wisconsin as elsewhere in the nation; that is, east-west roads have even numbers and north-south ones have odd numbers. Interstate exits are numbered by mileage from a starting point at a state boundary, making them useful reference points. Wisconsin has an exceptionally good system of state highways, which are numbered, and county highways, which are lettered. Designated Rustic Roads provide special off-the-beaten-path experiences. The state also has an extensive network of state trails designed for bicycle and foot travel. Finally, the Ice Age National Scenic Trail zigzags across the state along the southern limit of the last episode of glaciation, which takes its name from Wisconsin. Hikers can enjoy clear examples of glacial features along the completed segments of the trail, which in 2002 totaled about 400 miles of the proposed 1,000 miles. We note access points to portions of the trail that traverse easily recognized geological features, for example the northern and southern units of the Kettle Moraine in the Eastern Uplands, Ice Age National Scientific Reserves in the Northern Highlands and Eastern Uplands, and the Ice Age Interpretive Center in Interstate Park.

Besides the usual rest areas along interstate routes, there are many waysides and a few scenic overlooks along other highways in the state. Most have toilets, picnic tables, and old-fashioned hand-operated water pumps (made in Wisconsin, of course). Many rest areas and waysides also have interpretive signs, which explain highlights of the landscape, wildlife, or history. All are worth reading, and some are specifically geologic.

There are several local idiosyncrasies of names for topographic features. Most important is the term *mound*, which refers to any prominent hill, usually the highest in an area. This usage should not be confused with *effigy mound*, which refers to much smaller constructions in the form of animals or birds made by early Indians 1,000 or so years ago. *Coulee* is a French term commonly used for small tributary streams along the Mississippi Valley in western Wisconsin. Elsewhere, small streams are generally called *creeks* (often pronounced as "cricks"). A *flowage* is a lake produced by the damming of rivers, especially across the northern part of the state. The term apparently originated with the lumberjacks in the late 1800s and referred to the countless temporary impoundments of rivers that the lumberjacks created for floating logs downstream during spring thaws and for floating them from one drainage system to another.

We have drawn upon the work of many people, but we extend special thanks to several who have reviewed all or part of the book or have provided other assistance. We thank Bruce A. Brown, Charles W. Byers, Lee Clayton, William S. Cordua, Campbell Craddock, Tim Eaton, Nelson R. Ham, Mark T. Harris, James C. Knox, Gene L. LaBarge, Louis J. Maher, L. Gordon Medaris, Jr., David M. Mickelson, Michael G. Mudrey, Jr., Thomas S. Hooyer, Donald G. Mikulic, Roger Peters, Allan F. Schneider, and Antoni Simo. The University of Wisconsin Geology Museum, Frank Hoppe of the Wisconsin Department of Natural Resources, the Wisconsin Department of Tourism, and Paul Mayer of the Milwaukee Public Museum all provided photographs and helpful suggestions. Other photo sources are specified in captions. Graphics artist Mary E. Diman converted all photographs to digital format suitable for publication. We are deeply indebted to the Wisconsin Geological and Natural History Survey, especially to director James Robertson, graphics artist Susan Hunt, Deb Patterson for preparing landscape images, and editor Mindy James, for vital support of the preparation of this book. Lastly, we wish to pay tribute to the pioneering efforts of Richard A. and Rachel K. Paull for their 1977 guide for Wisconsin geology. Their book has been both an inspiration and a resource for our own project.

GEOLOGIC TIME SCALE

Age	Period	mya	Geologic Events in Wisconsin
CENOZOIC	Holocene Epoch	.01	Humans become agents of change
CENOZOIC	Pleistocene Epoch		Humans arrive 12,000 years ago as last glaciation wanes; landscape and vegetation become modern
CENOZOIC	Quaternary		Rapid draining of Glacial Lake Wisconsin carves the Wisconsin Dells about 14,000 years ago
CENOZOIC	Quaternary		Last advance of Laurentide Ice Sheet begins 26,000 years ago and reaches its maximum extent 18,000 years ago
CENOZOIC	Quaternary		Wisconsin Glaciation begins about 90,000 years ago
CENOZOIC	Quaternary	1.8	Multiple glaciations of all but southwestern Wisconsin with warmer interglacial periods
CENOZOIC	Tertiary	65	Erosion removes any record of deposition or of life forms; general cooling of climate
MESOZOIC	Cretaceous	145	Erosion removes any record of deposition or of life forms in Wisconsin during this Mesozoic "Age of Dinosaurs"
MESOZOIC	Jurassic	208	Erosion removes any record of deposition or of life forms in Wisconsin during this Mesozoic "Age of Dinosaurs"
MESOZOIC	Triassic	248	Erosion removes any record of deposition or of life forms in Wisconsin during this Mesozoic "Age of Dinosaurs"
PALEOZOIC	Permian	286	No deposits are preserved today in Wisconsin, but strata in adjacent states suggest former presence here
PALEOZOIC	Pennsylvanian	320	No deposits are preserved today in Wisconsin, but strata in adjacent states suggest former presence here
PALEOZOIC	Mississippian	360	No deposits are preserved today in Wisconsin, but strata in adjacent states suggest former presence here
PALEOZOIC	Devonian	417	Marine deposition over much of Wisconsin
PALEOZOIC	Silurian	443	Widespread deposition of dolomite, including the Niagara, with coral reefs in the Eastern Uplands
PALEOZOIC	Ordovician	495	Marine limestone and dolomite deposition, including the Prairie du Chien, interrupted by one interval of emergence from the sea during which the St. Peter sandstone was deposited
PALEOZOIC	Cambrian	545	Dominantly sandstone deposition, including the Mt. Simon, Tunnel City, Wonewoc, and Jordan sandstones, with an interval of emergence of the Wisconsin dome from the sea
PRECAMBRIAN	Proterozoic Eon		900 million years ago, St. Croix horst lifts up along the Douglas and Lake Owen faults
PRECAMBRIAN	Proterozoic Eon		1,100 million years ago, the Lake Superior rift and volcanism almost break the North American continent in two; Keweenaw basalts extruded and sediments deposited; Wisconsin dome uplifted
PRECAMBRIAN	Proterozoic Eon		1,450 million years ago Wolf River batholith forms
PRECAMBRIAN	Proterozoic Eon		1,650 million years ago folding and metamorphism of the Baraboo rocks
PRECAMBRIAN	Proterozoic Eon		1,700 million years ago Baraboo sandstones are deposited
PRECAMBRIAN	Proterozoic Eon		1,750 million years ago rhyolite volcanism at Baraboo; Montello batholith intrudes
PRECAMBRIAN	Proterozoic Eon		1,850 million years ago Penokean Mountains form during the tectonic plate collision between the Superior and Marshfield continents; granites intrude
PRECAMBRIAN	Proterozoic Eon	2,500	Banded iron of the Animikie strata is deposited in the sea between 2,100 and 1,650 million years ago
PRECAMBRIAN	Archean Eon		About 2,800 million years ago, granite gneisses form embryonic North America, called the Superior continent
PRECAMBRIAN	Archean Eon		Origin of the earth about 4,500 million years ago

mya=millions of years ago

Introduction to Wisconsin Geology

Wisconsin lies within the broad central part of the North American continent, that broad expanse between mountains on its eastern and western margins. There are no lofty mountains, active volcanoes, glaciers, or severe earthquakes here today, but all of these phenomena occurred in Wisconsin in the dim past. The geologic history of Wisconsin can be thought of in terms of three chapters. The first, or Precambrian chapter, spans geologic time from the origin of the earth around 4,500 million years ago to the first appearance of marine invertebrate animals around 545 million years ago. The oldest rocks in Wisconsin are granites in the central part of the state that were metamorphosed 2,800 million years ago. A variety of younger Precambrian rocks are exposed across the northern part of the state and lie buried beneath younger rocks in the southern part.

The second, or Paleozoic, chapter is represented by sedimentary rocks ranging in age in Wisconsin from about 520 to 400 million years old. Practically all of these were deposited in shallow seas that covered the stable central part of the continent several times during that interval. These rocks occur today in a U-shaped pattern surrounding the northern Precambrian rocks on the west, south, and east. In places, buried hills of Precambrian rocks peek through the younger strata in the south. Wisconsin has no preserved geologic record for the entire interval from about 400 to about 2.5 million years ago. We believe that strata were deposited here during at least the first part of this long interval, for such rocks still exist in the adjacent states. Erosion during the past 200 million years or so removed whatever record once existed.

During the third, or Quaternary, chapter of Wisconsin's history, climate cooled and great sheets of glacial ice flowed across the state from Canada several times during the last several million years. This was the great Quaternary Ice Age, the last phase of which was named the Wisconsin Glaciation because the features formed then are so clearly preserved here. Humans likely first entered Wisconsin about 12,000 years ago during the retreat of the last glacier.

Some Basic Background

There are three major categories of rocks. Igneous rocks form by the cooling and crystallization of molten magma; examples include coarse-grained, slowly cooled granite and fine-grained, rapidly cooled rhyolite, a volcanic rock of composition like that of granite. Sedimentary rocks form by the deposition of particles either worn from older rocks, as in a sandstone, or precipitated chemically from solution in water, as in salt and some limestones. Finally, metamorphic rocks form by the alteration of any preexisting rock through the action of heat and/or pressure, which causes chemical and physical changes in the rock necessary to adjust to new conditions; examples include quartzite, slate, schist, and gneiss.

The architecture of the earth consists of a metallic core surrounded by a mantle composed of a dark rock called peridotite. The mantle makes up 80 percent of our planet. The similarity of metallic meteorites to earth's core and stony meteorites to the mantle suggests the earth shares kinship with other bodies of the solar system. Because of intense pressure and the breakdown of radioactive atoms, the interior of the earth is very hot. The heat is not uniformly distributed, however, so there is a slow flow within the mantle of hotter material both upward and laterally toward cooler regions. The resulting turmoil is transmitted to the surface, where it is responsible for the movements of the earth's outer crust that cause earthquakes, volcanoes, and the raising of mountains.

The mantle is capped by a colder, less-pliable shell about 60 miles thick called the *lithosphere,* or "rocky sphere." The lithosphere beneath oceans is capped by basalt, a black volcanic rock much like the underlying mantle in composition. The basalt forms a layer called the *oceanic crust.* Continents are different, having a crust composed of granitic, volcanic, and sedimentary rocks richer in light-colored quartz and feldspar minerals than is basalt. The continental crust is also less dense than other parts of the solid earth, so the continents literally float like rafts on the denser mantle. The

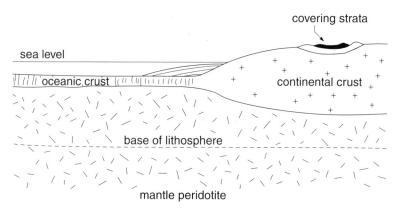

Oceanic and continental crust form the top of the lithosphere, a solid shell that caps the hotter, more-fluid mantle.

relatively light, granitic continental crust has been distilled from the mantle over geologic time by complicated structural and chemical processes. The Northern Highlands of Wisconsin contain much granitic rock, and the Precambrian history revealed there speaks to these distillation processes.

Overlying the granitic foundations or basement of the continent in Wisconsin are relatively young Paleozoic sedimentary rocks, which have not been deformed or metamorphosed like the older Precambrian ones. By the time these Paleozoic strata were passively deposited upon a deeply eroded Precambrian basement, the continent had become stabilized. Those strata once covered Wisconsin completely, but have been partially removed by erosion from the north-central part of the state during the past 200 million years or so.

How do we know that the erosion has gone on for 200 million rather than, say, 20 million or 20,000 years? Because geology deals with the history of the deep past, it needs a much longer calendar than our human one. The geological time scale, which is based upon stages of development of ancient life forms found as fossils, provides a standard calendar for comparing the relative ages of deposition of strata, or the span of occurrence of different life forms (such as dinosaurs), and for dating great mountain building events. The stacking arrangement determines the relative age of geologic strata and their fossils—any given stratum is younger than those beneath it. Similarly, an igneous rock is younger than all rocks it intruded or cut. But how do geologists determine the absolute numerical ages of geologic time? We measure radioactive atoms in certain minerals contained chiefly in igneous and metamorphic rocks. Sensitive instruments allow us to measure the amount of an unstable radioactive element (like uranium) as well as the stable product of breakdown or decay of that element (lead) within either a single mineral grain or a rock specimen containing many such grains. Knowing the rate of breakdown of the unstable element, we can then calculate how long it has been decaying in that mineral, or in other words how many years since the mineral first crystallized. This is the basis for the numerical ages we quote in this book for rocks older than a few million years.

For latest Quaternary history, which includes the end of the great Ice Age and later, a somewhat different technique provides numerical dates. If geologists can find organic material such as wood or bone buried in sediments, then a radioactive form of carbon (carbon-14) provides a means of dating. Radiocarbon makes up a minor but constant amount of the carbon in the atmosphere because it decays at the same rate that it is created by cosmic particle bombardment of atmospheric nitrogen. As long as a plant or animal is alive, it maintains a level of carbon-14 in its body that is the same as that in the atmosphere. When it dies, however, it ceases to gain new carbon-14 from the atmosphere and so the amount present in its tissues at death decreases through radioactive decay to nitrogen-14. About every 5,700 years, half of the carbon-14 then present in the tissue decays. By determining the ratio of carbon-14 to total carbon, we can calculate the time of death; that is, the time when the organic material ceased to maintain an exchange of carbon with the atmosphere. Geologists can use the radiocarbon method to date material that is younger than about 50,000 years, but for older material, too little radiocarbon remains for analysis.

Plate Tectonics and the Formation of Continents

Since 1970, the theory of plate tectonics has provided a powerful unifying concept for understanding and explaining many geological phenomena. Tectonics (from a Greek word meaning "to build") refers collectively to all large-scale deformations of the earth's outer shell. The lithosphere is not a uniform, continuous surface over the entire globe; it is divided into seven major plates and some smaller ones like the individual pieces of a jigsaw puzzle. These plates are all in motion relative to one other, being driven by the heat energy within the mantle below. They are separated from one another by tectonic zones of structural disturbance, which generate most of our planet's earthquakes and volcanoes. There are three

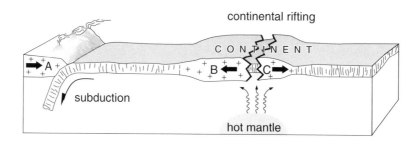

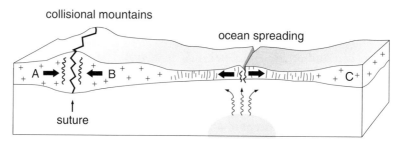

At lithosphere plate boundaries, plates move apart at continental rifts and ocean ridges and toward one another at ocean trenches and mountains.

kinds of lithosphere plate boundaries characterized by the relative motion between adjacent plates; either they move away from one another, move toward one another, or slide past one another.

Lithosphere plates move away from each other along boundaries marked by ocean ridges. Consider Iceland on the crest of the Mid-Atlantic Ridge today. A former huge plate split here and molten basaltic lava rose from the mantle to form the volcanoes of Iceland. The North Atlantic ocean basin was created and has gradually widened as North America and Europe, the fragments of a former supercontinent, have drifted apart while new oceanic crust formed along the ridge. If two plates move apart for millions of years, it stands to reason that somewhere else plates either must crash together and somehow disappear or else the surface of the earth must become larger as new plate material is generated at ocean ridges. We have no evidence that the earth has expanded through geologic time, but instead we find that beneath volcanic island chains like Japan, lithosphere is being disposed of by shoving the seafloor down beneath the islands into the mantle. This process, which we call *subduction*, balances the creation of new ocean crust along an eastern Pacific ridge. The subduction, characterized by a deep furrow or trench in the ocean floor, produces strong earthquakes, which shake the island region. All of this commotion within a subduction zone generates heat in the upper mantle, which melts some of the rock material; the magma so formed rises and erupts at the surface through volcanoes. An example of the third type of plate boundary is the famous San Andreas fault along which the western side of California is sliding northward relative to the North American continent. Intense shearing here between two plates causes earthquakes, but volcanoes are not formed.

How fast do plates move? The Atlantic seafloor today is spreading three-quarters of an inch per year, or about the rate of growth of your fingernails, while the impatient Pacific is spreading 2 inches per year. Over geologic time, such seemingly slow movements mean that subduction could consume an ocean basin 2,000 miles wide in about 66 million years, which equals the amount of time since the dinosaurs disappeared.

Because continental crust is less dense than any other part of the lithosphere, it refuses to sink into the mantle along subduction zones. Therefore, if two continents riding on separate plates meet, neither will sink, and the resulting collision crumples both continental margins to form a mountain range, which is a kind of suture along which two continents become welded together. Volcanic island chains or arcs like Japan also have relatively light crust, so the collision of a volcanic arc with a continent can also produce mountains. Examples of both types of mountain formation are recorded in the Precambrian rocks of Wisconsin. Also revealed are the effects of the burial and compression accompanying such collisions, which resulted in the intense deformation and metamorphism of the rocks.

One of the great benefits of the theory of plate tectonics was a long-awaited explanation of the origin of continental crust. The shoving or subduction of ocean floor sediments together with slabs of crust heats both materials together with contained water until melting occurs. This generates the magma that not only feeds volcanoes at the surface but also forms large granite masses at depth. Deeply buried sedimentary rocks become metamorphosed to schists and adjacent granites may be altered to gneisses, forming a complex plastic mixture that gets kneaded like bread dough into the makings of new continental crust.

Early in earth's history, new continental crust was generated rapidly. Subsequently, little new crust has been formed; rather, tectonic processes have repeatedly modified the continents. They have split or rifted apart, and the resulting fragments then rafted around to collide with one another only to tear apart again, much like bumper cars at an amusement park. The present continents are collages of old continental crustal fragments laced with deeply eroded mountain belts, which formed at different times along various collision boundaries. Once formed, continental crust is eroded, providing new sediments to ocean trenches that, through subduction and metamorphism, are converted back into continental crust. In this way, continental material has been recycled again and again throughout most of earth's history.

Precambrian Wisconsin

The earliest history of Wisconsin is closely linked with that of neighboring Minnesota and Michigan as well as Ontario to the north. The earliest record suggests that volcanic activity was rampant 3,500 million years ago. Intense deformation, metamorphism, and the injection of granitic magmas converted the ancient volcanic rocks to a complex of gneisses, which formed a small embryonic continent, called the Superior continent, by 2,500 million years ago. Wisconsin's oldest rocks were part of this continent. A variety of marine sediments were deposited in shallow seas on the southern margin of that continent, and they contain fossils of some of the earth's earliest life forms. Around 2,000 million years ago, here and on other continents, iron-rich sediments began to form in the oceans. The resulting banded iron formations are the world's principal iron ores, and all three states adjoining Lake Superior provided such ore to our nation's steel furnaces.

Beginning about 1,900 million years ago, everything changed when a volcanic island chain loomed out of the sea across central Wisconsin and erupted volcanic rocks. The surrounding sea was deeper than earlier seas—the remaining sediments are characteristic of deep water. The seafloor south of the early continent deepened as it was subducted, and the island chain

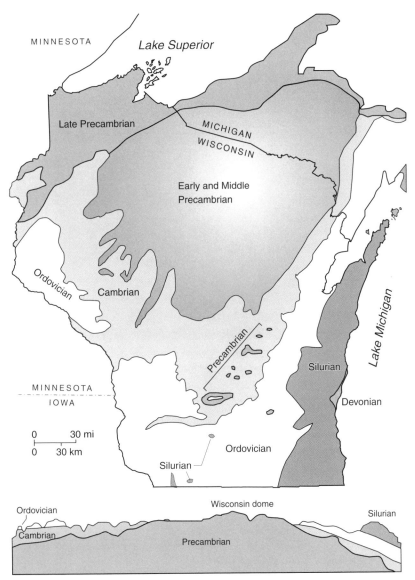

Bedrock geology of Wisconsin. Precambrian rocks in the north form a broad dome with Paleozoic strata inclined gently away from it.

moved northward, finally colliding with the margin of the old Superior continent to form the Penokean Mountains, Wisconsin's "Rocky Mountains." Granites that were intruded widely during this collision yield dates of from 1,890 to 1,815 million years. Geologists have traced the roots of those old mountains from Michigan across Wisconsin at least as far west as Minnesota, and they represent a major addition to the Superior continent.

Precambrian banded iron formation. View is 4 inches high. —R. H. Dott, Jr., photo

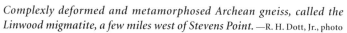

Complexly deformed and metamorphosed Archean gneiss, called the Linwood migmatite, a few miles west of Stevens Point. —R. H. Dott, Jr., photo

Nature was not through mangling Wisconsin, for less than 100 million years later, a new heating event produced more granite and the eruption of much rhyolitic volcanic material across the southern half of the state. When calm returned, a thick succession of red sandstones, black shales, and another banded iron formation were deposited across Wisconsin and Minnesota. These in turn were crumpled and metamorphosed around 1,650 million years ago. And 200 million years later a large granitic complex called the Wolf River batholith was intruded in east-central Wisconsin.

The final Precambrian episode involved a very different behavior of the earth's crust across northwestern Wisconsin and adjacent Minnesota. Continental rifting there, called the Lake Superior rift, threatened to tear North America in half, causing the two halves to drift apart. This crisis began with the eruption of enormous volumes of basaltic lavas along a great depression in northern Wisconsin and adjacent Minnesota around 1,100 million years ago. After the eruptions ceased, subsidence of the ruptured crust continued for at least 200 to 300 million years, and thick red conglomerates, sandstones, and shales were deposited within the rift. Hot solutions percolating through the basaltic lava rocks and overlying conglomerate deposited much pure copper, which was the basis for an important copper mining industry, especially in northern Michigan, for more than a century. This was the source for pieces of copper that Quaternary glaciers carried into Wisconsin hundreds of millions of years later.

Paleozoic Wisconsin

Following the great rifting episode, North America abandoned the turmoil of its youth and became a stable, mature continent. Since Precambrian time, Wisconsin has been near the center of the stable heartland of the continent, called by geologists the *craton* from a Greek word for "shield." Only the margins of North America have experienced violent tectonic events during the past 700 to 800 million years. A broad upwarping of the Precambrian crust called the Wisconsin dome, which includes the Northern Highlands region, influenced earliest Paleozoic paleogeography because it was a slightly higher area. This subtle feature probably originated as a complementary upwarping to the profound subsidence of the two arms of the Lake Superior rift on either side, and continued in Paleozoic time to be a dome between subsiding basins beneath Michigan to the east and Iowa to the southwest.

During the earliest Paleozoic period, the Cambrian, North America was situated very differently on earth than it is today. How can we say such a startling thing? The magnetic properties of certain iron minerals make them susceptible to the earth's magnetic field, so they orient themselves parallel with the field as they become frozen within certain rocks. These little fossil

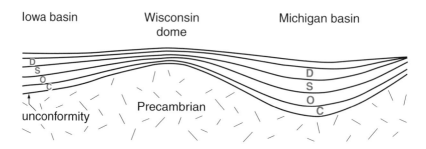

Strata are much thinner over the Wisconsin dome than in the adjacent basins. D, Devonian; S, Silurian; O, Ordovician; and C, Cambrian.

magnets then remember their original relationship to the field even if their containing rock gets moved around later. Fossil magnets tell us that North America was entirely tropical during Cambrian time and lay along the equator. Wisconsin was in the southern hemisphere at about 15 degrees south latitude.

Strange as it seems, Cambrian lands may have resembled the surface of Mars more than any modern earthly habitat. The climate must have been warm and wet, but land surfaces were virtually lifeless except for lowly algae and bacteria. We believe that microbes already lived above sea level in patchy, mosslike crusts on sandy or rocky surfaces as they do today on sterile sandy soils, especially in deserts. The possibility of drying out would challenge the organisms, but modern microbial crusts are able to shut down until the next rain, whether it comes next week or next year. Another major problem would be ultraviolet radiation from the sun. Again, microbes are the most tolerant of all organisms to ultraviolet light, and by Cambrian time, atmospheric ozone may have become abundant enough to filter out the radiation, making the land habitable for these tough creatures. Some suspicious-looking tracks reported at a couple of localities in North America suggest that adventurous crablike creatures took brief walks onto land to scavange on Cambrian beaches. Perhaps they did so by moonlighting to avoid an ultraviolet overdose.

Cambrian Seas

During latest Precambrian and early Cambrian time, a few hundred million years of tropical weathering and erosion had reduced all of North America to a low, nearly flat landscape with a veneer of sand dispersed widely by wind and rivers unimpeded by plants like ferns, grasses, or shrubs, all of which appeared much later. This sandy landscape was gradually sub-

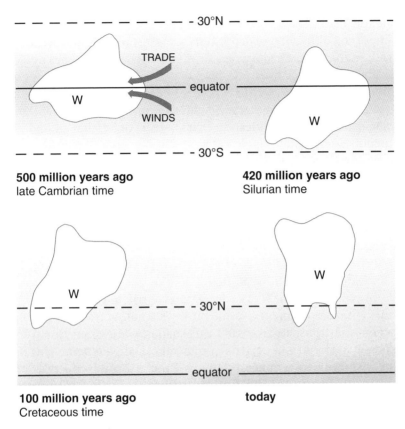

500 million years ago
late Cambrian time

420 million years ago
Silurian time

100 million years ago
Cretaceous time

today

The latitude of North America changed during the past 500 million years due to tectonic plate motions. W shows the location of Wisconsin.

merged by encroachment of the sea beginning around the margins of the continent about 600 million years ago, and reaching Wisconsin by 500 million years ago. Ocean waves and currents simply redeposited that loose sand, which had been abraded by wind and rivers for more than 100 million years. Wind abrasion produced remarkable rounding of many sand grains, which look like microscopic golf balls. The oldest sediments preserved in Wisconsin from that sea are exposed widely in the Western Uplands, and they consist mostly of sandstones of late Cambrian age. The sharp boundary between these flat-lying strata and the underlying, deeply eroded Precambrian rocks is exposed at many places in Wisconsin. A break such as this represents a buried landscape and a long gap in the rock record. Geologists call it an *unconformity* because the rocks above and below "do not conform to each other."

The seas that flooded North America during Cambrian and later times had important differences of depth, but they were probably nowhere deeper than a hundred feet. Their average depth changed several times as global sea level fluctuated relative to the level of our continent; several times the sea drained completely away to expose the entire continent for a few million years. The oldest Cambrian sediments to be preserved were coarse sands and fine pebbles with stratification characteristic of beaches and tidal environments; they contain ripple marks and impressions of crawling tracks made by animals such as trilobites and burrows made by worms and other soft-bodied animals. These were followed by sandy sediments with stratification indicative of deposition by migrating underwater dunes in a nearshore environment only a few tens of feet deep with vigorous current and wave action. Because the sand was moved so frequently, few fossils were preserved except for some animal burrows.

Farther offshore and in quieter water perhaps 50 to 100 feet deep, finer sand and some mud were deposited. These are the most fossiliferous deposits, containing the shells of such creatures as trilobites and brachiopods together with many more tracks and burrows. Another trademark of these deeper marine deposits is greensand, a nickname for fine-grained sandstones containing an abundance of a green mineral called *glauconite*. This iron- and potassium-bearing mineral akin to the micas forms by the reaction of seawater with clays and animal fecal material on the seafloor. The presence of abundant glauconite indicates that accumulation of sediment was very slow, because the chemical reaction that forms it is a very sluggish one. The deepest-water Cambrian deposits, which formed farthest from the shoreline where deposition was slowest, are the richest in glauconite. Other Cambrian sandstones that formed simultaneously nearer shore contain scattered glauconite pellets mixed with dominant quartz grains, giving the appearance of a sprinkling of pepper. These less-glauconitic sandstones were formed in a more agitated, shallow environment into which glauconite pellets were swept by storms from the glauconite factory in the deeper, offshore realm.

All of the marine Cambrian strata have features that indicate an important influence by infrequent storm waves. Being in the tropics a little south of the Cambrian equator, Wisconsin would have been in a zone of steady shallow currents driven by regular fair-weather trade winds and rare violent hurricanes. In these circumstances, powerful but infrequent and brief storms had a greater impact upon sedimentation than mild, everyday processes. British geologist Derek Ager once compared such circumstances with the life of a soldier— "long periods of boredom separated by brief periods of terror" (Ager, 1980).

The sea oscillated twice over Wisconsin during late Cambrian time. Near the middle of that interval, an abrupt change to coarser sand deposition by

Wave-formed ripple marks on a modern, sandy tidal flat in Georgia. Inset shows almost identical ancient ripples from the Baraboo quartzite.
—R. H. Dott, Jr., photos

Ancient

Late Cambrian trilobite (Dikelocephalus) *from Wisconsin.*
—Nigel Hughes photo

Cambrian greensand with flat pebbles of fine sandstone ripped up and redeposited by storm waves. —R. H. Dott, Jr., photo

wind and rivers indicates that the sea retreated from the central part of the state for a million years or so to expose a moderately wet but lifeless sandscape. When the land was flooded again, a second interval of fossiliferous, very fine sandstones and even limestone (or its cousin, dolomite) formed in offshore areas.

Ordovician History

The last Cambrian strata are sandstones that reveal a shallowing trend, which culminated with another drop of sea level at the end of Cambrian time. Once again Wisconsin was exposed as a very low, soggy, tropical land for a few million years. When the sea rose again about 490 million years ago, it spread far beyond Wisconsin to flood much of North America and introduce the Ordovician period. Although it was very shallow—probably less than 20 or 30 feet deep—the sand supply had finally been almost used up and limestone deposition now prevailed everywhere. This sediment was soon altered to dolomite. Limestone is composed of calcium plus carbon and oxygen, whereas its cousin, dolomite, contains both calcium and magnesium. Although magnesium is three times as abundant in seawater, calcium is less soluble so it precipitates more easily to make limestone. After deposition, concentrated, magnesium-rich, briny waters percolating

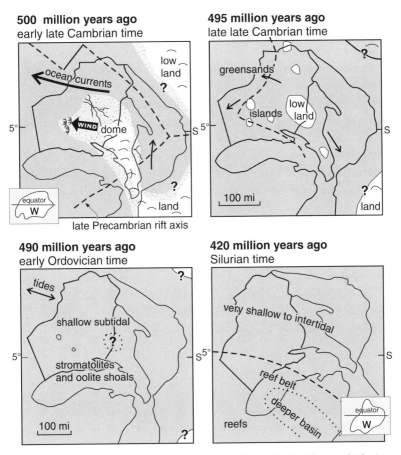

The ancient geography of Wisconsin during Cambrian, Ordovician, and Silurian times. Inset maps show North America relative to the equator. W, Wisconsin.

through the limestone precipitate magnesium, which displaces some of the calcium to convert the rock to dolomite. This process of recrystallization, which affected most Cambrian, Ordovician, and Silurian limestones in Wisconsin, also altered the texture of the original rock and blurred some details of fossil skeletons. Many of the Ordovician dolomites contain nodules or concretions of chert or flint, which also formed after original deposition of limestone by the precipitation of silica from pore fluids. The silica replaced original minerals to form chert nodules, which commonly preserve much of the original rock texture, including fossil shells.

The early Ordovician dolomite is named for Prairie du Chien on the Mississippi River, and it crops out more prominently than any other rock over much of the Western Uplands. The early Ordovician tropical sea was peculiar in that animals were scarce except for soft-bodied creatures, who left sporadic traces of their existence where they burrowed into fine sediments. Apparently the water was chemically inhospitable for most animals, probably being a little too salty. On the other hand, dome-shaped sedimentary masses formed by photosynthetic bacteria are common. These are called *stromatolites* and are composed of convex-upward laminations in dolomite, which were formed by entrapment of fine sediment particles on the mucous coating of bacterial colonies. Their form and size varies greatly from small biscuitlike surfaces to large turban-shaped domes. Another common feature is oolite, a rock made of little spheres like tiny ball bearings (about 1 millimeter in diameter), each containing microscopic concentric, onionskin-like laminations of limestone or dolomite surrounding a grain of sand or broken shell. Both stromatolites and oolites form today in very shallow, strongly agitated, warm, clear seawater that is saturated with calcium carbonate; tropical shoals washed by vigorous tidal currents are the favored sites. We know that Wisconsin still lay in the tropics 490 million years ago and by analogy with modern oolite-forming areas, we infer that the early Ordovician sea was less than 20 or 30 feet deep and was regularly flushed by strong tides.

Spaghetti-like animal burrows in Ordovician dolomite flagstones at Buena Vista Overlook in Alma, Wisconsin. —R. H. Dott, Jr., photo

Modern stromatolites growing in the intertidal area of Shark Bay, Australia, at low tide. Sand occupies the low areas between stromatolites. —P. Hoffman photo

About 480 million years ago, yet another fall of sea level again exposed the entire North American continent as a very low land. Streams eroded valleys into the early Ordovician dolomites and groundwater leached caves within them. In the central part of the continent, wind and rivers exhumed and redeposited the Cambrian sandstones, forming a new widespread blanket of quartz sand covering most of the central states, including Wisconsin. Then, as sea level rose again, shallow marine currents and waves redeposited most of this sand, but in southern Wisconsin and adjacent states, some of the wind deposits were preserved. This blanket of quartz sand, the St. Peter sandstone, is so pure that it is quarried locally for making glass and for molds for foundry castings; neither of these products can tolerate any impurities.

As sea level continued to rise during later Ordovician time, limestone deposition resumed. This time the water was deeper, perhaps as much as 100 feet. Stromatolites and oolites are lacking, but the environment was very hospitable to a diverse assemblage of calcareous bottom-dwelling, shell-forming animals, such as brachiopods, bryozoans, corals, clams, and crinoids. In fact, the late Ordovician formations are the most fossiliferous strata in Wisconsin. Deposition was not continuous, for shell-rich layers apparently concentrated by storm waves alternate with thin, dark bands

Large Ordovician stromatolite from Wisconsin. View shows the bottom of the stromatolite, which is about 3 feet in diameter.
—R. H. Dott, Jr., photo

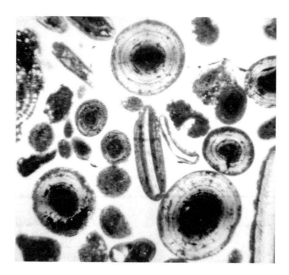

Modern oolite spheres, appoximately 1 millimeter in diameter, from the Bahama Banks.
—R. Ginsburg photo

Richly fossiliferous Ordovician limestone from southwestern Wisconsin. The fossils are brachiopods. —R. H. Dott, Jr., photo

altered by chemical reactions with seawater. These reactions act so slowly that deposition must have ceased for long periods just as with the formation of the greensands in some Cambrian sandstones. Also interstratified within the limestones are more than a dozen thin clay layers, which were formed by the alteration of volcanic ash. Volcanoes located along the eastern edge of the continent erupted the ash, which was blown into the sea and carried by currents as far as Wisconsin and Iowa. Age dates from minerals in the ash show that those volcanoes erupted about 455 to 450 million years ago.

The youngest Ordovician strata in the upper Mississippi Valley region belong to the gray Maquoketa shale, which contains only fossils of swimming and floating animals such as cephalopods and graptolites; apparently the sea bottom was too chemically foul for bottom-dwelling animals to thrive. Composed of soft shale, this formation erodes easily and rarely appears in outcrops, but many drill holes penetrate it. As is often true in geology, we must look far afield to understand the Maquoketa shale. Similar late Ordovician dark shales are much thicker in the eastern states and contain even more volcanic ash layers there. Together with Ordovician volcanic rocks in New England and Nova Scotia, these ashes indicate that a volcanic island chain like Japan was approaching the continent from the east 450 million years ago. It collided with North America about 5 to 10 million years later to form mountains, whose erosion provided the enormous volume of clay carried west across the inland sea to form the Maquoketa shale. Although 800 miles away, those ancient mountains left a mark even upon Wisconsin.

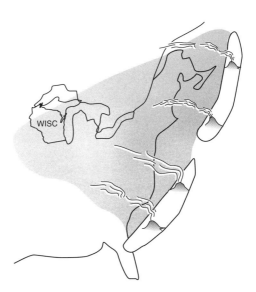

Fallout pattern of volcanic ash erupted along the eastern margin of North America about 450 million years ago, in Ordovician time.

Silurian and Devonian Seas

Silurian strata approximately 430 to 415 million years old are prominent in eastern Wisconsin, where dolomite of this period forms the backbone of the Door Peninsula on Lake Michigan and the ridges of eastern Wisconsin. These ridges are a continuation of the famous Niagara Escarpment, which can be traced from Niagara Falls, New York, where it was named, around the eastern side of Lake Huron to northern Michigan, and then southwest into eastern Wisconsin. There are considerable outcrops of Silurian dolomite on the Door Peninsula and islands to the north, but glacial deposits mostly cover these rocks farther south. The strata contain a diverse assemblage of marine animal fossils, but the alteration of the originally deposited limestone to the dolomite we see today has degraded the quality of preservation. Fossiliferous zones were deposited in normal seawater a few tens of feet deep, but many unfossiliferous zones were deposited right at sea level where the environment was inhospitable. The Silurian strata contain coral reefs that are among the earliest examples of reefs formed by marine animals. The tropical Silurian reefs occur at and south of Milwaukee and widely across Michigan, Indiana, Illinois, and Iowa.

The distribution of marine rocks today is a poor clue to the original extent of ancient seas, for erosion removes a great deal of the rock record. Isolated remnants of marine Silurian strata cap three high hills in southwestern Wisconsin. Their presence there as well as throughout eastern Wisconsin, together with the complete absence of Silurian sandstone, which would suggest a nearby shore, indicates that Silurian seas covered the entire state. A small area of Devonian dolomite (roughly 400 million years old) with marine fossils occurs within and just north of Milwaukee. Because Devonian marine strata are widespread in Michigan to the east and Iowa to the west, seawater probably covered Wisconsin during that period as well.

A 400-Million-Year Gap

Although no Paleozoic strata younger than Devonian exist anywhere in Wisconsin today, it seems inescapable that tropical marine conditions continued all across Wisconsin for perhaps another 100 million years because marine strata of that interval exist in adjacent states to the west, south, and east. After that, however, the seas probably never washed over Wisconsin. There is practically no rock record for a 400-million-year interval from Devonian time until the Quaternary Ice Age. The only possible deposits for the missing interval occur in western and central Wisconsin as widely scattered ridgetop remnants of very poorly dated river gravels. Although geologists have assigned them to the Cretaceous period, they could have formed anytime within the last 130 million years. So we can only wonder which dinosaurs wandered over Wisconsin and which ancestors of woolly mammoths grazed here during that long gap in our geological record.

Quaternary Ice Age

Ice ages when glaciers expanded to cover large parts of the earth have occurred several times during geological history, some before the continents broke apart and drifted to their present positions. We are living in the most recent of these ice ages. During the last 2.5 million years, glaciers have expanded repeatedly to cover the northern parts of North America. The terms *Quaternary Period* (a geologic term for the last 1.8 million years) and *Ice Age* (a term for a geologic event) are often used interchangeably in describing this most recent of the ice ages even though they are not strictly the same in meaning or time equivalence. Several of the glacier expansions during the last few million years reached the Midwest, covering all or part

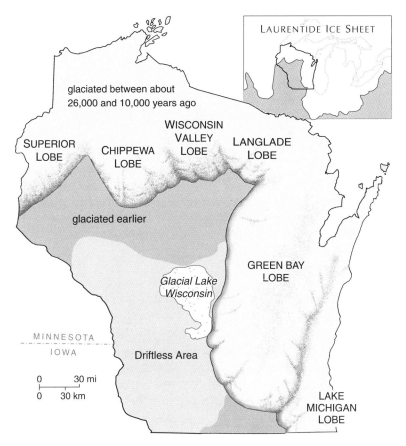

The extent of glaciation in Wisconsin, Glacial Lake Wisconsin, and the Driftless Area.

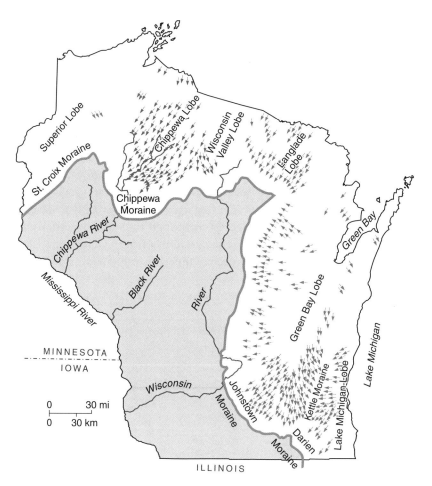

The orientation of drumlins indicates ice-flow directions of the late Wisconsin lobes of the Laurentide Ice Sheet. Moraines that mark the maximum extent of those lobes about 18,000 years ago and major outwash rivers are shown.

of northern and eastern Wisconsin and reaching southward to Indiana and Illinois. Only southwestern Wisconsin and adjacent parts of Illinois, Iowa, and Minnesota escaped glaciation. This region is known as the Driftless Area because it lacks glacial deposits, which in the past were collectively called "drift." Glaciers expanded to reach all sides of the Driftless Area at different times during the Quaternary Ice Age but are not known to have surrounded it completely at any one time.

North America was not the only area experiencing repeated glaciation during the last several million years. Climate changes, driven by cyclical changes in the shape of earth's orbit and the tilt of earth's axis, resulted in the expansion of glaciers in both high latitude and high altitude areas in many parts of the world; sea ice cover expanded as well. For much of the last 1 million years, alternating periods of warm and cold climate have resulted in a regular cycle of glacial and interglacial periods. During the cold periods in North America, glaciers expanded to reach into the Midwest a number of times. Interglacial periods were more like present conditions or even warmer. Evidence from cores of ocean-bottom sediments and from cores of ice from the Greenland and Antarctic Ice Sheets indicate that each climate cycle during much of the last 1 million years lasted about 100,000 years. Each cycle consisted of a long period of generally cooling climate, during which glaciers expanded, followed by a shorter interglacial period. We are now in an interglacial period but still in the Ice Age.

We do not know exactly how many times Wisconsin was glaciated during the Quaternary Ice Age. The geologic record of glaciation prior to the advance of the Laurentide Ice Sheet into Wisconsin about 26,000 years ago is incomplete and difficult to interpret. The landforms and materials that constitute the record of the earlier glaciations have been destroyed or altered by later glaciation, weathering, and erosion, or have been buried beneath younger landforms and materials. In contrast, the landforms and materials resulting from the most recent glaciation are well preserved and provide much insight into the history of the events and the geologic processes that formed the Wisconsin landscape that we see along the roadsides today. Why are there so many lakes in northern Wisconsin? Why is central Wisconsin so flat? What is the origin of the rolling hills of eastern Wisconsin? As we describe the geology of the regions of Wisconsin in later chapters, we shall explore these and many other questions about the geology of the state.

The most recent cycle of climate cooling and glacier expansion in North America is known as the Wisconsin Glaciation. It began about 100,000 years ago and had its most profound impact on Wisconsin when a huge sheet of ice advanced southward from Canada through the Lake Superior and Lake Michigan basins into Wisconsin about 26,000 years ago. The growth of this Laurentide Ice Sheet and other glaciers around the world tied up enough of the earth's water in ice to lower sea level about 400 feet, exposing large parts of the present continental shelf. The Laurentide Ice Sheet reached its maximum extent in Wisconsin about 18,000 years ago and retreated back to northernmost Wisconsin by about 10,000 years ago. How thick was it? Judging by the elevations of moraines that wrap around uplands like the Baraboo Hills, the ice sheet must have been several hundred feet thick near the margin, where the surface of the ice was quite steep. Farther from the margin, it flattened out to a gentle rise of only a few feet per mile toward the northeast. As with modern glaciers, the surface of the ice was probably steeper when it was advancing than when it was receding.

The margin of the ice sheet was lobate because the ice flowed farthest south in the Lake Superior, Lake Michigan, and Green Bay lowlands, and less far south where it had to flow over the highlands of northern Wisconsin and adjacent Michigan. At its maximum extent, the ice margin dammed Glacial Lake Wisconsin, a lake about the size of modern Great Salt Lake, in central Wisconsin, and as it melted back it dammed large, ice-marginal lakes in the Green Bay lowland as well as in the Superior and Michigan basins. The channeling of ice to the east and west by the deep Lake Superior and Lake Michigan basins protected the Driftless Area from glaciation.

The maximum extent of the Laurentide Ice Sheet in Wisconsin is marked by a nearly continuous moraine that accumulated along the ice margin. This ridge of rock debris varies in character from place to place, but everywhere forms a distinct dividing line between the most recently glaciated area of eastern and northern Wisconsin and the Driftless Area as well as areas that were glaciated earlier in the Ice Age. The landscapes of these areas are very different. The most recently glaciated area has many lakes and wetlands, as well as clearly glacial landforms such as moraines, drumlins, and eskers. In contrast, the Driftless Area has uplands of nearly flat-lying Paleozoic bedrock and deeply incised valleys. The area glaciated earlier in the Ice Age consists of gently rolling topography where erosion has greatly altered or obliterated the glacial landforms. This area has few lakes or wetlands.

Glaciers can modify the landscape over which they flow in a number of ways. The abrasion caused by rock debris carried in the base of a glacier as it slides over bedrock or other material can erode and shape the glacier's bed. This rock debris is deposited as *till*, a compact, unsorted mix of clay, silt, sand, and up-to-boulder-size gravel. As ice melts, some rock debris is released from the glacier's top surface and then moves downslope. This debris-flow sediment can appear very similar to till. Where these two types of sediment cannot be distinguished, we use the catchall terms *glacial material* or *glacial sediment*. Sediment-laden meltwater rivers flowing from glaciers deposit broad, sandy outwash plains that fill valleys from wall to wall. This outwash looks very different from till or glacial sediment because the running water has sorted the grains by size and deposited them in layers on the river bed. The glacier can also block valleys, resulting in the diversion of rivers and the formation of ice-marginal lakes. If a lake is large enough, deep enough, and exists long enough, clay, silt, and fine sand will settle out in fine layers to form broad, flat lake bottoms, which become local flat land areas after the lake drains.

Many areas of Wisconsin have distinct glacial landforms that both provide insight into how glaciers modify landscapes and reveal the glacial history of Wisconsin. Some of the most prominent types of landforms in glaciated landscapes are moraines, drumlins, eskers, and outwash plains. The ice in a glacier flows toward the glacier's margin and carries rock debris with it. At the margin, the melting of the ice releases this debris to form ridges called moraines. The margin of a glacier may stay in one place for a period of time because the amount of ice flowing to the margin equals the amount of ice that is melting. Moraines are important to geologists because they mark places where the margin of the glacier stood for some time. For example, the maximum extent of the Laurentide Ice Sheet in Wisconsin is marked in most places by a moraine ridge and a broad zone up to 10 or more miles wide of hummocky topography where piles of debris-rich ice melted.

The flowing glacier also shapes the landscape over which it passes. Drumlins are elongate hills that are lined up parallel to the direction of ice flow. They are formed by erosion or deposition or both at the bottom of the glacier. Rock debris in the bottom of the glacier can abrade underlying bedrock to make striations, or scratches. These striations are also lined up parallel to ice-flow direction. Drumlins and striations provide direct evidence of the direction former glaciers flowed.

Drumlins formed beneath the southern part of the Green Bay Lobe in eastern Wisconsin. —J. W. Attig photo

The glacial meltwater flowing within and beyond glaciers also produces distinct landforms, two of which are eskers and outwash plains. It is common for meltwater from the surface of a glacier to drain through holes and cracks to rivers flowing at the bottom of the glacier. These rivers flow in ice tunnels to the glacier margin. When the glacier recedes from an area, the sediment that accumulated in such a tunnel is left as a ridge of sand and gravel called an *esker*. Beyond the margin of the glacier, sediment-laden meltwater forms a broad, flat, sandy outwash plain. Meltwater rivers typically have a complex braided pattern of channels that extends across a broad floodplain. Blocks of ice commonly are left behind as a glacier recedes from an area. These may become buried in an outwash plain, and when they eventually melt, the overlying outwash collapses to form a pit or kettle on the plain. If buried ice blocks are abundant, so much of the outwash plain may collapse that the original nearly flat floodplain of the meltwater river may be nearly unrecognizable.

The cold climate that led to the growth of the ice sheet had an impact upon the landscape far beyond the edge of the glacier. Beyond the western edge of the Green Bay Lobe, including the Driftless Area, the land was nearly treeless tundra, whose surface thawed to depths of only a few feet during

Crossbedded sand and gravel typical of that deposited by braided meltwater rivers. —J. W. Attig photo

the warmest part of the year. Beneath this thin layer, the ground was frozen to a depth of tens or hundreds of feet as in permanently frozen, or permafrost, areas of today, such as northern Alaska and Canada. The frozen material beneath restricted the downward movement of water, resulting in very wet material near the surface during the summer that could easily move down even very gentle slopes. This accelerated movement of material on slopes beyond the ice sheet helped to obliterate glacial and other landforms that existed prior to the advance of the Laurentide Ice Sheet into the area. Another characteristic of permafrost is a polygonal pattern produced when the soil cracks as temperature fluctuates. This pattern is the surface expression of wedge-shaped masses of ice that form when water fills the cracks in the permafrost and freezes. Each time the crack opens, more water is added and the ice wedge grows. When climate warms and the ice wedges melt, silt or sand slump into the area formerly occupied by the ice. Such material that filled ice wedges has been observed at a number of sites in Wisconsin, where the wedges are typically about 3 feet wide at the top and extend downward about 3 to 6 feet before pinching out. Such patterns, clearly visible on air photos of several parts of Wisconsin, show us that permafrost once existed widely here. Because permafrost restricts the growth of trees, the lack of wood available for radiocarbon dating in southern Wisconsin for the time interval between about 26,000 and 14,000 years ago indicates when tundra existed.

Aerial photo of ice-wedge polygons in central Wisconsin. They are fossil traces of crack patterns formed in permafrost. The edges of the polygons, which had wedges of ice beneath them, show up as dark lines because the material that filled the void when the ice melted is silty and holds moisture well. Area shown is about one-quarter mile across.
—U.S. Department of Agriculture photo

Another impact of glaciation, which reached far beyond the ice margin, was the accumulation of a layer of windblown silt across the landscape. Called *loess*, this originated as thin layers of silt deposited on the beds of the Mississippi, Missouri, and other rivers carrying silt-rich meltwater from the ice sheet. Silt and clay were deposited over gravel bars when river flow

Cast of an ice wedge, clear evidence of the cold climate that produced the Quaternary glaciers. The dark material is silt that fills the area once filled by ice. Note how the growth of the ice wedge deformed the surrounding Cambrian sandstone. The ice-wedge cast is about 4 feet from top to bottom
—J. W. Attig photo

diminished. As this sediment dried, the prevailing westerly winds blew the fine material eastward. Just east of the Mississippi River, tens of feet of loess accumulated in some places, but the cover thins to a foot or two in most of central and eastern Wisconsin. This cover of loess is the foundation of the rich agricultural soils of the Midwest. When climate warmed and permafrost melted, the tundra home of the woolly mammoth, musk ox, and other grazing species gave way to spruce forest, the home of the American mastodon and other browsing animals, some of which were hunted by humans as early as 12,000 years ago. Spruce was slowly replaced by red and white pine as well as deciduous trees as the landscape evolved to the vegetation present at the time of settlement by European immigrants.

Diamonds, Meteorites, and Copper Nuggets

In a state where Paleozoic strata appear flat to the human eye, how can we explain a half dozen or so widely scattered small, circular areas of tilted and faulted strata? Were these disturbed by blasts from below or impacts from above, or does Wisconsin have examples of both?

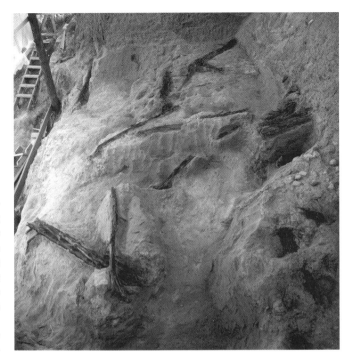

Two Creeks Forest Bed, the remains of a forest that grew 12,000 to 11,750 years ago in eastern Wisconsin before a glacial readvance buried it. The trees were spruce. —R. F. Black photo, circa 1970 during excavation

The Boaz Mastodon skeleton, discovered by farm boys in southwestern Wisconsin in 1897, is displayed in the University of Wisconsin Geology Museum in Madison.
—Photo courtesy of the University of Wisconsin Geology Museum

Diamonds found in glacial and river deposits between 1876 and 1913 at six localities in eastern Wisconsin stimulated eager searches for their source rock, but not until 1971 was a candidate found in northern Michigan about 20 miles from the Wisconsin border. Diamonds occur in an unusual rock called *kimberlite*, so named for the great diamond mines of Kimberley, South Africa. Kimberlite comes from the earth's mantle 70 to 100 miles beneath the surface and is intruded explosively up through the crust as vertical, pipe-shaped bodies called *diatremes*. Most diatremes are only about 1,000 to 2,000 feet in diameter, but they typically occur in groups; at least twenty diatremes are now known in northern Michigan. Kimberlites are generally magnetic, so magnetic surveys can detect them where exposures are poor. Another example was discovered near Racine in southeastern Wisconsin in 1994 by such a survey followed by drilling. Although no economically minable diatreme has yet been found, the distribution of diamonds in sediments in eastern Wisconsin strongly suggests a principal source in northern Michigan. Jumbled blocks of Paleozoic sedimentary and Precambrian metamorphic rocks occur within the diatremes, indicating they violently intruded up into the earth's crust during or after Paleozoic time.

Several other mysterious localities across Wisconsin and northern Michigan also have complexly jumbled and deformed Paleozoic strata, but no associated kimberlite. Were these also formed by diatreme blasts with their kimberlite not yet exposed by erosion? In two cases, unusual features suggest a different origin—the impact of meteoritic material falling from the sky. The Rock Elm disturbance in western Wisconsin has, besides jumbled rocks, quartz grains showing a microscopic structure caused by high-pressure shock. Together with the circular shape of the disturbance, this strongly supports an impact origin. In the center of the state the Glover Bluff disturbance is also circular and has shatter cones in Ordovician dolomite. The cones are also attributed to high-intensity shock. In neither case, however, has any meteoritic material been found, but large impacting bodies tend to disintegrate and vaporize completely when they hit.

Undisputed meteorites have also fallen across Wisconsin, but they were much too small to disrupt the bedrock. At least eleven meteorite falls have been documented since the 1860s. The meteorites range widely in size from the smallest weighing less than 1 pound to the largest around 200 pounds. The most famous is the Trenton meteorite found in 1868 on a farm 30 miles northwest of Milwaukee. Five pieces were recovered with a total weight of almost 96 pounds. This meteorite is displayed at the Milwaukee Public Museum.

Large pieces of nearly pure copper, some weighing hundreds of pounds, have been found in many parts of glaciated Wisconsin. Their source was in

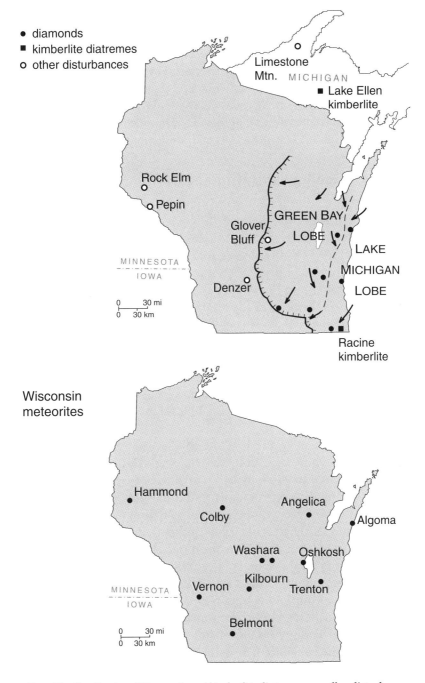

Top: *The distribution of diamonds and kimberlite diatremes as well as disturbances possibly formed by meteorite impacts.* Bottom: *Known meteorite occurrences.*

late Precambrian rocks that underlie some of the Upper Peninsula of Michigan and other parts of the Lake Superior basin. When the Quaternary ice sheets flowed through that basin into Wisconsin, they brought copper fragments along with many other rock materials. The surfaces of the large, soft copper masses were scratched and abraded by the abundant harder rocks that were also carried within the ice. Early peoples mined copper from the nuggets in the glacial sediment and from the source rocks in the Lake Superior basin, using it to fashion tools and implements as well as for trade.

Geology and Humans in Wisconsin

Geology has had a profound influence upon the human settlement of Wisconsin. The landscape itself dictated the best locations for ports and towns, land suitable for farming, routes for highways and railways, and the choicest recreational sites. Occurrences of rock and mineral raw materials have also been important, but perhaps even more critical has been water.

People first came into the Great Lakes region about 12,000 years ago, following close on the heels of the retreating glacier front. They exploited such geological materials as chert or flint, quartzite, and copper for making tools. They also quarried red claystones for making ceremonial pipes as well as the lead mineral galena and fossils for amulets. The Native Americans and the first Europeans, who were French explorers and traders in the 1600s, used the waterways for travel by canoe. Later settlers harnessed practically every waterfall for power to run mills for grinding grains and, later, for generating electricity.

The French learned of the lead ore in southwestern Wisconsin, and showed the natives how to smelt it. By 1800, Anglo-Americans had pushed out the French and soon came in droves to mine both lead and zinc. Farming and lumbering developed rapidly, and iron mining was under way in the far north by 1900. Most of the settlers came from the glaciated regions of northern Europe so had generations of experience in reading the landscape and climate of areas like Wisconsin. This helped them choose farm sites and exploit natural resources effectively. For example, Scandinavian immigrants were familiar with a limy lake deposit called *marl*, so they exploited it here for improving soils, for making firebrick for furnaces, as a paint additive, and for removing hair from hides before tanning them. They also were familiar with useful gravel and sand deposits, which are abundant in all glaciated regions. The early iron and steel industry used not only local ores, but also limestone for the smelting process and quartzite for lining blast furnaces. During the past century, lead, zinc, and iron mining have declined and ceased as has the use of marl, but geologists continue to locate a variety of essential construction materials. These include stone for buildings, crushed stone as well as sand and gravel for road surfaces

*Hydes Mill in southwestern Wisconsin established in the late
1800s at a waterfall on Mill Creek.* —R. H. Dott, Jr., photo

and for making concrete, and glacial lake clays and other clay sediments for making bricks. Finally, several Wisconsin sandstones provide unusually pure quartz sand for foundry mouldings and for use in drilling for petroleum; they could provide the silica for making glass as well.

Wisconsin has long been famous as a vacationland for the upper Midwest, especially for residents of large urban areas like Chicago, Milwaukee, and Minnesota's Twin Cities. It all began with the late-nineteenth-century decline of logging. Entrepreneurs began converting logging camps to rustic resorts for hunting and fishing, and the railroads helped promote travel to them. Ironically, where lumbering had destroyed much of nature, people now came to discover and enjoy it. At first only wealthy males came to "rough it," but in time their families also came. Some resorts were private clubs, a few of which were built by Chicago gangsters and bootleggers, who used them for refuges as well as recreation. With the advent of automobile travel in the 1920s, vacationing became accessible to middle-class families, and more modest resorts and campgrounds began to appear. During the 1930s, winter vacationing began as some resorts provided ski jumping, tobogganing, and ice skating. Today, cross-country skiing, snowmobiling, and ice fishing are popular.

We humans have greatly impacted the Wisconsin landscape as we have developed our farms, towns, and cities as well as the transportation networks that connect them. In clearing forest lands and draining wetlands for agriculture, factories, and housing developments, we have greatly modified the vegetation cover of the land and caused accelerated erosion with the resulting loss of precious topsoil. Covering a large share of the landscape with buildings, highways, and parking lots also has increased runoff of water, which further increases erosion and decreases the recharge of our vital groundwater. In recent years it has become clear that we are even impacting our climate.

Wisconsin has a tradition of concern for its natural environment, and several famous American conservationists were Wisconsinites. Geologist and University of Wisconsin president Charles R. Van Hise was one of the nation's earliest conservationists, in the early 1900s. John Muir grew up here and gained his interest in nature as a student at the university before migrating to California. Aldo Leopold, author of the famous *Sand County Almanac,* in which he proposed a land ethic, taught wildlife management at the university. Gaylord Nelson, creator of Earth Day and the National Wild and Scenic Rivers program, was both a Wisconsin governor and a U.S. senator. While the concerns of these pioneers focused primarily upon plants, animals, and water, they recognized as well that an understanding of geology is crucial to the resolution of most environmental problems.

A group of geologists in the Black River Falls area in 1916. —W. O. Hotchkiss photo

Northern Highlands

The Northern Highlands of Wisconsin, together with northern Minnesota and much of northern Michigan, make up the southern part of the Canadian Shield, a large, circular area of the continent dominated by Precambrian bedrock exposures. The Canadian Shield extends 1,500 miles north from central Wisconsin across Hudson Bay.

Pine trees, some as large as 6 feet in diameter and 200 feet tall, once covered large areas of the Northern Highlands. Logging between 1830 and 1915 denuded the region, but today a dense second-growth forest of mixed hardwood and coniferous trees covers most of it, enhancing the scenery but obscuring the geology. Quaternary glacial deposits also cover much of the bedrock of the Northern Highlands, and the topography largely reflects glaciation during the past 26,000 years or so. Therefore one must scratch beneath these deposits to discover the secrets of the state's oldest rocks. Such scratching has been economically rewarding over the years, for these rocks contain important deposits of iron and copper and a variety of building stones. The

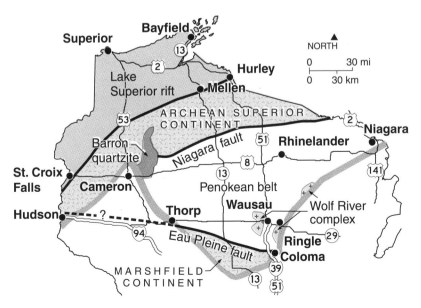

Roads and major tectonic divisions in the Northern Highlands.

economic importance of the Precambrian rocks of the Lake Superior region stimulated the early support of geological research there by both federal and state governments. It also nurtured the early development of strong geology programs in the major universities of the Great Lakes region.

Because of the scarcity of outcrops of geological materials and the many lakes, forests, and bloodthirsty insects, fieldwork in the north country has always been challenging, as two student fieldworkers of the early 1900s memorialized:

> No one can get a full measure of enjoyment who has not lived the life and has tasted its joys and its hardships. Who can forget the no-see-ums, the deer flies, the sand flies, and all the rest of the insatiable horde that from May to September make life exciting? Who can forget his first cedar swamp or the velvety deceptive muskeg, the foaming white water and the hard portage that follows? The somber beauty of the silent places, the barren burnt-overs and pestiferous slashings from logging? Or the moose, the deer, the bear, and the porkie who dined happily upon your boots? There was also the development of fundamental geological truths. Among these might be mentioned the proposition that a portage is the longest distance between two points; that all rocks should be classified as either aqueous or sedentary, aqueous rocks being those submerged and sedentary those in place above the water level; and the relation between occurrences of iron formation and great swarms of black flies and mosquitoes as well as the relation between blueberry patches and nickeliferous copper ore. (Priestly and Smith, 1924)

Combining fieldwork with geophysical techniques and drilling, geologists have discovered some of the region's concealed secrets. The Precambrian rocks of the Canadian Shield record several different outbreaks of volcanic activity interspersed with periods of deposition of sedimentary rocks, and several episodes of mountain making accompanied by the intrusion of large masses of igneous rocks such as granite into the earth's crust. We can present only a sampling of the variety of accessible Precambrian rocks and sketch only the highlights of Precambrian history. We shall consider in turn the following six subdivisions in order of decreasing age: the Archean Superior continent in the northeast, the Archean Marshfield continent of central Wisconsin, the Penokean belt, the post-Penokean red quartzites and rhyolites, the Wolf River igneous complex, and the Lake Superior rift of northwestern Wisconsin.

Archean Continents

An embryonic North America had formed during early Precambrian, or Archean, time. A part of this in northeastern Wisconsin is called the Superior continent. Another area of Archean rocks in central Wisconsin is called the Marshfield continent. Both contained a wide variety of original rock types that were metamorphosed during a series of deformations resulting from lithosphere plate interactions. The original relationship between the Marshfield and Superior continents is uncertain. Was the Marshfield torn away from the Superior or was it a separate continent from far away? All that we know is that a plate collision joined the two after Archean time.

Our Archean rocks, gneisses between 2,700 and 3,000 million years old, make up Wisconsin's earliest recognizable crust. These banded and much-contorted rocks must have been metamorphosed at depths exceeding 15 miles, where old continental crust became soft and pliable. Partial melting produced some fluid magma, which formed light-colored bands of granitic material mixed with darker banded gneiss. Such a rock is called

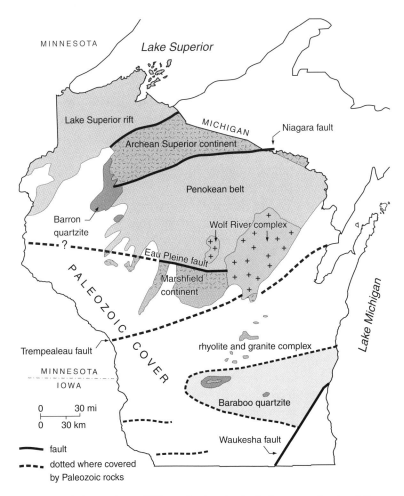

Precambrian geology of Wisconsin showing both the exposed rocks of the Northern Highlands and some buried Precambrian rocks farther south.

migmatite or "mixed rock," because it is partly metamorphic and partly igneous. Some of the magma rose to higher levels of the crust like giant bubbles to form simple granitic intrusions. Where we find migmatites exposed today, we know that erosion has removed a great deal of overlying crust.

Proterozoic Sediments

At the beginning of the next division of Precambrian time, called *Proterozoic* for "primitive life," the southern margin of the Superior continent lay across northern Wisconsin, while the central part of the state was an ocean basin. A thick sequence of quartz sandstones, dolomite, and ancient glacial sediment was deposited on the margin of the continent from about 2,400 to 2,200 million years ago. We know the early ocean was very shallow because the dolomite contains structures called stromatolites formed by photosynthetic microorganisms and by the calcium sulfate minerals gypsum and anhydrite precipitated during the evaporation of large amounts of seawater. Shallow-water, wave-formed ripple marks are also common in the sandstones, which are now metamorphic quartzites. Some tilting and erosion followed the deposition of those early Proterozoic strata, after which younger strata roughly 2,100 to 1,900 million years old were deposited unconformably upon the older rocks. This younger sequence is called Animikie after the Indian name for Thunder Bay on the north shore of Lake Superior in Canada. The first deposits of the Animikie sequence were also shallow marine sandstones and stromatolitic dolomites. These were followed by iron-rich sediments called *banded iron formation*, which were to become the famous Lake Superior iron ores of Minnesota, Michigan, and Wisconsin. These ores consist of alternating iron-rich and iron-poor sediment in very even layers averaging about a quarter of an inch thick each.

Precambrian Banded Iron Formation

The banded iron formations of Precambrian time are among the most puzzling rocks known to geologists, and their origin is still being debated 150 years after their first discovery in Michigan. Although such rocks are now known from most continents and are the world's principal ore of iron, their geological investigation began in the Great Lakes region of North America in the 1850s. The problem is that, unlike most other types of sedimentary rocks, no deposits like these are forming today for us to study. The solution to the mystery must be that the chemistry of the earth's surface was very different 2,000 to 1,500 million years ago than what it is today. The most likely factor has seemed to be oxygen. Iron is chemically unstable in the presence of oxygen, so today it quickly combines at the earth's surface with oxygen to form minerals like hematite and magnetite, which are relatively insoluble. In an environment poor in oxygen, however, iron is relatively soluble; therefore, if the early Proterozoic atmosphere and ocean were oxygen-poor, dissolved iron could have been abundant because it is such a common constituent of rocks and so much of it would have been released by weathering and erosion. Where other sedimentation was very slow, iron could become concentrated enough to form iron formations. That this occurred in a variety of environments is indicated by a diversity of associated sedimentary features. For example, some iron formations are associated with stromatolites and oolites, which are known to form only in very shallow, agitated water. Other examples occur with dark, very evenly laminated, sulfur-rich sediments, which must have been deposited in very quiet, perhaps deeper, oxygen-free environments.

The worldwide absence of iron formations from strata younger than 1,000 million years seems to support the long-held view that iron formation deposition ceased when atmospheric oxygen had become so abundant that it prevented the deposition of the banded iron sediments. A newer idea that microbes may have played a key role in iron deposition, however, offers the alternative explanation that the cessation of their deposition might be due more to biological than atmospheric changes. In the 1950s, Wisconsin

Banded iron formation, Negaunee, Michigan. —R. H. Dott, Jr., photo

geologist Stanley Tyler discovered well-preserved microscopic structures in chert closely associated with an iron formation on the north shore of Lake Superior at Schreiber, Ontario. These proved to be hitherto unknown microscopic plant and bacterial remains, and the discovery launched a worldwide search for Precambrian fossils that continues today. We now know that more diverse life was around than was previously believed. Tyler's discovery also suggested the possibility that microbes played a role in precipitating the iron formations.

Penokean Mountain Building Event

After the deposition of iron-rich sediments, conditions changed. Faulting fragmented the margin of the Superior continent, and it subsided to greater depths below sea level. Later deposits were dark shales and impure sandstones called *graywacke*. Such sediments reflect the erosion of new, unstable lands, whose presence is also indicated by associated volcanic rocks of various types. We conclude that a volcanic island chain like today's Aleutian or Indonesian Islands appeared across central Wisconsin and that an oceanic lithosphere plate was being shoved or subducted beneath that volcanic chain. The process of subduction of one lithosphere plate beneath another generates a lot of heat, which causes melting deep within the crust to produce magma for repeated volcanic eruptions at the surface and intrusions of granitic rocks at depth. Volcanic ash was also erupted and scattered widely by winds. As the ocean basin between became narrower due to the subduction of oceanic crust, the volcanic islands at the edge of the Marshfield continent moved nearer to the old Superior continental margin.

Finally the inevitable happened. The volcanoes and the Marshfield continent were crushed against that old continent like rafts of driftwood cast ashore by storm waves. This calamity caused crumpling and metamorphism and the upheaval of a lofty mountain range across central and northern Wisconsin. The Niagara fault zone, named for a small town in northeastern Wisconsin, marks the main collision boundary, or suture, but even north of that fault a 30- to 40-mile-wide portion of the Superior continent of Archean age with overlying Proterozoic strata was folded and faulted. We refer to the cataclysm as the Penokean mountain building episode, which is named for the Penokee Range of north-central Wisconsin. It spanned the interval from 1,890 to 1,815 million years ago, with some granites forming during the long period of subduction and others intruding at the end of the collision and metamorphism. The eroded roots of the old Penokean Mountains can be traced westward across Minnesota and beyond as well as eastward across Michigan, proving that this was a big-time event in North America's geologic history. Rich metallic ore deposits formed within the roots of the old Penokean volcanoes but were concealed and unknown until

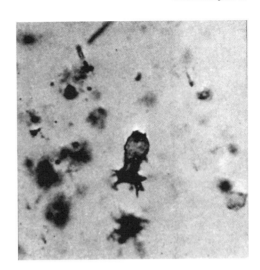

*Microfossils associated
with stromatolites in
the 1,900-million-year-
old Gunflint chert.*
—S. A. Tyler photo

the 1970s. Their discovery came only after geophysical surveys and drill cores gave hints of rich copper deposits and lesser amounts of zinc, silver, and gold. Moreover, new knowledge gained elsewhere about ore formation within much younger volcanic regions gave added impetus for exploiting these newly recognized ancient deposits.

Post-Penokean Volcanism and Quartzites

For 70 million years or so, the Penokean Mountains were eroded, and then three more disturbances topped off the Precambrian history of Wisconsin. A new heating of the crust around 1,750 million years ago caused the intrusion of a large granite complex, the Montello batholith, at depths of 4 to 6 miles, and the eruption of vast sheets of rhyolitic volcanic rocks, which are concentrated today across southern Wisconsin. These did not form from ordinary liquid lavas, but rather from very hot gaseous flows of volcanic ash that spread rapidly across the landscape. The flows cooled so slowly that some of the ash fragments melted partially and fused together.

Erosion and intense weathering then leveled most of the mountains, and a widespread blanket of red quartz-rich sandstone, another iron formation, and then black shales were deposited across both the deeply eroded roots of the former Penokean Mountains and the post-Penokean granites and rhyolites. These strata were thickest near the new southern margin of the continent, which lay in the vicinity of present northern Illinois. Around 1,650 million years ago, both the sediments and underlying rhyolites were deformed and metamorphosed within a new, smaller mountain range raised across southern Wisconsin; these we call the Baraboo Mountains. The cause

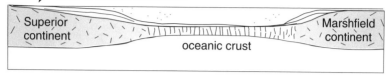

NORTH   SOUTH

2,000 million years ago

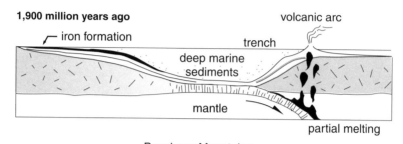

1,900 million years ago

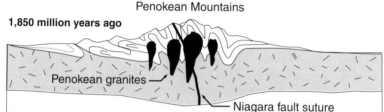

1,850 million years ago

Penokean Mountains

*Formation of the Penokean Mountains by the closing
of an ocean basin and the collision of two continents.*

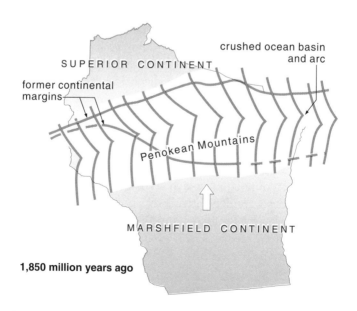

The Penokean Mountains formed when the Superior and Marshfield continents collided.

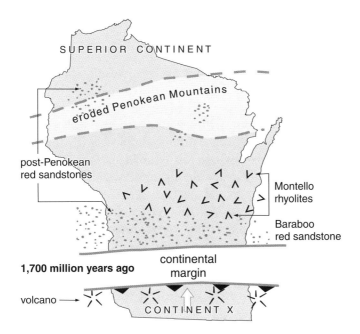

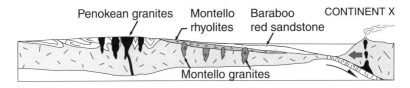

The depositional setting of the Baraboo sandstone approximately 1,700 million years ago.

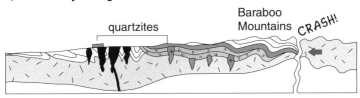

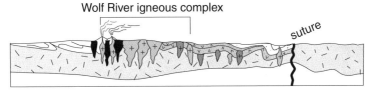

Sequence of deformations between 1,700 and 1,450 million years ago.

of this disturbance is uncertain, but likely a volcanic island chain or another continent collided from the south with the North American margin. Then tranquillity and erosion prevailed for 200 million years before nature jolted Wisconsin once again with igneous activity around 1,450 million years ago. This new heating event produced the Wolf River igneous complex of east-central Wisconsin and related volcanoes near Wausau. Similar granites and rhyolites of like age also occur very widely from Missouri to Colorado and Arizona, suggesting that they were all part of some continent-wide phenomenon. The cause of this very widespread igneous event is mysterious for no known plate collision was involved.

The chemistry of Wisconsin's igneous rocks provides important fingerprint clues to their origins. Laboratory experiments at high temperatures and pressures and theoretical chemistry allow us to estimate temperature and pressure of formation of magmas, which can then be translated to depth of formation. Basalts and gabbros form by the direct melting of mantle material rich in calcium, magnesium, and iron. Granitic and rhyolitic rocks, on the other hand, form through the partial melting of older crustal rocks, which were richer than the mantle in potassium, sodium, and silica. Granitic magmas themselves differ according to tectonic setting. Granitic rocks like the Penokean granites and rhyolites of Wisconsin, which are related to subduction beneath volcanic chains, are rich in calcium but poor in the alkaline elements potassium and sodium. On the other hand, so-called alkaline granites like the Montello and the Wolf River, which occur within the interior of continents and were not associated with subduction, are richer in potassium and sodium and poorer in calcium. Their magmas originated by melting near the base of the continental crust, but they scavenged additional materials by melting some crust as they rose.

Blackstones, Brownstones, and Fieldstones of the Lake Superior Rift

Rocks beneath northwestern Wisconsin record a unique tectonic crisis in the history of North America. A great rising plume of hot mantle arched and pulled apart, or rifted, the crust, threatening to tear the continent in half and send the two halves adrift. Around 1,100 million years ago during late Precambrian time, enormous volumes of mostly basaltic lavas, which ordinarily are found in oceanic areas, were erupted in the middle of the continent as untold numbers of earthquakes shook the region. Melting in the upper part of the earth's mantle, at least 25 miles below the surface of the continent, produced basaltic magmas rich in iron and calcium. The earliest magmas were intruded as dikes along great fissures parallel to present-day Lake Superior. Then magma began to spill out across the landscape as huge, fluid lava flows like those of Hawaii. Meanwhile, a black igneous rock called *gabbro* was intruded into the base of the basalt sequence. Although of the same composition as basalt, its coarse-grained crystalline texture tells us that it cooled slowly at depth. It is more than 1,000 feet thick where exposed today in north-central Wisconsin near Mellen and in Minnesota at Duluth. Known commercially as "black granite," the rock makes a handsome decorative stone.

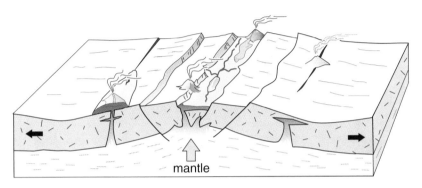

In a continental rift, hot mantle swells up, warping, cracking, and faulting the crust and erupting molten magma.

For about 20 million years, magma poured again and again from fissures to accumulate a thickness of more than 25,000 feet of basalt within the rift. Then volcanism ceased, and a similar thickness of river and lake sediments filled and spread beyond the rift. These two rock sequences together have been named for the Keweenaw Peninsula of northern Michigan, where they are well exposed and from which copper was long mined. Eventually, rifting ceased before the continent was torn in half. A two-branched rift scar in the center of the continent extends southwestward 1,400 miles from Lake Superior to Kansas and 500 miles southeastward beneath Michigan. Between these, the crust warped up, becoming the Wisconsin dome. The East African rift valleys and New Mexico's Rio Grande rift valley today show us what central North America was like 1,000 million years ago. These modern rift systems have many earthquakes, volcanoes, and enormous fault scarps. The tearing away of Africa from Arabia and the opening of the Red Sea between produced the East African valleys during the past 35 million years as part of the breakup of a former Gondwana supercontinent. The Lake Superior rift, however, aborted and our continent remained whole.

The enormous volume of basalt and gabbro, which are more dense than typical continental rocks, caused the crust to subside along the rift. The

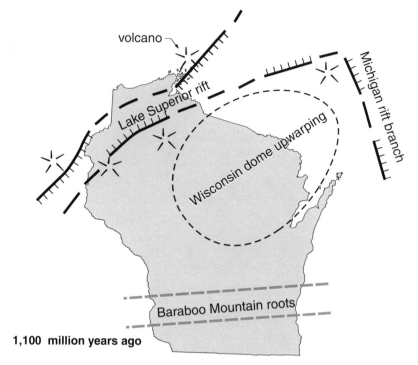

1,100 million years ago

Relationship of the Lake Superior rift and the Wisconsin dome approximately 1,100 million years ago.

The late Precambrian Keweenaw rocks within the Lake Superior rift valley, the basin now occupied by Lake Superior. Different types of copper ore are also shown.

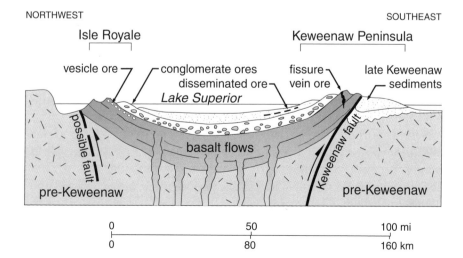

broad, downwarped synclinal structure of the rift is still present beneath Lake Superior today. The presence of basalt and gabbro can be detected beneath a cover of sediments with an instrument called a gravity meter, which is sensitive to the relative densities of underlying rocks. In the 1950s, the buried extension of the rift system was traced from its surface exposure around Lake Superior all the way to Kansas using the gravity meter. Later, drilling confirmed its presence there.

The rapid eruption of so much volcanic material introduced a great deal of heat into the crust. Hot, mineral-rich solutions percolated through the cooling lavas and deposited a variety of minerals in gas bubble holes in the basalts and along fractures cutting through them. The bubble holes, called *vesicles*, are filled primarily with silica, but other minerals also occur sparingly. Some of the siliceous fillings have beautifully colored, concentric laminations, and when basalts containing them were later eroded, these resistant little nodules accumulated in river and beach gravels as today's much sought-after Lake Superior agates. Some of the hot fluids also deposited metallic copper within some of the basalts and between the pebbles in overlying conglomerate, especially in the Keweenaw Peninsula of Michigan and on Isle Royale near the Minnesota shore. As they cooled, the basalts commonly developed a conspicuous columnar structure. Shrinkage during cooling produced evenly spaced cracks perpendicular to the top and bottom surfaces of the basalt layers. The cracked basalt resembles a series of closely spaced columns or pillars.

Native Americans mined the copper and traded implements made from it down the Mississippi Valley. European immigrants were interested in the source of copper because the United States had to import the ore. At first the newcomers found only some remarkable glacial fieldstone boulders composed of pure, metallic copper. It was not until the 1840s that minable copper was finally located in the Keweenaw Peninsula. An important 1848 discovery turned out to be a rediscovery of an old Indian mine in which a 6-ton mass of pure copper, which the Indians had detached from a vein, was supported by oak logs. The logs and copper mass showed evidence of chipping and hammer stones were present.

From about 1850 to 1950, copper production boomed, but after 1970, only one mine was still active. The Lake Superior copper deposits are unique for the predominance of pure, metallic copper rather than more typical ores in which copper is combined with sulfur or other elements. The largest masses of pure copper were more of a bane than a blessing, however, because they were difficult to mine. Copper is so soft that these nuggets refused to split when dynamited, so miners had to laboriously chisel them down to manageable pieces. Sadly for Wisconsin, commercially significant mineralization was confined to Michigan even though the copper-bearing rocks do extend across the border. Ironically, Michigan instead of Wisconsin got the Keweenaw country only through a political compromise when Michigan gained statehood—its consolation for giving up the harbor at Toledo to Ohio.

Most of the Keweenaw sediments were deposited by rivers, but some accumulated in large lakes similar to several modern East African rift valley lakes. An unusual billion-year-old, organic-rich lake deposit, the black Nonesuch shale in Michigan, has generated a thick, tarry petroleum. During the early 1980s, oil companies drilled several wildcat wells along the Lake Superior rift system in the hope of finding commercially significant accumulations of Nonesuch oil, perhaps the oldest on earth. Although it was a great gamble, they were encouraged by the production of late Precambrian oil in Siberia, Saudi Arabia, and China. Except for this unusual black shale, however, most of the Keweenaw sediments are red or brown due to cementation by small amounts of iron oxide. In the late 1800s when brownstone was popular for buildings and bridge supports, the red sandstones were quarried in the Apostle Islands region of Wisconsin and in eastern Minnesota.

Beginning about 1,000 million years ago, the former rift was turned inside out; that is, this long, narrow subsiding feature was converted into a long, narrow series of uplifted fault blocks. Distant compression of the continent along its southeastern margin reactivated many of the buried rift-margin faults, but reversed their motion. Whereas previously the axis of the rift had dropped along such faults, now it was raised thousands of feet to bring older rocks up against younger ones. The fault blocks then became stabilized, and the thick late Keweenaw strata were eroded to expose the older basalts. Beginning about 500 million years ago, Cambrian strata were

A large erratic boulder of pure copper from glacial deposits in east-central Wisconsin.
—Photo courtesy of the University of Wisconsin Geology Museum

1,100 million years ago

gabbro intrusions — basalts — rhyolite

mantle — gabbro

subsidence

0 ———— 50 mi
0 ———— 80 km

1,000 million years ago

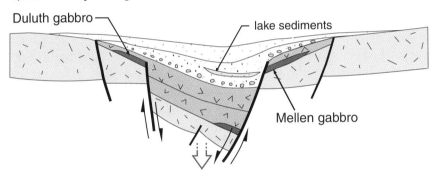

Duluth gabbro — lake sediments

Mellen gabbro

900 million years ago

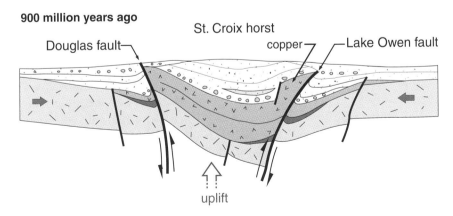

St. Croix horst

Douglas fault — copper — Lake Owen fault

uplift

Three stages in the evolution of the Lake Superior rift. Initial faulting, subsidence, and lava eruptions 1,100 million years ago were followed by a thick accumulation of sediments 1,000 million years ago. A continental plate collision far away compressed and raised the rift along existing faults 900 million years ago.

deposited unconformably upon these rocks. Then, sometime after the Ordovician period, some of the faults were again reactivated, probably by a new compression of the southeastern margin of North America due to collisions with island chains or other continents. In some places, the Keweenaw rocks were not only raised vertically but were also thrust outward over Cambrian and Ordovician strata.

Quaternary Glaciation

Traveling the roads of the Northern Highlands, you will see two very different landscapes. The northern part of the region is rugged and hilly, a forested land of many lakes and wetlands. Only in places does the shape of the underlying bedrock surface control the shape of the landscape. In contrast, the southern part of the region is gently rolling with few lakes or wetlands, and much of this area is cultivated. Here, the bedrock surface shapes the landscape. The strikingly different landscapes of these two parts of the Northern Highlands are largely a result of how recently they were glaciated. The northern part was glaciated between about 26,000 and 10,000 years ago, but the southern part was glaciated much earlier, some areas as much as hundreds of thousands of years ago.

The more time that has passed since glaciation, the longer erosion has had to modify the landscape. A recently glaciated landscape like that of the northern part of the Northern Highlands still has well-preserved glacial landforms, such as moraines, drumlins, and eskers, as well as numerous lakes and wetlands in low, closed depressions. In contrast, in an area glaciated longer ago, like the southern part of the highlands, erosion has obliterated the glacial landforms, and lakes and wetlands have mostly been filled with sediment or drained as river tributaries slowly extended into more and more of the landscape.

Early Glaciations

In the southern part of the Northern Highlands, bedrock is overlain by a patchy cover of material derived from the weathering of the underlying rock. Sediment up to several tens of feet thick, deposited during several early glaciations of the area, overlies the patchy cover in places. These early glaciations occurred too long ago for radiocarbon dating to help discern their history, and much of the sedimentary record has been removed by erosion or altered by weathering. The earliest glaciers advanced into the area from the west, carrying fragments of fossiliferous limestone and gray shale. The deposits containing these tend to be gray to light brown with a lot of silt because the glacier was eroding and incorporating much shale or lake sediment as it flowed across Manitoba and Minnesota before reaching Wisconsin. The extent of these early glaciations from the northwest is poorly

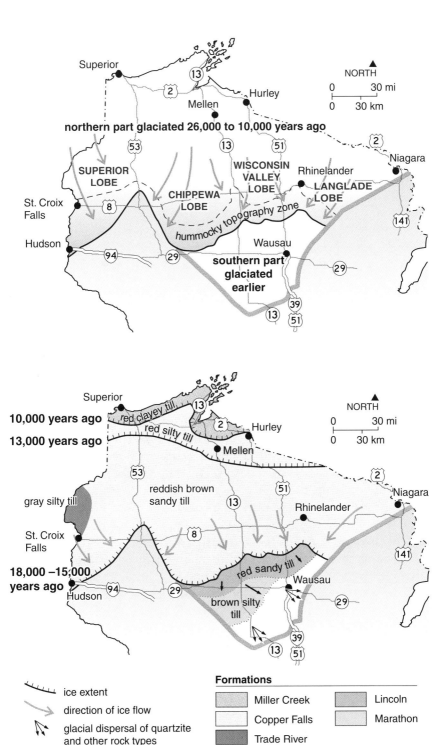

Top: *Timing and extent of glaciation in the Northern Highlands. The zone of hummocky topography marks the southern extent of late Wisconsin Glaciation.* Bottom: *The characteristics of till in different parts of the Northern Highlands and three successive ice-margin positions in late Wisconsin time.*

known because erosion has removed most of their deposits. The distribution of pieces of quartzite derived from a source near Wausau indicates that one or more of the early glaciers reached southeastward at least to the Wisconsin River. Although the exact timing of these early glaciations is unknown, the lack of preserved glacial landforms where these old northwesterly derived deposits are at the surface suggests that they were deposited at least one hundred thousand years ago and some at least several hundred thousand years ago.

Following the glacial advances from the northwest, a series of advances from the north reached as far as the southern part of the Northern Highlands. In contrast to the earlier advances, these deposited reddish brown, sandy glacial deposits that contain fragments of banded iron formation, Keweenaw volcanic rock, reddish brown sandstone, and other rock types derived from the Lake Superior area. In the southern part of the highlands, these northerly derived glacial materials occur as isolated patches in the western part of the area and as a nearly continuous cover in a band about 10 miles wide across the northern part of the area. The landscape here consists of gently rolling hills that reflect the topography of the underlying bedrock, subdued moraines and drumlins, and some natural wetlands. A nearly continuous till cover along with some preserved wetlands and glacial landforms indicate that this landscape was glaciated much more recently than areas covered with the northwesterly derived, silt-rich glacial sediment. Several radiocarbon dates of organic material that accumulated in bogs on top of the reddish brown glacial sediment indicate the latest of these advances melted from the area no later than about 50,000 years ago.

Late Wisconsin Glaciation—The Most Recent

Beginning about 26,000 years ago, the southern margin of the Laurentide Ice Sheet advanced out of the Lake Superior basin into Wisconsin and covered the northern part of the Northern Highlands with reddish brown, sandy glacial sediment rich in rocks carried from the Lake Superior basin. The ice sheet reached its maximum extent by about 18,000 years ago. Lobes shaped by the form of the broad regional lowlands flowed over northern Wisconsin. The ice sheet advanced farthest south in the large regional lowlands now partly occupied by Green Bay and Lake Superior. Between these large lobes, high bedrock ridges that straddle the Michigan-Wisconsin border retarded the flow of ice. By about 15,000 years ago, the ice sheet began to shrink northward and, following several limited readvances, finally receded from northernmost Wisconsin about 10,000 years ago. This last ice sheet to advance into Wisconsin left in its wake a landscape dotted with lakes and wetlands, a landscape rich in well-preserved moraines, drumlins, eskers, and many other glacial landforms. The area is mostly forested—it is the area of Wisconsin's northwoods.

Across northern Wisconsin the maximum extent of the Laurentide Ice Sheet is marked by a conspicuous zone, in places more than 5 to 10 miles wide, of very hilly or hummocky topography. The melting of a thick sequence of rock debris and ice that accumulated along the margin of the ice sheet formed this topography. Near the edge of the glacier, slabs of debris-rich ice were stacked up when the glacier repeatedly advanced over slightly older stagnant slabs of debris-rich ice. This stacking was likely enhanced by the compression produced when flowing ice encountered ice near the margin that was frozen solidly to its bed. Near its margin, the glacier was thinner, so cold temperatures penetrated to the bottom of the ice. The same cold conditions produced permafrost beyond the glacier margin.

How did hummocky topography form from a pile of debris-rich ice? The process is the same as the one you can watch happening each spring when the pile of dirty snow at the end of your driveway melts. Where the dirt is thick it insulates the snow beneath so most melting occurs where the dirt is thin or absent. Sooner or later the melting produces a low spot and the wet dirt from adjacent high spots slumps into the low spot, exposing

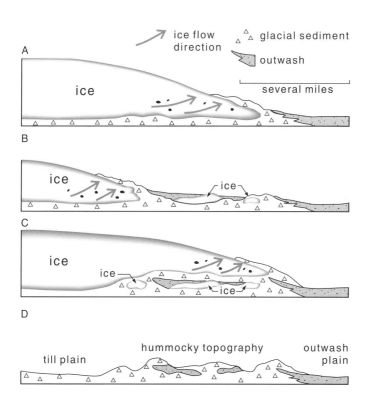

The formation of hummocky topography.

the surrounding snow that it had covered and protected from melting. This process repeats until all of the snow has melted, leaving an irregular pile of dirt. The same thing happened along the margin of the Laurentide Ice Sheet at a grand scale, and rather than just sand and a few pebbles like you might see at the end of your driveway, everything from clay to boulders was mixed with the ice.

Hummocky topography covers thousands of square miles in northern Wisconsin. Individual hummocks are typically hundreds of feet in diam-

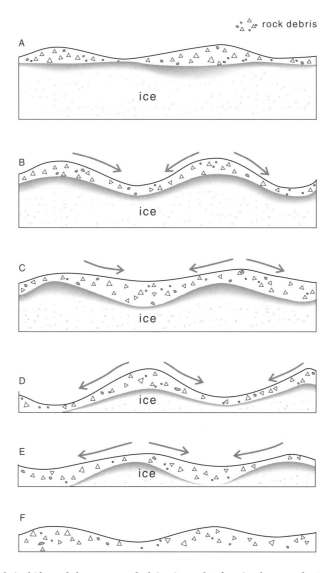

Rock debris shifts and slumps as underlying ice melts, forming hummocky topography.

eter and tens of feet high, but many exceed one hundred feet. The low parts of these hummocky areas contain thousands of lakes and wetlands. Although geologists believe the margin of the ice sheet receded from this pile of debris-rich ice by about 15,000 years ago in northern Wisconsin, it may have been a few thousand years more before climate warmed enough for all of the buried ice to melt. In many places the outer edge of the hummocky zone is marked by a distinct, sharp-crested moraine ridge tens of feet wide and high. These ridges probably formed in part by stacking of debris-rich ice and in part by slumping of rock debris from adjacent disintegrating ice.

Some high parts of the hummocky topography were formerly small lakes that filled depressions in the ice surface and were walled by the ice itself. Water flowing into the lakes from the surrounding ice carried sediment that accumulated as it does in any lake. The coarse sediment settled out near the shore and some was reworked by waves. The fine sediment settled to the bottom farther offshore in deeper, quieter water. When the ice surrounding the lakes melted, the sediments that accumulated in the lakes were left as high, flat-topped areas on the landscape. Many ice-walled lake plains have a dish-shaped surface with the coarse material deposited near the ice wall forming a rim ridge around the lake plain. These ice-walled lake plains are commonly a mile or more across and result in a distinctive land-use pattern in northern Wisconsin—roughly circular areas of agriculture surrounded by extensive forest. The lake plains are nearly flat and boulder free, their elevated positions in the landscape have somewhat longer

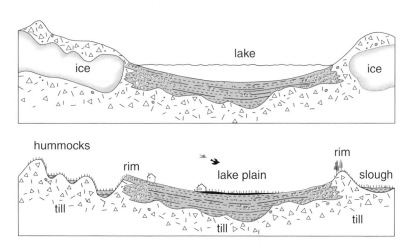

The formation of an ice-walled lake plain. **Top:** *A lake forms on the debris-covered part of a glacier and sediment accumulates on the lake floor.* **Bottom:** *After the ice melts the lake sediment is left as a high, nearly flat area usually surrounded by hummocky topography.*

frost-free growing seasons, and the fine-grained sediment holds moisture well. This is about as good as it gets for farming in the northern part of the Northern Highlands! Farm buildings are typically located on the ridges of the ice-walled lake plains.

Ice-walled lakes on the Tokositna Glacier in Alaska. A thin layer of rock debris covers the ice. The steep, dark slopes around the lakes are ice. —J. W. Attig photo

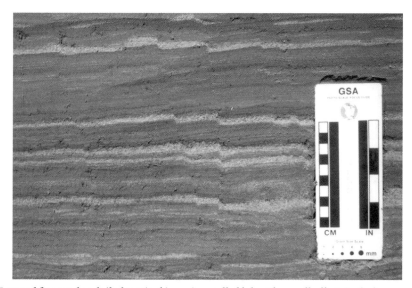

Layered fine sand and silt deposited in an ice-walled lake. The small offsets in the layers are faults that probably formed when buried and surrounding ice melted. —J. W. Attig photo

Tunnel channels are also common features of the hummocky zone. Broad troughs up to half a mile wide that cut through the hummocky zone at right angles are the present-day surface expression of deep channels cut beneath the margin of the glacier by meltwater. Accumulations of very large boulders, some in excess of 10 feet across indicate that large, short-lived outbursts of meltwater exited these tunnels.

When climate began to warm near the end of the last glaciation around 15,000 years ago, the amount of ice flowing to the margin of the Laurentide Ice Sheet was no longer sufficient to replace the ice lost to melting. Therefore, the margin of the ice sheet began to retreat northward. The general retreat of the ice from Wisconsin was interrupted by times when the margin stayed in one place for some time and by times when the margin readvanced. Significant readvances of the ice margin out of the Lake Superior basin into Wisconsin occurred about 13,000 and 10,000 years ago. The last of these readvances, which just reached northernmost Wisconsin, is well dated. The ice overran a forest, and the wood from buried trees has yielded many radiocarbon dates of about 10,000 years.

In northern Wisconsin, narrow moraines and extensive outwash plains mark places where the melting ice margin stabilized for a period of time. The readvance 13,000 years ago, however, formed a broad, hummocky zone similar to, but smaller than, the one marking the maximum extent of the ice sheet. Rivers carrying vast quantities of meltwater and sediment deposited the outwash plains. These outwash rivers did not flow in a single channel as most rivers in Wisconsin do today but instead flowed in a vast system of channels forming a braided pattern across floodplains that were miles wide in places. They filled the landscape from valley wall to valley wall with gravelly sand, forming broad, nearly flat sand plains. In many

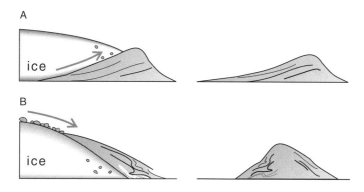

Two methods of moraine formation. A. Debris-rich slabs of ice from the bottom of the glacier are stacked at the edge of the glacier. B. Debris slumping off the glacier accumulates at the edge of the glacier. A combination of these processes formed most moraines.

parts of northern Wisconsin, outwash sediment was deposited on top of and around masses of ice left behind as the ice sheet melted. When this ice melted, the overlying and surrounding outwash collapsed, forming the depressions, called *kettles* or *pits*, that hold the thousands of lakes and wetlands characteristic of northern Wisconsin.

Glacial Lake Duluth

Whenever the Superior Lobe advanced westward in the Lake Superior basin, it blocked the eastern outlets of the basin, and water ponded between the ice front and the rim of the basin. The elevation of the lowest available outlet controlled water levels in lakes at the margin of the ice. These lakes formed a number of times in the western Lake Superior basin during the retreat of the Superior Lobe at the end of the Wisconsin Glaciation.

The final advance of the Superior Lobe into Wisconsin 10,000 years ago dammed several small lakes between the ice margin and the southern rim of the Lake Superior basin in northwestern Wisconsin and adjacent Minnesota and Michigan. As the lobe retreated northeastward, these small lakes coalesced to form Glacial Lake Duluth, which extended along much of the southwestern part of the ice margin. This lake drained southward through

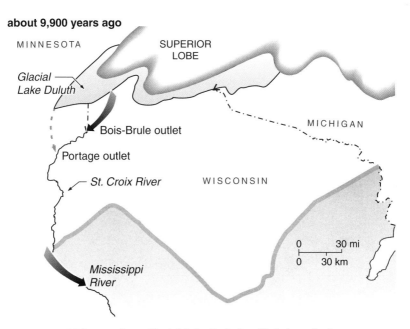

Meltwater from Glacial Lake Duluth spilled through the Bois-Brule outlet. Bold arrows show direction of water flow.

the Bois-Brule outlet. Today, the Bois Brule River 25 miles east of Superior flows north into Lake Superior, but Glacial Lake Duluth rose about 500 feet higher than the modern lake so it drained south through the upper Brule valley, at a low point along a ridge of Precambrian basalt. The water then flowed into the upper St. Croix River, which drains into the Mississippi River. Another outlet southwest of Duluth also drained the lake when the Superior Lobe blocked the Bois-Brule outlet. The elevation of Glacial Lake Duluth beaches indicates that the highest level of the lake was around 1,100 feet above sea level. The water spilling out of Lake Duluth through the Bois-Brule outlet cut a deep, steep-walled channel that is over 1 mile wide in most places. Lake Duluth drained through the Bois-Brule outlet between about 10,000 and 9,500 years ago. Earlier ice-marginal lakes also undoubtedly drained through both the Portage and Bois-Brule outlets. Today, the St. Croix River flows in this broad, steep-walled channel, which is as much as 100 feet deep. It was certainly much deeper prior to being partly filled with outwash and postglacial river sediment.

There are many uncertainties in reconstructing the history of ice-marginal lakes like Glacial Lake Duluth. The precise mapping and correlation of beach elevations over great distances is difficult. Geologists do not know how much the outlets were downcut by the water spilling through them, or exactly how deep the water in the outlet was at any time. In addition, differential rise or rebound of the earth's crust following the removal of the weight of the glacier has tilted the shorelines of the glacial lakes—the shoreline of Glacial Lake Duluth rises eastward. The modern outlet of Lake Superior, the St. Marys River at Sault Sainte Marie, continues to rise a little over a half foot per century faster than the western end of the basin. As the Superior Lobe retreated eastward, Glacial Lake Duluth expanded until lower-level outlets were opened in the eastern part of the basin.

Interstate 39/U.S. 51
Stevens Point—Hurley
155 miles (250 km)

Interstate 39 leaves the Central Plain at Stevens Point and enters the Northern Highlands, although the change is not obvious on the highway because Quaternary deposits conceal the bedrock. On the Wisconsin River to the west, however, the boundary between the regions actually occurs 25 miles farther southwest at Wisconsin Rapids, where Precambrian rocks appear along the river beneath Cambrian sandstones. After lumbering declined in the early 1900s with the leveling of the great pine forests across northern and central Wisconsin, paper mills appeared along this part of the Wisconsin River to exploit small trees unsuitable for lumber. Such mills needed both water and electric power, so dams were built at half a dozen rapids in this area. Today, the best rock exposures are found below some of those dams, for example at Conants Rapids near Stevens Point.

At Stevens Point, the highway crosses a broad outwash plain that slopes gently westward away from the Green Bay Lobe, which reached its maximum late Wisconsin position about 6 miles to the east. At Stevens Point the outwash plain beyond the Green Bay Lobe merges with the outwash plain of the Wisconsin River, which in turn merges with the lake bottom of Glacial Lake Wisconsin about 5 miles to the south.

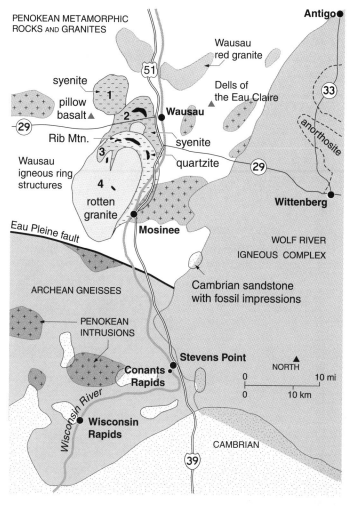

Bedrock of the Wausau–Stevens Point area along I-39/U.S. 51. Numbers 1 through 4 show the position of four former volcanoes in the Rib Mountain area.

Between Stevens Point and Wausau, I-39/U.S. 51 crosses several bedrock uplands and flat outwash terraces. The Central Wisconsin Airport on the east side of the highway near Mosinee is on one of these bedrock uplands. The thin and patchy material overlying bedrock in this area is derived from the weathering of the underlying rock. Although this area may have been glaciated during the early advances from the northwest, early glacial features and debris are not preserved this far east. North of Mosinee the road crosses a high outwash terrace along the Wisconsin River. The gravelly sand from these outwash terraces along the river is mined in many places for construction aggregate.

Archean Marshfield Continent

The ancient rocks of the Stevens Point area were part of the Marshfield continent of Archean age. Throughout this area, 2,800-million-year-old Archean gneisses were intruded by a variety of Penokean granites and other types of rocks that are around 1,850 million years old. All have been complexly deformed and metamorphosed. The most accessible exposures of the rocks occur along the Wisconsin River.

Approximately 12 miles north of Stevens Point at the Portage-Marathon County border (mile 171.5), the highway crosses a major boundary between the Marshfield continent and the Penokean belt. It is concealed along

Intensely sheared rock from the Eau Pleine fault zone, the boundary between the Marshfield continent and the Penokean belt. Sample is from a quarry at Dancy on Lake Du Bay west of I-39 near the Portage-Marathon County border. —M. Diman scan of polished rock slab

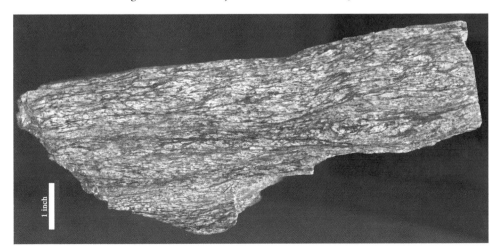

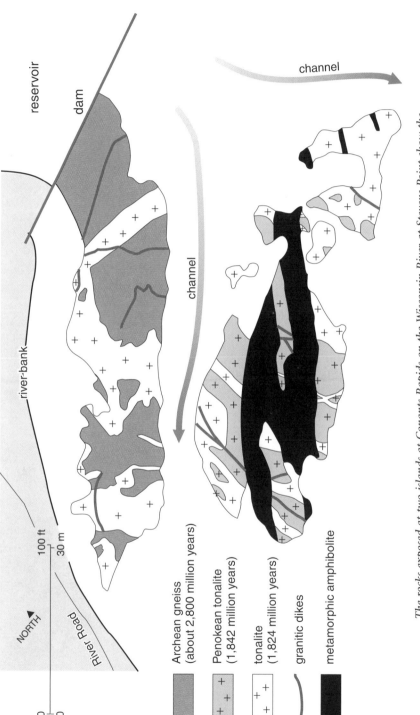

NORTH

River Road

100 ft
30 m

0
0

river-bank

reservoir

dam

channel

channel

Archean gneiss
(about 2,800 million years)

Penokean tonalite
(1,842 million years)

tonalite
(1,824 million years)

granitic dikes

metamorphic amphibolite

The rocks exposed at two islands at Conants Rapids on the Wisconsin River at Stevens Point show the complexity typical of the Archean Marshfield continent. —After Maas, Medaris, and Van Schmus, 1980 the highway, but in scattered exposures to the west along the Big Eau Pleine River, a zone of intense shearing marks the fault zone suture between these two provinces. The faulted boundary is traceable from a little east of I-39 for 100 miles northwest, where it disappears beneath flat-lying Cambrian strata. North of the boundary, Archean rocks are absent and Penokean volcanic and granitic rocks predominate. Regardless of where the Marshfield Archean rocks originated, they must have been close to their present position during the Penokean episode for them to have been intruded by various Penokean-age igneous rocks around 1,850 to 1,830 million years ago. At Mosinee, Penokean granitic and other igneous rocks are exposed. For example just north of the Wisconsin 153 interchange, dark dikes cut granitic rock.

A Patch of Cambrian Sandstones

About 10 miles southeast of Mosinee and east of I-39, one of the most northerly patches of Cambrian sandstone occurs and is quarried for flagstones. Spectacular fossil impressions and tracks of several kinds of animals occur in the quarries, but no actual skeletons are present. Most interesting are circular, dinner-plate-size impressions of hundreds of jellyfish that were stranded on an ancient seashore by tropical hurricanes, which

Impressions of jellyfish stranded on a ripple-marked Cambrian shoreline near Mosinee, Wisconsin. —J. W. Hagadorn photos

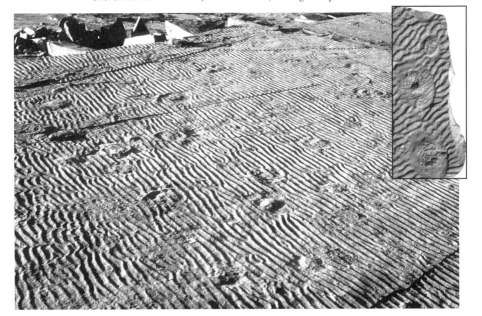

blew the helpless creatures landward on at least seven different occasions. Other impressions that resemble auto tire tracks were formed by some extinct animal who crept across wet sand in search of a microbial feast. Associated wave-formed ripple marks indicate a very shallow, sandy environment, which was exposed at low tide.

Wausau Area and Rib Mountain State Park

As you approach Wausau from the south, you can see first Mosinee Hill and then Rib Mountain to the west of the highway. County N to the west provides access to Rib Mountain State Park. From the top, a clear day provides a view of the broad, low-relief glaciated landscape to the west and southwest, the moraine deposited when the Green Bay Lobe stood at its maximum late Wisconsin extent to the east, and the outwash plains along the Wisconsin River to the south and east. To the north you can see the moraine deposited when the Wisconsin Valley Lobe stood at its maximum position.

Just south of Wausau the Rib River flows into the Wisconsin River from the west. I-39/U.S. 51 crosses a broad wetland at the confluence. The

View looking south across the Rib River at Rib Mountain near Wausau. Once thought to be the highest point in the state, it is now known to be the fourth, at 1,940 feet. —Photo courtesy of the Wisconsin Department of Natural Resources

Wisconsin River drainage reaches far to the north, therefore it carried sediment-rich meltwater from the last ice sheet longer and much later than did the Rib River, which only drained the ice sheet when it was near its maximum extent northwest of Wausau. The outwash sediment accumulating along the Wisconsin River built its floodplain to a higher level than the floodplain of the Rib River. The higher Wisconsin River floodplain dammed the lower Rib River valley, producing the low gradient and broad wetlands of the Rib River near the confluence.

The Wausau area is a geological cornucopia. Besides the effects of glaciation upon the landscape, there is a complete suite of different Penokean rocks nearby and a sampling of the younger Wolf River igneous complex. Penokean rocks include rhyolitic and basaltic volcanic rocks, sedimentary rocks, and a variety of granitic intrusions. All were deformed and metamorphosed to varying degrees by Penokean mountain building, which culminated around 1,850 million years ago. Wisconsin's state rock, the Wausau Red Granite, is not metamorphosed and is probably post-Penokean (perhaps 1,750 million years old). It has long been quarried north of the city.

You can see slightly metamorphosed rhyolitic volcanic and sedimentary rocks at the north edge of Wausau at the intersection of I-39/U.S. 51 with County WW. East of the river on County W, 1.5 miles south of WW, a long roadcut exposes sedimentary rocks rich in rhyolitic ash derived from the volcanic chain. Half a mile farther south, a cemetery contains many headstones made from Wausau Red Granite. Metamorphosed rhyolite is very well exposed in the beautiful Dells of the Eau Claire River, a county park 12 miles northeast of Wausau at a bridge on County Y. Meltwater flowing from the late Wisconsin Green Bay and Langlade Lobes cut this little gorge. Upstream and downstream from the dells, broad outwash plains flank the river. Metamorphosed basalts occur west of the Wisconsin River, but you can only see these along county roads.

Wolf River igneous eruptions created a line of volcanoes in the Rib Mountain area about 1,450 million years ago. A class of igneous rocks poor in silica, called *syenite*, together with more normal granite, was intruded beneath these volcanoes, only the eroded roots of which are preserved today. Try to imagine several belching craters just west of the highway between Mosinee and Wausau. Just west of I-39, syenite is exposed behind the east parking lot of the prominent white Wausau Insurance Buildings on Stewart Street, which is accessible from the Wisconsin 29 interchange (exit 192). Syenite also is exposed along the interstate just north of this interchange. The Wolf River igneous rocks differ from Penokean ones in composition—they are richer, for example, in the alkali elements potassium and sodium. They also differ tectonically because no compressional folding was associated with their intrusion.

Rib Mountain is near the center of the roots of the volcanoes of Wolf River age. Resistant white, vertical quartzite forms the long ridge of the mountain. Like several other equivalent quartzites scattered widely over Wisconsin, it postdates Penokean mountain building, owing its origin to the deep erosion of the Penokean Mountains. Later metamorphic events converted the eroded sediment into quartzite. Today, the Rib Mountain quartzite crops out in a nearly circular pattern that formed when a ring-shaped mass of syenite that was intruded beneath the Wolf River volcanoes engulfed some sandstone, changing it to quartzite. An early glaciation carried pieces of this quartzite eastward.

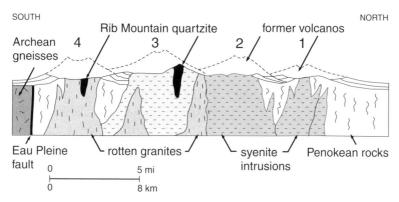

The roots of four former volcanoes in the Rib Mountain area. Heat and pressure from the intruding syenite metamorphosed sandstone into the hard, resistant quartzite that forms the long ridge of Rib Mountain.

Southwest of Rib Mountain, the quartzite is surrounded by an unusual granite that underlay the southern half of the youngest volcano. The composition of the dominant mineral, feldspar, changed markedly as the granite cooled; the cores of the crystals are of one feldspar variety rich in potassium, but the outer rims are of another variety richer in sodium. This change was due to a complex chemical response to changing water pressure as magma rose through the crust. This unusual texture of granite was named *rapakivi*, which means "rotten granite" in Finnish, reflecting a peculiarity of weathering by crumbling physically to a fine rubble without altering very much chemically. The severe glacial climate during several Quaternary glacial advances may have produced the rubble. The expansive force of water freezing frequently in fine cracks in the rock probably broke it up without causing noticeable chemical change. Whatever the explanation, rotten granite rubble has long been excavated west of Rib Mountain for use in landscaping.

Large feldspar crystals in a Wolf River granite at Tigerton showing rapakivi texture. Crystal cores are potassium feldspar; the rims are sodium feldspar. —L. G. Medaris photo

The rotten granite has some of the highest radon values in Wisconsin. Radon gas is formed by natural radioactivity in rocks and may cause lung cancer if inhaled over a long period. It is only a hazard in poorly ventilated spaces in buildings constructed upon radon-emitting rocks. Also of environmental importance in the Rib Mountain area is that the groundwater has an unusually high fluorine content. The good news is that the local folks' teeth are very resistant to decay, but the bad news is that the abundant fluorine causes mottling of their teeth.

The dark screens you will see covering many farm fields in central Wisconsin shade the herb ginseng, which is native to the local forests, from the bright sun. The root of ginseng is thought by many people, especially the Chinese, to have beneficial health effects. Most of the local crop is exported to Asia. The fields must be abandoned after harvesting only a few crops because the spores of organisms that cause root rot build up in the soil.

Wausau to Woodruff

Between Wausau and Brokaw the highway crosses a bedrock upland before descending back onto the outwash plain along the Wisconsin River. Two miles north of Wausau, roadcuts along I-39/U.S. 51 expose pre-Penokean rhyolite. The Wausau Red Granite is exposed nearby and is quarried west of the highway 4 miles farther north. It was intruded into the surrounding Penokean volcanic rocks perhaps 1,750 million years ago.

From Brokaw northward, a nearly continuous cover of reddish brown, sandy glacial sediment mantles the hills flanking the Wisconsin River. With the exception of subdued drumlins and moraines, glacial landforms are absent from this landscape, which is part of the area glaciated prior to the late Wisconsin advance, which did not reach this far south.

North of Merrill the highway continues to cross the old glacial landscape for about 6 miles before crossing into the area glaciated by the Wisconsin Valley Lobe near the end of the Wisconsin Glaciation. The ice margin probably stood here as recently as 15,000 years ago. Between here and Irma, the highway crosses the hummocky topography formed as debris-rich ice melted. Note the abundant wetlands along the roadside. Contrast this hummocky landscape with the uplands south of Merrill, where glaciation occurred much earlier. The flat areas the highway crosses just south and north of Larson Lake are ice-walled lake plains, which are a common part of this hummocky landscape.

Harrison Hills

We recommend a side trip on Wisconsin 17 northeast from Merrill to the Harrison Hills. The total loop is about 50 miles, but it will take you to some of the most spectacular hummocky glacial topography you will see anywhere. Even if you are not a big fan of glacial hummocks, this is a great trip for scenery, fall color, spring wildflowers, and hiking. Take Wisconsin 17 northeast from its intersection with Wisconsin 64 and I-39/U.S. 51 in Merrill. Follow Wisconsin 17 about 8 miles to Bloomville where the road crosses the outwash plain deposited beyond the margin of the Wisconsin Valley Lobe. The maximum extent of the lobe was about 2 miles west of Bloomville. You can get excellent views of the moraine marking the eastern edge of the hummocky zone and the position of the maximum extent of the Wisconsin Valley Lobe by taking County J west from Bloomville for 3

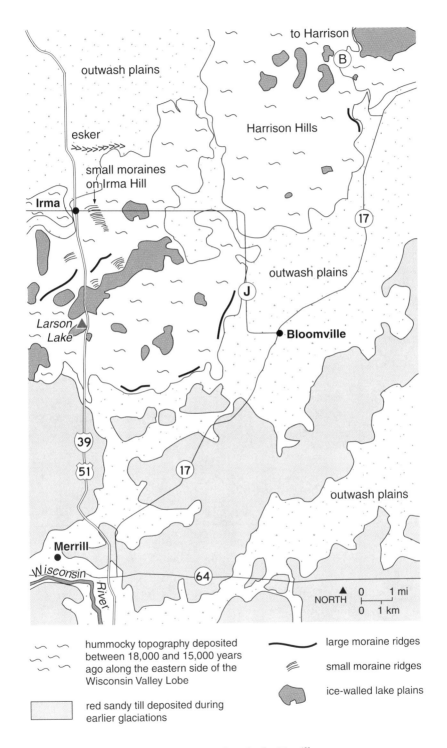

Geology along I-39/U.S. 51 in the Merrill area.

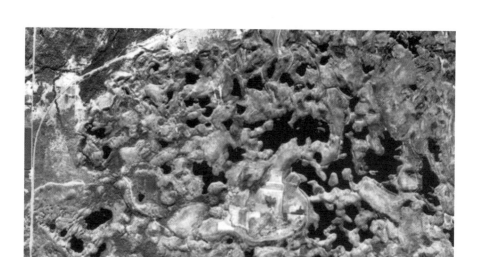

Aerial view of part of the Harrison Hills shows hummocky topography and lakes. The oval feature near the center of the photo is an ice-walled lake plain.
—U.S. Geological Survey National High Altitude Photography program

miles. Return and continue north on Wisconsin 17 for another 8.5 miles across the outwash plain to the intersection with County B to the west. For about a half mile, County B heads westward across the outwash plain and then turns sharply northward into the hummocky topography of the Harrison Hills. Watch for access to the Ice Age National Scenic Trail on the west side of the road. Follow County B for several miles as it winds through the spectacular high-relief hummocky topography and the many lakes and wetlands of the Harrison Hills. Although hard to see from the road, many of the high points in this landscape are ice-walled lake plains. Rejoin I-39/U.S. 51 by following County B for about 4 miles to its junction with County D in Harrison and taking County D west about 10 miles to Tomahawk, or simply backtrack to Merrill.

Irma and Tomahawk

Sixteen miles north of Merrill (8 miles south of Tomahawk) at the village of Irma, there is another small patch of Cambrian sandstone, which was deposited upon deeply eroded Penokean rocks of Precambrian age. You can see flat-lying sandstones on Irma Hill half a mile east of I-39/U.S. 51 along County J. This is the most isolated patch of such strata, being near the center of the Wisconsin dome, which was higher in the landscape during Paleozoic time. This patch, which is 50 miles north of the nearest Cambrian outcrop, contains ripple marks and faint fossil impressions, including jellyfish and tire-track-like animal trails similar to those in quarries southeast of Mosinee. Such patches of sandstone prove that the Cambrian sea covered most, if not all, of the Northern Highlands, which today is overwhelmingly dominated by Precambrian bedrock exposures thanks to erosion of all but these small patches of whatever younger strata once covered the dome.

Enjoy the great view from the top of Irma Hill. The upland to the south is the hummocky zone marking the maximum extent of the last ice sheet. If you drive about a half mile to the south or north on County H, you will notice that the banks on the side of the road look as if they have been cut through a wavy surface. Indeed they have—each one of the "waves" is an east-west-trending moraine deposited along the margin of the Wisconsin Valley Lobe as it receded northward. These moraines are clearly visible on aerial photographs. Their pattern shows how the retreating ice margin wrapped around Irma Hill. These may be annual moraines deposited as

Aerial view of the sequence of parallel moraine ridges on Irma Hill. Each moraine ridge is about 10 feet high and about 150 feet wide. They were deposited at the margin of the Wisconsin Valley Lobe as it receded from the area. Irma is at the intersection at the far left-center of the area shown. —U.S. Department of Agriculture photo

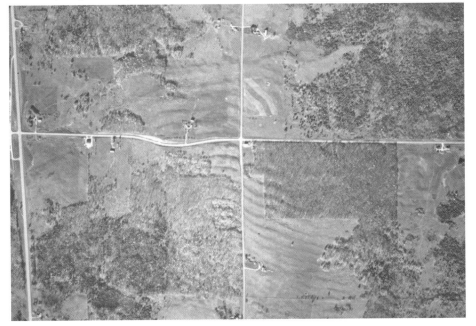

Gravel pit exposing the cross section of an esker. —David M. Mickelson photo

the ice advanced a short distance each winter when melting of the ice margin lessened. A fresh roadcut several years ago showed that each of the moraines is composed of till deposited when the ice margin advanced a few tens of feet over outwash.

Between Irma and Tomahawk, I-39/U.S. 51 crosses an extensive area of outwash deposited by streams draining the eastern part of the Wisconsin Valley Lobe. Two east-west-trending eskers cross this stretch of road, one about 2 miles north of Irma, and another about 1 mile south of Tomahawk just north of where the highway crosses over Kaphaem Road. The esker just south of Tomahawk is being extensively mined for sand and gravel. Between Tomahawk and Minocqua, the highway crosses a series of sandy moraines and outwash plains. Much of the outwash in this part of Wisconsin was deposited on top of masses of stagnant glacial ice. The eventual melting of this buried ice formed the basins that now hold the many lakes that have drawn fishermen and vacationers to the area for years.

Woodruff to Hurley

A few miles north of Woodruff, geophysical measurements indicate that the Niagara fault zone crosses the highway beneath a cover of thick glacial deposits. This, perhaps Wisconsin's single greatest fault zone, is the collisional boundary between the southern margin of the Superior continent of Archean age to the north and the main part of the Penokean volcanic island chain of Proterozoic age to the south. The collision between these two great tectonic features elevated the Penokean Mountains 1,890 to 1,815 million years ago. Rocks of the former volcanic chain and the margin of the old continent were crushed together, metamorphosed, and intruded by countless bodies of granitic rocks. The collision affected a 25-mile-wide zone within which Proterozoic rocks surround large elliptical areas of older Archean gneiss, which are like chocolate chips in a cookie.

About 10 miles north of Woodruff, near the Diamond Lake boat landing on the west side of the road, the highway passes between several high hills, which are northeast-southwest-trending drumlins formed beneath the Wisconsin Valley Lobe. The broad, pitted outwash plain that the highway

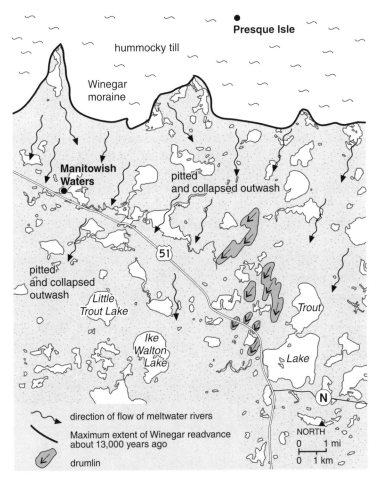

Geology along U.S. 51 southeast of Manitowish Waters. Note the large area of pitted and collapsed outwash and the many lakes.

crosses between these drumlins and Manitowish Waters was deposited about 13,000 years ago when ice readvanced out of the Lake Superior basin into northern Wisconsin. This readvance reached its maximum southern extent about 3 miles north of Manitowish Waters, where it deposited the Winegar moraine.

Bedrock exposures are rare north of Woodruff, but 6 miles southwest of Manitowish Waters, a roadcut along Wisconsin 182 (2 miles west of its junction with Wisconsin 47) exposes a schist containing the mineral kyanite, which indicates intense metamorphism at a depth of about 15 miles; the rocks have also been intensely deformed. About 5 miles to the northwest of the roadcut is a zone of unusually high electrical conductivity in the crust. The zone is about 10 miles wide and extends for more than 60 miles westward across northern Wisconsin and to a depth of at least 10 miles. Drill samples suggest that this zone owes its electrical character to the presence of carbon-rich metamorphosed sediments containing the mineral graphite, which is pure carbon and an excellent electrical conductor. This zone must mark a concealed major faulted boundary between intensely metamorphosed rocks to the south and less disturbed Penokean volcanic rocks to the north, which are exposed in Turtle-Flambeau County Park at Lake of the Falls, 6 miles west of U.S. 51 via County FF.

A depression forming in a modern outwash plain where a buried block of ice is melting. The depression is about 30 feet wide. —J. W. Attig photo

About 2.5 miles north of the junction of County FF and a mile north of Pike Lake, U.S. 51 rises onto the hummocky topography of the Winegar moraine. Here, the hummocky zone is about 8 miles wide. This east-west-trending upland is also the Lake Superior–Mississippi River drainage divide. Long before automobiles and U.S. 51 existed, this divide had to be traversed by the Flambeau Trail, which climbed 900 feet in elevation from Lake Superior over the Penokee Range a few miles west of present Hurley, and then south to the wetlands of the Turtle Flambeau Flowage. Though travelers followed waterways for much of the trail, they had to portage 6 miles to reach the headwaters of the Flambeau River, which was an important route across northern Wisconsin for Native Americans and fur traders. It is sobering to consider that trek as we speed effortlessly across this area in the comfort of our modern automobile. Keep in mind that, besides the sheer physical effort to clamber over such terrain, our rugged fore-runners also would have been barraged by countless blood-thirsty insects as they lugged heavy canoes and baggage across the divide. Besides mosquitoes and blackflies, there was the infamous no-see-um, a fitting name said to have been derived from an Indian word, *moseeums,* which was adopted by frontier lumberjacks. The no-see-um is immortalized today in four Wisconsin place-names.

Hurley and the Penokee-Gogebic Iron Range

The Hurley area provides an opportunity to sample the geology of the southern margin of the ancient Superior continent as well as a century of iron mining. Bedrock is at or near the surface along the highway for the last 6 miles south of Hurley. Many of the bedrock outcrops in this area have been glacially polished and striated. The bedrock exposures are of pink and gray Archean granite older than 2,500 million years and part of the crust of the old Superior continent.

At the south edge of Hurley on the west side of the highway is a section of a large rock cylinder 5.5 feet in diameter of this granite. Several more sections of the same huge rock core are displayed outside the Wisconsin border visitor center at the junction of U.S. 51 and U.S. 2 on the north side of town. The core was cut in the 1940s by a large drill at the Cary Iron Mine on the south edge of town. The visitor center has an excellent display about the history of mining on the Penokee-Gogebic iron range, which extends across the Wisconsin-Michigan border through Hurley.

The Wisconsin side of the mining district occurs along a northeast-southwest-trending prominent ridge known as the Penokee Range, which is described in one tourist brochure as "rising teton-like with its breathtaking skyline and vistas, and offering unlimited opportunities for adventure." Overstated? Well, perhaps a trifle. In 1852, early government geologist

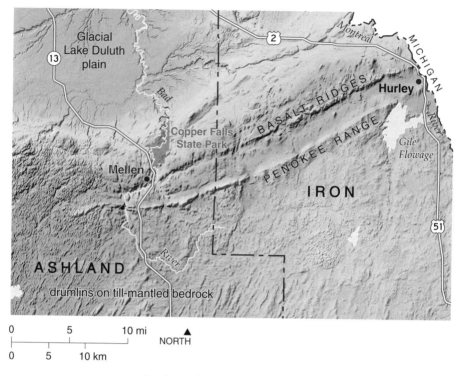

Landscape image of the Hurley area.

Charles Whittlesey intended to name this the "Pewabic Range" for the Chippewa word for "iron," but a government printer somehow misspelled it as "Penokie," which became "Penokee."

Magnetic properties of iron-bearing sedimentary rocks in an area 20 miles west of Hurley, near Penokee and Mellen, had attracted attention in 1848, but it was not until 1883 that mining began in Michigan on the Gogebic part of the range. Although the Ironwood banded iron formation had first been discovered in the western Penokee Range in Wisconsin, metamorphism rendered it unsuitable there for ore. Whittlesey wryly observed that these "rocks have been the sport of giant forces which tossed and tilted them about at various angles and elevations realizing the fable of Atlas" (Whittlesey, 1862–63). The metamorphism decreased eastward, however, so that minable ore was found from Upson, 10 miles west of Hurley, eastward into Michigan. By 1885 there were six mines, by 1886 thirteen, and in 1895 twenty mines dotting the Penokee-Gogebic iron range. Because the strata containing the iron formation dip steeply, mining had to utilize underground shafts and tunnels. After World War II, underground mining could no longer compete with cheaper open pits in Minnesota, where the strata are nearly flat lying. The Cary Mine at Hurley, Wisconsin's last, closed in 1967.

In the heyday of iron mining, Hurley earned a reputation as Wisconsin's city of sin, with the motto "Where Highway 51 ends, the fun begins." Hard-drinking, fist-swinging miners, tough ladies of the night, and a touch of exaggeration created a legend, which persisted long after the miners and ladies had departed. Around 1970, the old county jail was converted to an

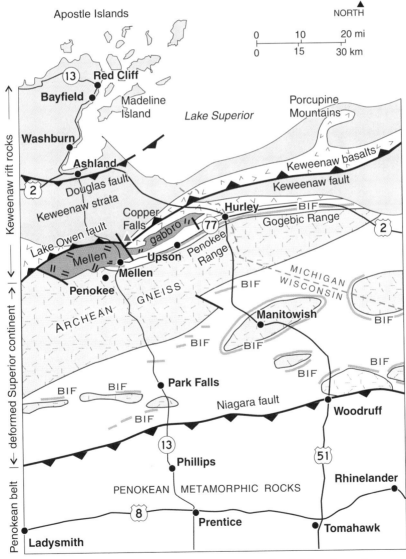

Bedrock geology of north-central Wisconsin. BIF, *banded iron formation.*

Large core of Archean gneiss displayed at the highway information center along U.S. 51 on the north edge of Hurley. Dark, angular fragments are of older metamorphic rock that was intruded by granite. —N. Dott photo

unusual hotel. In 1977, a group of touring international geologists was treated to a memorable night in converted jail cells. A Russian was delighted to be lodged in the solitary confinement cell, while an Argentinean made a jailbreak to visit infamous Silver Street and meet a Spanish-speaking exotic dancer who had taken his fancy.

Animikie Strata

The Ironwood banded iron formation is part of the Animikie sequence of sedimentary rocks that also includes the Palms quartzite and the Tyler formation. These sediments were deposited upon eroded Archean granites. To the east in Michigan, however, a slightly older Proterozoic sedimentary sequence is present between the Palms quartzite and the Archean rocks; presumably these older sediments were also deposited in Wisconsin, but tilting and erosion removed them from here before deposition of the Palms sands.

The Palms quartzite was initially sand and mud deposited by tidal currents as a very shallow ocean first flooded the southern margin of the deeply eroded ancient Superior continent about 2,200 million years ago. The iron-rich sediments in Hurley overlie the Palms, and above them is the Tyler formation, a thick sequence of black mudrock, now slate, and interstratified

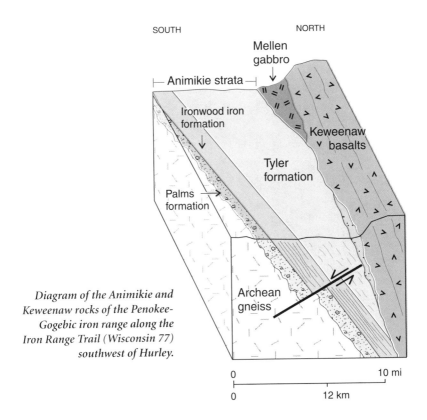

Diagram of the Animikie and Keweenaw rocks of the Penokee-Gogebic iron range along the Iron Range Trail (Wisconsin 77) southwest of Hurley.

dark, impure sandstone. You can see examples of the Tyler formation at the junction of U.S. 51 and U.S. 2 and along Wisconsin 77, especially 1 mile east of Iron Belt, in Upson at Upson Falls Park.

Whereas the Palms quartzite and the Ironwood banded iron formation were deposited in shallow ocean environments on a continental shelf, the Tyler sediments reflect a deepening of the environment, which favored the accumulation of fine muddy sediments relatively rich in organic matter, which contributes to their dark color. Occasional influxes of heterogeneous sand were carried into the deeper water environment by turbulent flows of muddy and sandy water driven down sloping sea bottoms by gravity. Unlike the sand of the Palms formation, which was derived from the old Superior continent to the north, some of the sand of the Tyler came from the south. Therefore, we believe that a profound structural change faulted and depressed the old continental margin to deepen the ocean environment there and simultaneously to raise land farther south, which shed sand into the deepened ocean. What could this change have been? It was the approach of the Penokean volcanic island chain, the roots of which are crossed on U.S. 51 to the south of Hurley between Manitowish Waters and Mosinee.

Impure sandstone and shales of the Precambrian Tyler formation exposed at the U.S. 2–U.S. 51 interchange on the north side of Hurley. These strata were deposited during the deepening of the Penokean Ocean between the Superior continent and the Penokean volcanic island chain. —R. H. Dott, Jr., photo

The collision of the volcanic chain with the Superior continental margin deformed and metamorphosed the Penokee-Gogebic strata slightly, but not nearly so severely as the mangled rocks farther south, especially south of Woodruff. The steep northward dip of about 60 degrees of the Penokee-Gogebic strata was imposed by the much later tilting and thrust faulting of the younger Keweenaw basalts just north of Hurley and at Copper Falls near Mellen to the west. These basalts form a prominent ridge that parallels the Penokee-Gogebic iron range from Hurley west to Mellen.

Penokee Iron Range Trail

The Ironwood banded iron formation is exposed in Hurley at the corner of Iron Street and Third Avenue only two blocks south of Silver Street, the city center. The outcrop is beside the old courthouse, which now houses a county museum with some mining lore. Within Hurley and adjacent Ironwood, Michigan, collapsed mine tunnels have created a bit of a problem, which has been solved by creating city parks over some of them.

Wisconsin 77 southwest of Hurley is the Penokee Iron Range Trail with several historical heritage sites. Montreal, 3.5 miles southwest of Hurley, had the largest mining operation in Wisconsin. It was a town designed by a benevolent company with rows of identical company houses and an elegant community center, the Hamilton Club. The Montreal Mine was 4,335 feet deep, said to be the deepest iron mine in the world around 1900. It produced 45,747,708 tons of ore from 1886 to 1962.

Half a mile east of Montreal, Giles Falls provides excellent exposures of the Palms quartzite, which underlies the Ironwood banded iron formation. West of Montreal at Pence, the old Flambeau Trail crosses Wisconsin 77. Just west of Pence, Plummer Road leads 0.1 miles south to the Plummer Mine site with its photogenic headframe still standing, the only one left in the district. This mine was 2,367 feet deep and operated from 1904 to 1924. The Iron Range Trail continues another 15 miles to Mellen, with several outcrops of the Tyler slate along the way, especially around Upson. The Ironwood banded iron formation occurs on the west end of Mount Whittlesey, 2 miles southeast of Mellen via County P.

U.S. 2
Superior—Hurley
104 miles (170 km)

U.S. 2 across northern Wisconsin is part of the Lake Superior Circle Tour, which also traverses Minnesota, Michigan, and Ontario. At Superior, St. Louis Bay provides clear evidence of the ongoing drowning of the western end of the Lake Superior shoreline caused by differential rebound of the earth's crust after glaciation. The outlet of Lake Superior at its eastern end is rising more rapidly than the western end of the basin, so the water level is slowly rising in the Superior area. St. Louis Bay is the drowned mouth of the St. Louis River. Sand spits extend nearly all the way across the head of the lake and protect the harbor at Superior-Duluth. The most spectacular spits, the combined Wisconsin and Minnesota Points, are about 1 mile offshore and are more than one-quarter mile wide in places. The highest points on them are more than 20 feet above lake level. They formed where the shallow bottom of St. Louis Bay interfered with incoming waves, building a sandbar on the lake floor several thousand years ago. Sand moved by shore currents extended the bars completely across the mouth of the bay except for the inlet to the harbor, which lies nearer the Wisconsin shore.

U.S. 2 crosses the Lake Superior rift of late Precambrian time. Opposite Superior at Duluth, Minnesota, Keweenaw basalts and gabbro form cliffs along the northwest shore of Lake Superior—the west side of the rift. Some

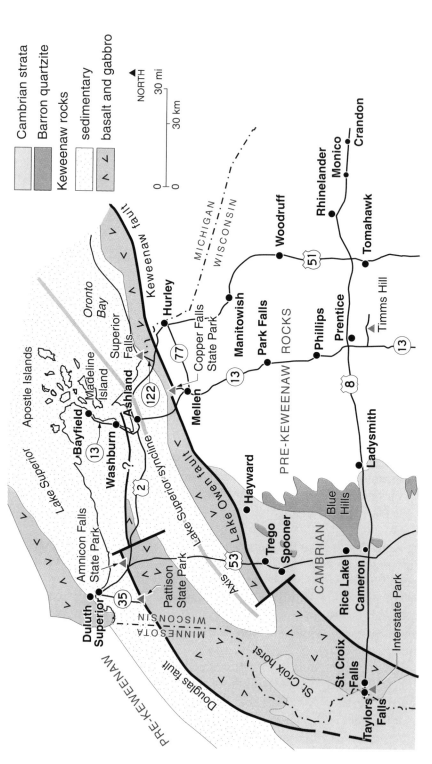

Bedrock geology of the Lake Superior rift in northernmost Wisconsin.

of the same basalts appear just south of Superior, where the Douglas fault has raised them, forming an escarpment on the skyline south of the city. Much of the route from Superior to Hurley, however, is across the Lake Superior lowland draped with red Glacial Lake Duluth sediments, which overlie the Keweenaw sedimentary and volcanic rocks. The old rift rocks are exposed only at scattered localities such as Pattison State Park, Amnicon Falls State Park, on the Bayfield Peninsula, the Apostle Islands, and along the Lake Superior shore near the Michigan border. Still older Precambrian rocks, which pre-date the Lake Superior rift, are exposed around Hurley.

Pattison State Park

Follow Wisconsin 35 for 15 miles south of Superior to see the spectacular Big and Little Manitou Falls in Pattison State Park, where river erosion has cut through clayey Glacial Lake Duluth sediment to reveal the bedrock. At 165 feet, Big Manitou is Wisconsin's highest waterfall. Although concealed here, the Douglas fault passes through this park as it does at Amnicon

Big Manitou Falls over late Precambrian basalt in Pattison State Park south of Superior.
—Photo courtesy of the Wisconsin Department of Natural Resources

Falls State Park 15 miles northeast on U.S. 2. About 900 million years ago, it raised and tilted the Keweenaw basalts of the Lake Superior rift. The faulted basalts form the escarpment that overlooks the Lake Superior lowlands to the north. The basalts were faulted against younger, late Precambrian red sandstones, which you can see in the walls of the canyon below Big Manitou Falls. Beneath both falls, prospectors in the nineteenth century dug shallow caves and pits in search of copper minerals, which were known to occur in similar rocks in northern Michigan; yields here were very poor.

From Wisconsin 35 just above Big Manitou Falls, you can look north across the lowlands to see the city of Superior and the cliffs at Duluth, formed by the same resistant basalts. The lowland between is underlain by less-resistant late Precambrian sedimentary rocks like those in the canyon below Big Falls and by the deposits of Glacial Lake Duluth. Sandy beach deposits between Little Manitou Falls and Interfalls Lake mark the southeastern shoreline of Glacial Lake Duluth.

Superior to Amnicon Falls State Park

From Superior eastward to the intersection with U.S. 53, U.S. 2 crosses an area of red clayey till and Glacial Lake Duluth sediment that were washed by waves of later, and lower, ice-marginal lakes in the Lake Superior basin. At Amnicon Falls State Park, 15 miles southeast of Superior and just east of the U.S. 53/U.S. 2 junction, the Amnicon River has eroded through Quaternary sediments and cascades over the Douglas fault escarpment, exposing tilted and faulted basalts. All along its southwest-to-northeast trend, the fault has raised the hard Keweenaw basalts several thousand feet both upward and northward against the late Precambrian sandstones. The topographic escarpment owes its origin to the fact that the basalts are more resistant to erosion than the sedimentary strata. A guide to the geology of Amnicon Falls State Park is available at the park entrance.

There are three waterfalls in the park, the upper two of which flow over resistant basalts, whereas the Lower Falls is over red sandstones. The steeply inclined Douglas fault crosses the river just below the Upper Falls and adjacent Snake Pit Falls. A zone of shattered rock, or breccia, which crosses the river about 80 feet in front of the Upper Falls, marks the fault. Downstream the red sandstone is inclined about 10 degrees toward Lake Superior. If the Douglas fault did not exist here, the basalt would lie several thousand feet below the sandstone and, like it, would only be inclined 10 degrees. Downstream from the falls at the end of a nature trail, the sandstone was quarried long ago when brownstone was in fashion for buildings.

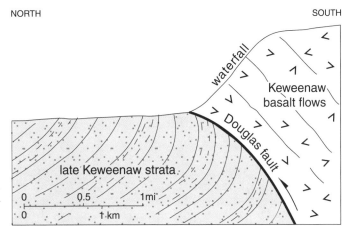

NORTH   SOUTH

Keweenaw basalt flows

Douglas fault

The Douglas fault at Amnicon Falls State Park along U.S. 2 east of Superior.

late Keweenaw strata

waterfall

| 0 | 0.5 | 1mi |
| 0 | | 1 km |

Lake Superior Lowland

Between Amnicon Falls State Park and Hurley on the Michigan border, U.S. 2 mostly passes over Glacial Lake Duluth sediments and crosses the shoreline several times. The steep banks along the rivers flowing north to Lake Superior expose clayey till and lake sediment in many places, and some have eroded through soft sediment to bedrock, forming many waterfalls. Between Amnicon Falls State Park and Poplar, the route passes over a wave-washed surface of Glacial Lake Duluth. At Maple, U.S. 2 crosses several low, sandy beach ridges a few hundred feet west of the center of town at an elevation of about 1,080 feet. Then the highway climbs above the level of Glacial Lake Duluth just east of Maple.

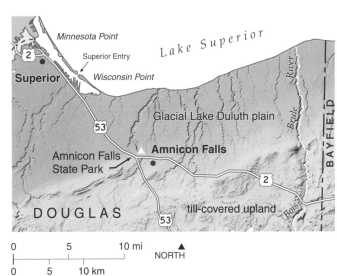

Landscape image showing the deep valleys that rivers have cut into the clayey till and lake sediment of the Glacial Lake Duluth plain.

Minnesota Point

Superior Entry

Wisconsin Point

Superior

Lake Superior

Glacial Lake Duluth plain

Amnicon Falls State Park

Amnicon Falls

till-covered upland

DOUGLAS

BAYFIELD

Brule River

Bois

| 0 | 5 | 10 mi |
| 0 | 5 | 10 km |

NORTH

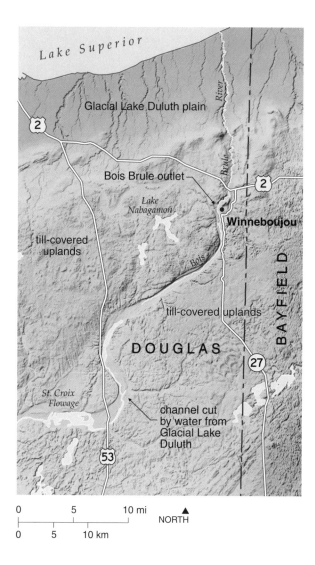

Landscape image of the Bois-Brule outlet of Glacial Lake Duluth that funneled the overflowing lake water south to the St. Croix River.

East of Maple, U. S. 2 crosses a hilly upland of bouldery till and outwash before descending into the mouth of the Bois-Brule outlet of Glacial Lake Duluth at Brule. A side trip of a few miles south of Brule on Wisconsin 27 follows the outlet channel cut by the outflow from the lake. Although the area is forested, and views are limited, the walls of the channel can be seen in a few places. For early explorers and fur traders, the Bois Brule River provided relatively easy access between Lake Superior and the Mississippi River drainage by a portage 30 miles to the south into the headwaters of the St. Croix River.

From Maple east through Iron River and beyond, U.S. 2 crosses a broad hilly upland of pre–Glacial Lake Duluth bouldery till and outwash before dropping back down to the Glacial Lake Duluth shoreline about 2 miles west of Ino, where the road crosses the flat top of a delta deposited into Glacial Lake Duluth, as well as several beach ridges of that lake. Between Ino and Ashland, the highway descends onto wave-washed till and lake plain. The Lake Superior shore bluffs in the Ashland area are composed mostly of red clayey till and lake sediment.

Three miles west of Ashland at the junction of U.S. 2 and Wisconsin 13 is the Northern Great Lakes Visitor Center, which provides interpretations of both natural and cultural history as well as recreational information about the Lake Superior region. There are some geological displays of interest.

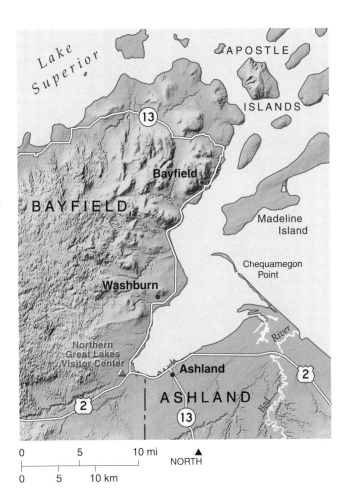

Landscape image of the Ashland-Bayfield area.

Chequamegon Bay and the Apostle Islands to the north have figured in Chippewa tribal legends and also in Henry Wadsworth Longfellow's *The Song of Hiawatha*. At the mouth of Chequamegon Bay 10 miles to the northeast, a long sand spit, Chequamegon Point, and Long Island provide the protection for a fine harbor. These formed in a similar way to Wisconsin Point at Superior, beginning as an offshore bar several thousand years ago and then growing lakeward as sand was added by longshore currents. One Chippewa legend, however, said that a powerful spirit constructed the spit to trap the Great Beaver of Lake Superior. Ashland's protected harbor made it an important port for the shipment of iron ore mined along the Penokee-

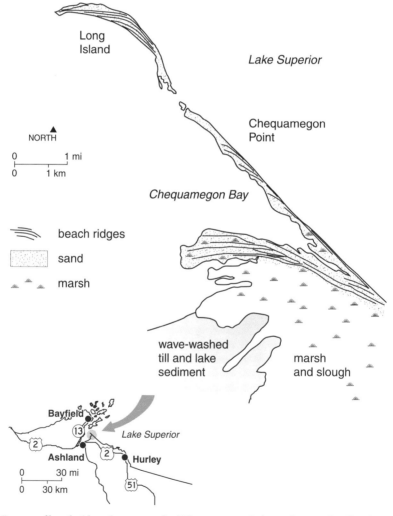

Pattern of beach ridges shows growth of Chequamegon Point and Long Island by the addition of sand by shore current. Wisconsin Point at Superior formed in a similar way.

Gogebic iron range to the southeast until the late 1960s. A single, large ore-loading dock facility still looms silently over the harbor where there were four in the heyday of iron mining. Beginning in the 1870s, Ashland also became a popular resort area. A large hotel and nearby resorts hosted such notables as Theodore Roosevelt, Calvin Coolidge, and Chicago's Marshall Field. On nearby Madeline Island, a cluster of cottages built by wealthy Nebraska families earned the nickname Nebraska Row. See the road guide **Wisconsin 13: Abbotsford—Bayfield** for a discussion of the Keweenaw rocks of the Bayfield Peninsula and Apostle Islands.

East of Ashland, U.S. 2 continues over Glacial Lake Duluth deposits. For 30 miles it passes through the Bad River Indian Reservation, the second largest of Wisconsin's several reservations. Near Odanah, U.S. 2 crosses the broad floodplain near the confluence of the White and Bad Rivers. The clayey, wave-washed plain east of Odanah has small northeast-southwest-trending drumlins indicating sedimentation in Glacial Lake Duluth here was not sufficient to completely obliterate features on the pre-lake till surface.

Two miles west of Cedar, U.S. 2 crosses an area of east-west-trending sand dunes deposited near the shore of Glacial Lake Duluth. The dunes are up to 20 feet high. Beaches, which formed as the water level of Glacial Lake Duluth dropped from its maximum elevation of about 1,100 feet, wrap around the northern end of the upland on which the dunes formed. The 1,100-foot shoreline is just north of Cedar.

At Cedar, a 4-mile side trip south on Wisconsin 169 takes you to Gurney, which sits on the flat, sandy surface of a delta built into Glacial Lake Duluth. Two miles farther south at the 90-foot-high Potato River Falls, erosion has cut down through red clayey till and Glacial Lake Duluth sediments to expose Keweenaw conglomerate, shale, and sandstone of late Precambrian age. These same sedimentary rocks are also exposed at Copper Falls State Park, which is about 7 miles farther southwest via Wisconsin 169, but is described in **Wisconsin 13: Abbotsford—Bayfield**.

Three and a half miles east of Cedar along U.S. 2, the Lake View Cemetery sits on the moraine that marks the maximum extent of the ice readvance that blocked the eastern outlets of Lake Superior to form Glacial Lake Duluth. The Lake View moraine, which formed about 10,000 years ago, is the low ridge just south of the highway, and it crosses the road about 1 mile to the east of the cemetery. About 1 mile east of the intersection with Wisconsin 122, U.S. 2 crosses a low swampy area and a railroad. This lowland is part of a system of channels cut by water draining westward from Glacial Lake Ontonagon on the Upper Peninsula of Michigan into Glacial Lake Duluth. After another 2 miles the highway descends into another low swampy part of this channel system before rising onto bedrock with a very patchy cover of glacial sediment in the Hurley area.

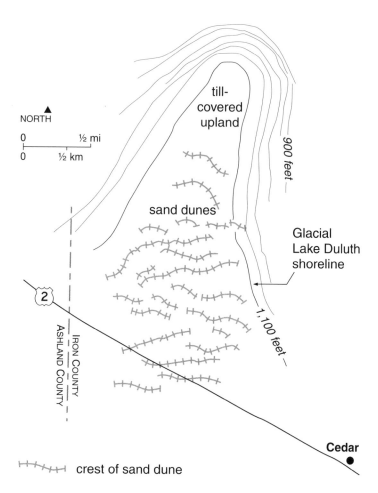

NORTH

0   ½ mi
0   ½ km

till-covered upland

sand dunes

900 feet

Glacial Lake Duluth shoreline

1,100 feet

2

ASHLAND COUNTY | IRON COUNTY

Cedar

⊢⊢⊢⊢⊢⊣   crest of sand dune

Glacial Lake Duluth shoreline and shorelines of lower ice-marginal lakes
wrap around an upland west of Cedar. Sand dunes formed near the shore.

Montreal River and Hurley

From Saxon, 11 miles west of Hurley, a 5-mile side trip north on Wisconsin 122 provides access to a viewpoint for scenic rock exposures and waterfalls on the Montreal River, which here separates Wisconsin and Michigan. To view the 90-foot-high Superior Falls tumbling over resistant red Keweenaw sandstone, cross into Michigan for a short distance and park at a power plant substation. A short walk from here takes you to the Lake Superior shore on Oronto Bay, where red sandstone is exposed. These sandstones overlie the Keweenaw basalts. More than 100 feet of red till and clayey Glacial Lake Duluth sediments are also exposed in the higher parts of the bluffs above Oronto Bay.

Between Wisconsin 122 and Hurley, U.S. 2 crosses obliquely over the entire Keweenaw basalt sequence, which is inclined steeply northward toward Lake Superior. Hurley lies at the base of this more than 20,000-foot-thick volcanic sequence. A major unconformity separates the Keweenaw rocks from older Precambrian metamorphosed sedimentary rocks. Steeply inclined dark sandstones and thin slates (Tyler formation) are exposed in roadcuts at the junction of U.S. 2 and U.S. 51 on the north edge of Hurley. The base of the Keweenaw rocks lies just north of the junction but is not clearly visible here. Eagle Bluff Scenic Overlook on the Hurley golf course just west of town (via County D) is very near the base and provides an excellent view north toward Lake Superior. The first basalt flows have pillow structures, which indicate that they were erupted into water, presumably a large lake within the Lake Superior rift depression.

Although once a brawling city of sin echoing with a cacophony of drunken miners, gamblers, and prostitutes, Hurley is today a quiet shadow of its former self. The pre-Keweenaw geology of the area and the Penokee-Gogebic iron range extending from here to the southwest is described in **I-39/U.S. 51: Stevens Point—Hurley**.

U.S. 8
St. Croix Falls—Pembine
246 miles (396 km)

St. Croix Falls is within the area glaciated by the late Wisconsin advance of the Superior Lobe across northwestern Wisconsin. The subtle upland crossed by U.S. 8 about one-half mile east of St. Croix Falls is a moraine deposited by the advance of the Grantsburg Lobe into the area from the west after the Superior Lobe had receded from the area. By advancing beyond the St. Croix River, the Grantsburg Lobe dammed the river north of St. Croix Falls, resulting in the formation of Glacial Lake Grantsburg in western Wisconsin and adjacent Minnesota.

Interstate Park and the St. Croix Horst
Wisconsin and Minnesota jointly created Interstate Park in 1900 because of the 300-foot-deep scenic gorge, the Dalles of the St. Croix River, cut through a series of resistant Keweenaw basalt lava flows. It is Wisconsin's oldest park, which an 1850 visitor judged to be "One of God's beauteous spots on earth." St. Croix Falls, Wisconsin, and Taylors Falls, Minnesota, were established around 1840 at the falls, which marked the upriver limit of steamboat navigation. It was an opportune site for damming the river

*Late Precambrian basalt
exposed in the Dalles of
the St. Croix River at
Interstate Park. View
looking upstream at the
U.S. 8 bridge and dam in
distance.* —Photo courtesy
of the Wisconsin Department
of Tourism

for milling; the dam is upstream from the U.S. 8 bridge across the river. During the lumbering days of the late nineteenth century and before the first dam was built in 1905, the Dalles experienced many spectacular logjams.

St. Croix Falls lies at the western end of the Ice Age National Scenic Trail and the park's interpretive center features special exhibits relating to glaciation of the region. This area is a unit of the Ice Age National Scientific Reserve and also lies within a National Scenic Riverway. Interstate Park is especially noted for many potholes worn in the basalt by turbulent eddies in which stones were whirled around and around, carving circular or cylindrical pockets in the rock. You can see these along trails on both sides of the river a short distance below the U.S. 8 bridge. Some of the potholes are more than 100 feet above the present river level, so must have been cut by the huge torrent of glacial meltwater that swept down the St. Croix Valley when Glacial Lake Duluth drained through the Bois-Brule outlet about 80 miles northeast, which is discussed in roadguides for **U.S. 2: Haugen—Superior and U.S. 53: Superior—Hurley**.

The park is located on a raised fault block called the St. Croix horst. About 1,000 million years ago, some of the boundary faults along the Lake Superior rift were reactivated, but with reversed motion, raising the axis of the former down-faulted rift. Erosion stripped off all of the late Keweenaw sedimentary rocks and exposed the older basalts. Geologists have identified at least ten separate lava flows within the park. The top of each flow has many pore holes formed by gas bubbles trapped when the lava congealed; many of these were later filled with light-colored minerals precipitated from percolating water.

When the Cambrian sea flooded this part of the Great Lakes region around 500 million years ago, hills of basalt a few hundred feet high became islands. The setting was like that in the Baraboo District of south-central Wisconsin, although the islands in the Cambrian sea there were higher and were composed of quartzite rather than basalt. At Interstate Park, Cambrian conglomerate contains huge boulders of basalt that are as much as 10 feet in diameter; they simply fell from the sea cliffs during storms and were buried without being moved by waves, thus retaining an angular shape. Smaller cobbles and boulders up to 3 feet in diameter are

Pothole eroded into basalt by a whirlpool with trapped pebbles as abrasive. Interstate Park, St. Croix, Wisconsin. —Photo courtesy of the Wisconsin Department of Natural Resources

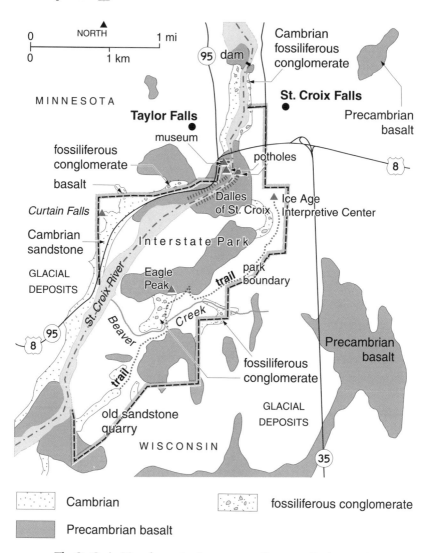

*The St. Croix River has cut a deep gorge at Interstate Park, exposing
Precambrian basalt and Cambrian sandstone and conglomerate.*

mostly rounded, indicating that storm waves could tumble and roll these
smaller sizes enough to wear off their corners. As at Baraboo, the Interstate
Park area also experienced occasional violent tropical storms, which generated waves as much as 20 feet high that pounded the basaltic islands. At
Interstate Park, unlike Baraboo, the Cambrian conglomerates and sandstones
deposited against the ancient sea cliffs contain fossil brachiopod shells and
trilobite fragments. As might be expected for such a rigorous environment
at the base of sea cliffs, most of this material was broken and concentrated
in thin shelly layers.

You can see Cambrian conglomerate and fossiliferous sandstones along trails on both sides of the river. On the Wisconsin side, for example, look for them in Beaver Creek valley, crossed by the Silverbrook Trail about one-quarter mile south of Eagle Peak. On the Minnesota side, they are exposed just south of the town of Taylors Falls and west of U.S. 8 behind a commercial miniature railroad facility. One-half mile farther south is Curtain Falls Trail, the northern branch of which passes an exposure of fossiliferous

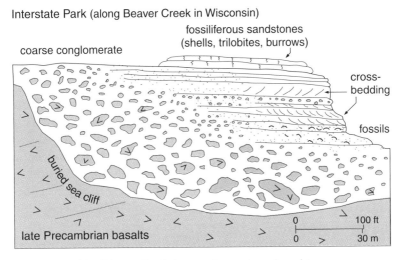

Fossiliferous Cambrian conglomerate and sandstone deposited against sea cliffs of late Precambrian basalt.

Cambrian sandstone, which is in direct contact with the Precambrian basalt—surprisingly without any coarse conglomerate between them. The southern branch of this trail climbs higher and exposes a cliff of Cambrian sandstone, which forms Curtain Falls. This sandstone contains no conglomerate but has undulatory or hummocky lamination characteristic of deposition by storm waves. This sandstone also contains some scattered shells and zones with animal burrows. In its lower part, it also contains grains of the green mineral glauconite. Although this mineral formed on the seafloor where deposition was, on the average, very slow, it was moved and redeposited by brief episodes of violent storm waves.

St. Croix Falls to Cameron

About 12 miles east of St. Croix Falls, near the eastern junction with Wisconsin 46, U.S. 8 crosses the buried Lake Owen fault zone, which marks the eastern boundary of the Lake Superior rift. Between St. Croix Falls and

Upper and Lower Turtle Lakes, U.S. 8 crosses about 25 miles of pitted and unpitted outwash and hummocky glacial topography. Many of the erratic boulders here were derived from the Keweenaw basalts, which occur between St. Croix Falls and Lake Superior. The moraine ridge marking the maximum extent of the late Wisconsin advance of the Superior Lobe crosses the highway just west of the junction with County T, 1 mile west of the town of Turtle Lake.

For the next 25 miles east from Turtle Lake, U.S. 8 crosses a gently rolling landscape. Till was deposited here during an earlier advance of the Superior Lobe into the northern part of the Western Uplands, which may have occurred just shortly before the major late Wisconsin advance. The lowlands are pitted outwash plains; a wayside park at Turtle Lake is on one such plain. The Turtle Lakes are large pits formed where buried ice melted. From Barron to Cameron, the road traverses a broad area of pitted outwash. Cameron, at the junction with U.S. 53, is on a broad area of pitted outwash deposited by meltwater rivers flowing from the Chippewa Lobe to the east and the Superior Lobe to the west. Much of the outwash in this area was deposited by rivers flowing from the area of the junction between these two lobes, which was about 15 miles north of Cameron.

Glacial geology of the Cameron area.

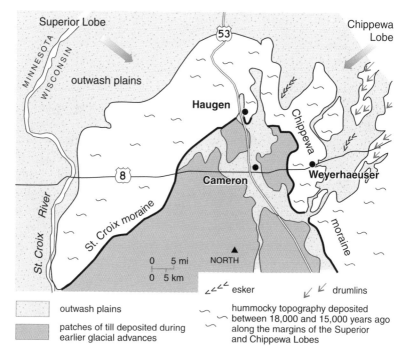

Cameron to Pembine

Cameron lies within the northern edge of the Western Uplands just south of the terminal moraines of the last glaciation. About 4 miles east of Cameron, U.S. 8 crosses Pokegama Creek, which flows in a meltwater channel, before rising onto an area of thin, patchy till on bedrock. This till was deposited prior to the late Wisconsin advance of ice that deposited the Chippewa moraine about 19,000 years ago.

The bedrock near Cameron is Cambrian and Ordovician and was deposited over an irregular topography eroded from Precambrian quartzite. In the Blue Hills northeast of Cameron, a 1,300-foot-thick sequence of gently tilted, red Barron quartzite of Precambrian age unconformably overlies the complexly deformed Penokean rocks, which include granites 1,850 to 1,765 million years old. This quartzite appears to be identical with the Baraboo quartzite 160 miles to the southeast. In turn, these seem to be equivalent with the red Sioux quartzite in southwestern Minnesota, suggesting that an enormous volume of quartz sand was deposited as a vast blanket across the deeply eroded roots of the Penokean Mountains between 1,700 and 1,600 million years ago. All three contain thin layers of red, orange, or purple, fine-grained mudstones that Native Americans quarried for making their ceremonial pipes called *calumets*.

Five miles east of Cameron, a low roadcut exposes flat-lying, fine-grained Cambrian sandstones containing many brachiopod fossils together with animal burrows. At the west end of the cut are poorly exposed conglomerates with angular red quartzite fragments up to 3 or 4 feet long. A patch of red quartzite low in the exposure was the apparent source of the fragments. Better exposures a mile or so to the south show a greater thickness of coarse conglomerate, which is identical with the Cambrian quartzite-bearing conglomerates in the Baraboo area. These two areas are remarkably similar.

Just before the Barron-Rusk County line, U.S. 8 crosses into the Chippewa moraine, which marks the edge of the Northern Highlands. The moraine here consists of high-relief, hummocky topography with many ice-walled lake plains. Weyerhaeuser is on one of these. The Chippewa Moraine Unit of the Ice Age National Scientific Reserve has displays and informational materials describing the Ice Age, glaciers, and glacial landscapes. It also provides access to the Ice Age National Scenic Trail. To reach the unit, take Wisconsin 40 south from Bruce about 20 miles to County M and head east on it for about 4 miles; watch for Ice Age Drive to the south.

At Bruce, U.S. 8 crosses the Chippewa River 12 miles north of its confluence with the Flambeau River, which rises in northeastern Wisconsin and drains much of the north-central part of the state. Both rivers were important highways for Native Americans, trappers, and the lumbering industry. East of Bruce, U.S. 8 leaves the hummocky zone of the Chippewa Lobe. Faint drumlins occur on till-covered uplands separated by wetlands.

At Ladysmith, the highway crosses the Flambeau River, which flows in an outwash plain of the Chippewa Lobe.

The open-pit Flambeau Copper Mine operated 1 mile southwest of Ladysmith for ten years until 1996. The deposit was small but rich in copper minerals plus some zinc, gold, and silver. It occurred within a complex of metamorphosed Penokean volcanic rocks, which are overlain by Cambrian sandstone. This type of deposit is commonly associated with rhyolitic volcanism. Metal-bearing solutions rise through the flanks of volcanic islands to form seafloor hot springs, where metal-charged solutions react with seawater to deposit the ore minerals. The Flambeau Mine extracted the richest ore and then the land was reclaimed by filling the pit and replanting the surface, which can be seen on the west side of Wisconsin 27 only 1.25 miles south of U.S. 8.

Between Ladysmith and Prentice, U.S. 8 traverses a broad area of low-relief drumlins on till-covered uplands separated by wetlands. From the road, it is difficult to recognize the hills as drumlins, but maps and air photos show that they trend northeast-southwest, formed by the southwestward-flowing ice of the Chippewa Lobe. About 2 miles west of the junction with Wisconsin 13 near Prentice, U.S. 8 crosses an esker that is mined for sand and gravel. The outwash plain along the South Fork of the Jump River at Prentice is also mined for sand and gravel.

Eight miles southeast of Prentice via County C is Timms Hill, the highest point in Wisconsin at 1,952 feet above sea level. Timms Hill consists of a complex of sediments deposited between the Wisconsin Valley and Chippewa Lobes. Included are lake sediments, till, and outwash. The hill is at least in part a remnant of an ice-walled lake. About 8 miles east of Prentice, near Brantwood, the landscape of low-relief, poorly formed drumlins separated by wetlands continues, but the orientation of the drumlins is different. Here, they trend northwest-southeast because they were formed by the southeastward flowing ice of the Wisconsin Valley Lobe. Eighteen miles east of Prentice, U.S. 8 crosses the Somo River. A long esker, which begins north of the highway, can be traced southeastward along this river for about 15 miles, crossing I-39/U.S. 51 just south of Tomahawk. East of the Somo River, U.S. 8 crosses several more miles of drumlins and a broad pitted outwash plain before reaching the junction with I-39/U.S. 51. The many large lakes in this area occupy collapse depressions (kettles) in the outwash plain where isolated blocks of ice left by the receding glacier slowly melted.

Between the I-39/U.S. 51 intersection and Rhinelander, U.S. 8 crosses a broad area of pitted and collapsed outwash. Our route crosses the Wisconsin River at Rhinelander, gateway to northeastern Wisconsin's northwoods and lakes country. This is true Paul Bunyan land as commemorated by the Logging Museum at Pioneer Park on the south side of the city. The irregular, hilly landscape that extends for many miles on both sides of the river is mostly pitted outwash and collapsed outwash and till deposited as the Wisconsin Valley and Langlade glacial lobes wasted from the area. Some of the high areas of collapsed outwash are linear features with a strong northwest-southeast trend. They mark recessional positions of the Langlade Lobe. The roadside rest area on the north side of the road about 3 miles east of George Lake is on a northeast-southwest-trending drumlin shaped beneath the Langlade Lobe.

At Monico, Precambrian volcanic rocks of the Penokean volcanic island chain appear again. At the southwest corner of the junction with U.S. 45/ Wisconsin 47, glacially striated and grooved pillow basalt is exposed beside the highway. Beneath the Pelican River wetlands about 5 miles west of Monico, a copper deposit was discovered in the 1970s, but it was too small to be worth mining. It is of the same type as at Ladysmith. South of Monico 2 miles on the west side of U.S. 45/Wisconsin 47, there is an outcrop of granite that is about 1,765 million years old. It must have been intruded into the Penokean volcanic complex after the completion of Penokean

Precambrian pillow basalt erupted on the floor of the Penokean ocean basin. Outcrop is in Monico. —R. H. Dott, Jr., photo

mountain building. Monico is also approximately at the divide between westward drainage to the Wisconsin River and eastward drainage to Lake Michigan.

Between Monico and the Wolf River crossing about 7 miles east, U.S. 8 crosses several poorly formed drumlins separated by broad wetlands. Immediately east of the Wolf River, the road crosses an upland area with spectacular long drumlins. Many of these narrow, northeast-southwest-trending drumlins of the Langlade Lobe are over 1 mile long. The highway crosses them almost at a right angle.

South of Crandon is Mole Lake, the site of another copper-zinc deposit associated with Penokean volcanic rocks. This large, rich deposit was discovered by drilling in 1975, but twenty-eight years later when this book was completed, the site was sold to local Indian tribes and no mining is planned. The deposit, which is one of the largest of its type in the world, lies in the headwaters region of the Wolf River, which is Wisconsin's most treasured whitewater trout stream and is designated a National Wild and Scenic River. It is also adjacent to the Mole Lake and Potawatomi Indian Reservations, and is upstream from the Menominee and Stockbridge-Munsee Reservations. There are many recreational homes in the area, too. Because the ore contains sulfur, there is fear of the formation of sulfuric acid through the interaction of groundwater with the ore during mining. In addition, waste or spoil piles at the surface would have to be carefully designed and monitored to avoid the release of toxic metals and acids into surface waters. Finally, because the deposit extends 1,700 feet below the surface, it would have to be mined through underground workings, so there is fear that the necessary pumping of water from the mine might lower the groundwater table and lake levels within the surrounding region. The state has imposed such severe environmental requirements that it is questionable if mining will ever occur at Mole Lake.

At Crandon, U.S. 8 descends onto an outwash plain deposited beyond the wasting Langlade Lobe, then climbs into another upland with drumlins just east of town. Lake Metonga on the south edge of Crandon is a large kettle lake in the outwash plain. East of Crandon, U.S. 8 crosses a drumlin-bearing upland for about 5 miles before entering a broad area of pitted and collapsed outwash, which continues to Laona and beyond to Cavour and Armstrong Creek.

South of Laona about 15 miles via Wisconsin 32 is a series of ridges of gray and red Precambrian quartzite on McCaslin Mountain. This quartzite contains sand grains of 1,760-million-year-old zircon minerals and was intruded by Wolf River granite that is 1,450 million years old. Therefore, this quartzite is about the same age as the Baraboo, Barron, and probably also the Rib Mountain quartzites. A vast blanket of pure quartz sand must

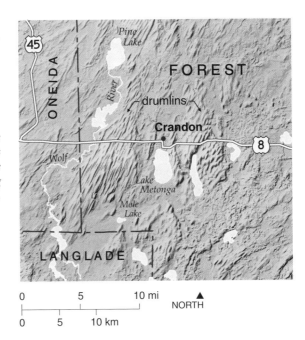

Landscape image showing drumlins formed beneath the southward-flowing Langlade Lobe.

have been spread across all of Wisconsin and buried the deeply eroded roots of the Penokean Mountains prior to Wolf River igneous events.

Near Armstrong Creek several drumlins project above the outwash. U.S. 8 continues over pitted outwash and till uplands to the intersection with U.S. 141. Several north-south-trending moraines of the Green Bay Lobe cross this area, but they are hard to see from the road.

Bedrock reappears again along U.S. 8 about 2 miles west of Dunbar, where a large outcrop north of the highway and railroad track shows salmon pink granite with some very coarse veins. Similar outcrops appear intermittently in the 10 miles between Dunbar and the junction with U.S. 141 just south of Pembine. These date from the Penokean mountain building episode about 1,860 million years ago. For waterfall addicts, Twelve Foot Falls County Park about 7 miles southeast of Dunbar has a series of four falls, which expose related granitic rocks.

The intersection with U.S. 141 is on a westward-sloping outwash plain deposited by meltwater flowing from the Green Bay Lobe when it stood at the moraine that is located about 1 mile east of the intersection. It is the wooded ridge that you can see in the distance to the east of the intersection. This north-south-trending moraine can be traced for many miles. U.S. 141 continues northward to Niagara, crossing several pitted outwash plains and an area of thin glacial sediment on bedrock.

U.S. 8/U.S. 141/U.S. 2
Pembine—Florence via Niagara and Iron Mountain
35 miles (52 km)

Exposures of metamorphosed volcanic and associated sedimentary rocks occur from 2 miles north of Pembine to the border at Niagara, Wisconsin. Other exposures occur east of U.S. 8/U.S. 141, especially along the Menominee River. The most accessible of these is at scenic Long Slide Falls, which you can reach by a side road 5 miles north of Pembine, then 2 miles east. These volcanic rocks are also visible in the eastern part of Niagara looking across to the north (Michigan) side of the Menominee River from U.S. 141. Here, they have been steeply tilted and sheared by the major Niagara fault zone, which lies just to the north. This fault is the boundary between Penokean belt rocks and the old Superior continental margin to the north. As in so many other towns in the state, a dam obscures Niagara's waterfall. Nonetheless, the town claims to be Wisconsin's waterfall capital because Marinette County possesses over a dozen falls.

U.S. 141 crosses from Niagara north to Iron Mountain, Michigan, where it joins U.S. 2, and the two merged roads then reenter Wisconsin, paralleling the Niagara fault zone for 13 miles between the border and Florence.

Menominee Iron Region

Iron Mountain was the center of the Menominee Range iron mining region, which included Norway and Crystal Falls in Michigan as well as the Florence area of Wisconsin. Iron was first discovered here in 1880, and the ore was transported east by rail to Lake Michigan to be loaded on ships at Escanaba, Michigan. Precambrian 2,100- to 1,900-million-year-old Animikie rocks similar to those at Hurley occur in this district, although here the sequence is more complete in its upper part and is more complexly folded and metamorphosed; 1,860-million-year-old granites have intruded it. The basement comprises 2,600- to 2,300-million-year-old gneisses of the old Superior continental margin. Unconformably overlying these is a quartzite, a dolomite, an iron formation, and then a thick succession of metamorphosed volcanic rocks alternating with slates, graywackes, and finally another iron formation. The highway route west from Iron Mountain through Florence crosses complexly folded rocks of the upper part of this sequence. The first roadcut west of the U.S. 2 Menominee River bridge exposes metamorphosed volcanic rocks, and there are a few small exposures of slaty, metamorphosed sediments west of Florence. Six mines operated southeast of Florence between 1880 and 1932, mining the upper of the two iron formations.

The combined frustration of geological complexity and poor exposures in the Florence district was eloquently portrayed in 1880 by geologist W. B. Brooks:

> When facts are so scarce, one is so rejoiced in finding them that he almost forgets that he has perhaps waded swamps or clambered through windfalls with intense labor and found only a single outcrop. He may have passed within a few rods of others and not observed them, because of trees and brush and fallen timber. The same labor would have carried him a hundred miles comfortably on horseback in the far west. (Brooks 1880)

Around Iron Mountain, Michigan, the lower iron formation was mined at several localities. At Norway, tours of an old mine are offered, and there is a Menominee Range Historical Museum in Iron Mountain. Flat-lying Cambrian sandstone and Ordovician dolomite overlie the Precambrian sequence in the high hill just northwest of Iron Mountain. These small, outlying patches of Paleozoic strata lie only 20 miles west of a continuous belt of such rocks, which extend south into eastern Wisconsin.

Precambrian stromatolites, which are structures formed by photosynthetic cyano-bacteria, near Iron Mountain, Michigan. The convexity of the laminations indicate that the top of these vertical strata is toward the top of the photo. —R. H. Dott, Jr., photo

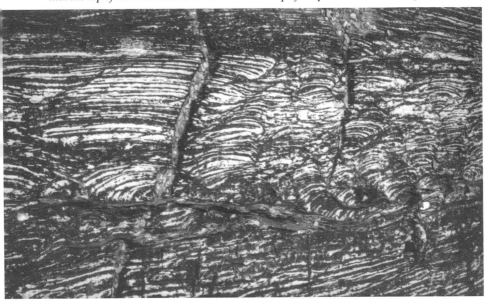

U.S. 53
Haugen—Superior
85 miles (138 km)

At Haugen, U.S. 53 rises onto an area of hummocky topography up to 10 miles wide deposited along the late Wisconsin margin of the Superior Lobe. Ice-walled lake plains a mile or more across are a prominent part of this hummocky zone where a thick pile of debris-rich ice melted. Where U.S. 53 crosses the Washburn-Barron County line about 2 miles north of Haugen, it is on a broad ice-walled lake plain. The highway continues across more hummocky topography then crosses another ice-walled lake plain at Sarona. The well-developed hummocky topography ends about 3 miles north of Sarona. Near Spooner, broad hills composed of till from several glacial advances dominate the landscape. Geologists believe the Spooner Hills are remnants left between channels eroded by water flowing beneath the ice toward the margin of the last ice sheet. South of the Spooner area, the water probably escaped the ice margin through tunnel channels.

At Trego, U.S. 53 crosses the Namekagon River. This portion of the river is part of the St. Croix National Scenic Riverway and is a very popular canoeing area. Trego is on the south edge of the nearly 2-mile-wide outwash plain along the river. About 2 miles north of Trego, the road climbs onto an upland mantled by till and areas of outwash.

A few miles east and west of Trego, small outcrops of Cambrian conglomerate and sandstone surround areas of Barron quartzite. These Cambrian sediments must have been deposited near islands of bedrock, as they were at Interstate Park to the west near Cameron and in the Baraboo area farther south. Practically no bedrock is visible along U.S. 53 for 50 miles north of Trego. From drilling and geophysical measurements, we know that the underlying bedrock changes approximately where the highway rises north of Trego. Here, the route crosses into the Lake Superior rift, which is dominated by late Precambrian Keweenaw bedrock. The boundary between the two types of bedrock is the Lake Owen fault along which the Keweenaw volcanic rocks were raised thousands of feet against Cambrian strata. Quaternary glacial and glacially related deposits conceal the Lake Owen fault here.

Between Minong and the Washburn-Douglas County line, the road crosses several ice-walled lake plains, which are part of an area of hummocky topography that extends to Gordon.

At Gordon, 25 miles north of Trego, U.S. 53 crosses the St. Croix Flowage in the headwater region of the St. Croix River, which, farther downstream, separates Wisconsin from Minnesota for more than 100 miles. The bedrock concealed beneath this area is the Keweenaw sedimentary sequence.

Immediately north of Gordon, U.S. 53 descends into the St. Croix River trench, a channel cut by meltwater draining from Glacial Lake Duluth through the Bois-Brule outlet to the St. Croix River and then to the Mississippi River. Cranberries are grown commercially on the flats north of the river just east of Gordon. About 2 miles farther north, U.S. 53 climbs the cutbank on the north side of the St. Croix trench and rises onto a broad outwash terrace. The Solon Springs Airport is on this terrace. A wayside park just north of the airport provides a view across the St. Croix trench to the east. The wayside is near the top of the west cutbank of the trench, which is about 100 feet deep. Imagine what it would have been like to see this trench filled from wall to wall with roiling meltwater draining from Glacial Lake Duluth. Glacial deposits in this area are overlain by fine sands that wind winnowed from the sandy material in till exposed as the ice retreated and from outwash plains; this was before vegetation became established.

North of Solon Springs, U.S. 53 crosses several miles of outwash before rising onto an upland area with wetlands interspersed between slightly hummocky till patches. This terrain stretches to within a few miles of the intersection with U.S. 2. About 7 miles south of that intersection, in the area of the junction with County B just east of the village of Hawthorne, U.S. 53 crosses the shoreline of Glacial Lake Duluth and then descends northward onto a nearly flat plain of wave-washed clayey till. This till plain extends to the intersection with U.S. 2. County B at Hawthorne provides an alternate route west 14 miles to Pattison State Park.

Glacial Lake Duluth sediments conceal the Douglas fault, which runs along the base of the escarpment near the junction with U.S. 2. About 900 million years ago, this fault raised Precambrian volcanic basalts against younger Precambrian sandstones, which also lie beneath the Gordon area to the south, where they are 400 feet higher in elevation than they are here. The sandstones are less resistant to erosion, so here lie about 50 feet lower than the adjacent basalts of the escarpment. You can see these effects of the Douglas fault best at Amnicon Falls State Park just a mile east of the junction of U.S. 53 with U.S. 2 and at Pattison State Park, a few minutes drive south of Superior. Both parks are described in **U.S. 2: Superior—Hurley**.

To the north, across the lowlands beyond the city of Superior, Duluth, Minnesota, is built on a similar basalt escarpment. About 10,000 years ago, as the glacier was retreating from this region, Glacial Lake Duluth flooded the lowland between the two escarpments. It was ancestral to present Lake Superior and was at least 500 feet higher than the surface of Lake Superior. In the glacial lake were deposited red clay sediments, which cover the different Precambrian rocks like a blanket. As the lake shrank to become present Lake Superior, streams quickly eroded the soft lake sediments, exposing the underlying hard bedrock in many of the valleys that drain the uplands.

Glacial Lake Duluth and details of the Superior-Duluth lowland are described more fully in **U.S. 2: Superior—Hurley**.

Wisconsin 13
Abbotsford—Bayfield
155 miles (224 km)

Abbotsford lies at the eastern eroded edge of Paleozoic strata, which dominate to the west and south. Like U.S. 51 from Wausau to Woodruff, Wisconsin 13 north from Abbotsford to Phillips lies entirely within the Precambrian Penokean belt, but exposures are few. From water wells and other scant evidence, we can say that the bedrock consists of metamorphosed volcanic and sedimentary rocks intruded by scattered granitic bodies, all of which were formed within the Penokean volcanic island complex around 1,900 million years ago. At Medford, for example, volcanic rocks underlie the city with Penokean-age gneiss a few miles to the south. Around 1,850 million years ago during the Penokean mountain building episode, the entire volcanic belt was caught in a vicelike squeeze between the Superior continent to the north and the Marshfield microcontinent, which lies just to the south of Abbotsford.

Between Abbotsford and Medford, Wisconsin 13 crosses a low-relief, gently rolling landscape blanketed by glacial sediment deposited during several of the early glaciations. Glacial landforms are absent in this area because of a long period of erosion since the early glaciers covered the area. About a mile north of Stetsonville, Wisconsin 13 leaves the area of brown, silty glacial sediment derived from the northwest and crosses onto reddish brown, sandy glacial sediment derived from the Lake Superior basin. There are no clear exposures of these materials along this section of road, but look for the color of the sediment in foundation holes or other excavations you may chance upon.

Although the glacial sediment here is virtually identical in color, grain size, and the composition of rock fragments to that deposited north of Medford during the late Wisconsin Glaciation, the landscape is much different. Here, there are no well-preserved glacial landforms, only a few subdued moraines, and lakes and wetlands are not common. In contrast the landscape changes dramatically about 2 miles north of Medford, where the southeastern margin of the late Wisconsin Chippewa Lobe reached its maximum extent about 18,000 years ago. A 6- to 8-mile-wide zone of hummocky topography with abundant ice-walled lake plains marks the late Wisconsin maximum. During the late 1800s, a brickyard located about 3

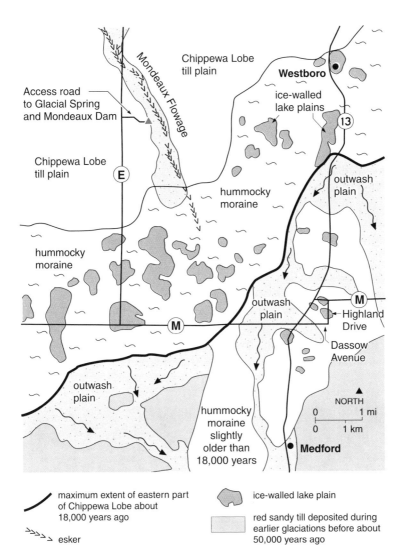

Glacial geology of the Medford and Mondeaux Flowage areas.

miles north of town was making brick from the clayey sediment deposited in one of these ice-walled lakes. The flat-topped hills that Wisconsin 13 passes through about 3 miles north of Medford are all ice-walled lake plains. On some you can see the raised rim around the margin of the plain.

Mondeaux Flowage

At the junction with County M, 4 miles north of Medford, Wisconsin 13 crosses an ice-walled lake plain. County M to the west provides access to the Mondeaux Flowage area of the Chequamegon National Forest. The Mondeaux Flowage occupies a tunnel channel cut at the base of the Chippewa Lobe when it stood at its maximum extent. An esker later formed down the center of the channel. It is common in this part of Wisconsin for eskers to occupy the center of broad erosional channels. The eskers are typically flanked by broad wetlands that fill much of the remainder of the channel zone.

To see the Mondeaux Flowage, take County M west for about 7 miles to the intersection with County E to the north. The intersection is on a large ice-walled lake plain. The buildings to the northwest of the intersection are on the rim of the lake plain. The flat-topped hills along County E are small ice-walled lake plains. Take County E north about 8 miles and then turn east on the access road to Mondeaux Dam and Glacial Spring. In about 1 mile, shortly after Glacial Spring, this road intersects a north-south road that closely follows the west side of the flowage and provides access to Mondeaux Dam to the north and Spearhead Point, West Point, and Picnic Point Campgrounds to the south. Spearhead Point, West Point, and many of the islands in the flowage are esker segments. A continuous esker forms the west edge of the flowage throughout this area. The Ice Age National Scenic Trail follows the crest of the esker here.

Air photo showing the moraine and hummocky topography that mark the maximum extent of the eastern part of the Chippewa Lobe in the Medford area about 18,000 to 15,000 years ago. The flat area to the south is outwash plains and old till plains. The farm fields in the northern two-thirds of the photo are on ice-walled lake plains. The intersection of County M and County E is on a lake plain at left-center —U.S. Geological Survey National High Altitude Photography Program

Esker forming a long narrow point and islands in the Mondeaux Flowage. —J. W. Attig photo

Low-angle air photo of an ice-walled lake plain near Medford. The detour via Dassow Avenue crosses the center of this plain. —J. W. Attig photo

Medford to Mellen

A short detour east on Dassow Avenue, which intersects Wisconsin 13 across from County M 4 miles north of Medford, provides another good opportunity to see a well-preserved ice-walled lake plain. Take Dassow Avenue about 1.5 miles east to the intersection with Highland Drive, then turn north on Highland Drive. The slope you climb is where the ice stood holding the south side of an ice-walled lake plain. When the ice melted, the lake sediment collapsed to form the slope. The road then crosses the south rim ridge of the lake plain and descends into the central basin of the lake, which is about a half mile wide. The central former lake basin is filled with about 30 feet of laminated, silty lake sediment, which was soft enough in places to sink a drill truck and four-wheel drive pickup truck to the floorboards. Fortunately a friendly farmer with a large tractor was there to help us! Continuing north, Highland Drive crosses over the north rim ridge of the lake and descends the northern sloping edge of the lake plain. Turn left at the intersection of County M and travel about one-half mile west to rejoin Wisconsin 13.

Between Medford and Westboro, Wisconsin 13 passes diagonally through the hummocky zone marking the maximum extent of the Chippewa Lobe. The hummocks in this area are composed of the reddish brown, sandy, bouldery glacial sediment typical of the area. The flat areas along this section are outwash plains and ice-walled lake plains. Timms Hill 5 miles east of Ogema on Wisconsin 86 is the highest point in Wisconsin, with an elevation of 1,952 feet, which is deceptive given the general flatness of the terrain along this route. Timms Hill is composed of a thick sequence of till, outwash, and lake sediment deposited between the Wisconsin Valley and Chippewa Lobes of the Laurentide Ice Sheet.

The landscape from Prentice to Glidden along Wisconsin 13 is a low-relief, swampy terrain of till plains and outwash plains. There are many low northeast-southwest-trending drumlins shaped by the southwestward flowing Chippewa Lobe.

Phillips is home of the remarkable Concrete Park, where a quaint collection of some two hundred life-size concrete human and animal figures depict the settlement of the northwoods. By a slight stretch, one can argue some geological significance here because concrete is made from limestone and some of the figures are decorated with chips of local rock rather than the more common broken glass and bric-a-brac. Also displayed in some pillars and a fireplace are some fine igneous rocks with large mineral crystals, and interesting glacial erratic boulders decorate the edges of the driveway and parking lot.

Between Phillips and Park Falls, Wisconsin 13 crosses the important Niagara fault zone, but there is no hint along the highway; only subsurface drilling and geophysical information have traced it here. At Park Falls, a Precambrian granite of the Penokean belt and some coarse veins are exposed just below the Flambeau Paper Company dam. Park Falls and the remainder of Wisconsin 13 north to Mellen lie within the southern part of the old Superior continental margin, which was profoundly deformed and metamorphosed 1,850 million years ago during the Penokean upheaval. In the vicinity of Morse, about 10 miles south of Mellen, Archean gneiss of the Superior margin is exposed. Penokean sedimentary and volcanic rocks got complexly jumbled together with the edge of the Superior continent here across a zone at least 25 miles wide.

About 3 miles north of Glidden, Wisconsin 13 enters a 6- to 7-mile-wide zone of hummocky topography with a distinct ridge, the Winegar moraine, along its southern margin. This moraine marks the maximum extent of a readvance of the ice margin out of the Lake Superior basin about 13,000 years ago. The sediment deposited by this readvance contains more silt than the sediment deposited by earlier advances in this part of northern Wisconsin. The ice margin had wasted far enough northward prior to readvancing that lakes formed between the ice margin and the southern edge of the Lake Superior basin. The readvancing ice incorporated silt that had accumulated in these lake basins. Although ice paused and readvanced several times during the general recession of the Laurentide Ice Sheet from northern Wisconsin, most of the moraines or other ice-marginal features are not easily recognized along the roadsides.

North of the Winegar moraine, bedrock controls the landscape for several miles north and south of Mellen. A few small drumlins composed of till are present on the bedrock. A marker in a wayside on the west side of Wisconsin 13 just north of the junction with Wisconsin 77 is titled "Great Divide." It marks the drainage divide between the Great Lakes–St. Lawrence River and Mississippi River basins.

Two miles south of Mellen, the highway crosses the western end of the Penokee Range, for which the Penokean mountain building event was named. It extends northeastward to Hurley and becomes the Gogebic Range in Michigan. The rock sequence in this range begins with a quartzite that was deposited upon eroded Archean gneisses. It is overlain by the Ironwood banded iron formation, which was first discovered in the Mellen area because of its magnetic character. We include more details of the Penokee-Gogebic iron range in **I-39/U.S. 51: Stevens Point—Hurley.**

Mellen Area

From Mellen north to Lake Superior, Wisconsin 13 is within the Lake Superior rift. The Lake Owen fault zone, which marks this boundary farther southwest, lies a few miles to the north within late Precambrian volcanic basalt. The Keweenaw fault extends from northern Michigan southwestward and somehow connects with the Lake Owen fault zone north of Mellen. The compression that formed these faults was also responsible for tilting the Keweenaw basalts and sedimentary strata steeply in the region from Mellen to Hurley.

At Mellen a thick gabbro mass was intruded along the base of the lowest volcanic rocks. The Mellen gabbro extends east and west of town for a total distance of 40 miles. Metamorphism by this intrusion made the Ironwood banded iron formation unsuitable for ore in the western Penokee Range. The gabbro is zoned internally so that its composition varies from true gabbro at the base to granite at the top; the first minerals to crystallize, which are richer in heavy elements like iron, sank to form dense gabbro, and minerals with lighter elements crystallized later to form less-dense granite.

The Mellen gabbro has long been quarried and marketed as a handsome "black granite." It is exposed along Wisconsin 13 for 1 mile just north of the junction with Wisconsin 169. The first roadcuts are gabbro, but the most northerly ones expose a slightly younger, intrusive granite containing spectacular angular inclusions of black gabbro. You can also see coarse gabbro at a large quarry on Wisconsin 169 about 1 mile northeast of the junction with Wisconsin 13, near the south end of Loon Lake just before the entrance to Copper Falls State Park.

Copper Falls State Park

Six miles north of Mellen via Wisconsin 169 is picturesque and geologically important Copper Falls State Park. The short side trip is worthwhile for the opportunity to see two spectacular waterfalls where forks of the Bad River join and then race through a gorge cut across steeply tilted Keweenaw basalt flows and overlying Keweenaw sedimentary rocks. Copper Falls is only about 20 feet high, but its companion Brownstone Falls on the Tyler Fork of the Bad River is 30 feet; the gorge downstream is 60 to 100 feet deep. An easy 1.5-mile trail takes the visitor past all of this with excellent interpretive signs to explain the geology. Builders made interesting use of Mellen gabbro in the massive fireplace at the concession stand and in stairs and a bridge nearby. Slabs of pre-Keweenaw Tyler slate were used for the walkways near the concession stand, and glacial erratic boulders or fieldstones of varied compositions were used for walls and stairways downstream from the falls near Devil's Gate. A thick sequence of glacial deposits is exposed in the hillside above the river north of the main parking lot. The reddish brown till, called the Copper Falls formation, is typical of the late Wisconsin sandy till deposited in this area by the most recent ice sheet.

The name of the park reflects the fact that, from the 1860s to the early 1900s, attempts were made to mine copper from the basalts between the two falls. The booming copper mines of northern Michigan were exploiting

Brownstone Falls over late Precambrian basalt in Copper Falls State Park. —Photo courtesy of the Wisconsin Department of Natural Resources

the same rock interval only 100 miles to the northeast. The miners even diverted the Bad River from a channel still visible east of the picnic grounds to prevent frequent flooding of their workings. All of the effort was poorly rewarded, however, for little copper was found.

Lake Superior Lowlands

North of the gabbro exposures along Wisconsin 13, bedrock is mostly concealed all the way to Ashland. For 5 miles north from Mellen, the route is over the Keweenaw basalts, which are well exposed at nearby Copper Falls State Park. In the remaining 18 miles to Ashland, Quaternary deposits conceal the Keweenaw sedimentary rocks that overlie the basalts. Near Highbridge the highway crosses several beaches deposited along the southern margin of Glacial Lake Duluth. Here, the shoreline was at an elevation of about 1,100 feet. The road then descends to the Lake Superior lowland where extensive areas of clayey till and lake sediment were washed by the waves of Glacial Lake Duluth. This lake plain, which extends to Ashland, is flat in most areas but is locally deeply dissected by rivers such as the Marengo and the White, which cross the highway. The deep, steep-walled channels that these rivers have cut into the till plain are typical of river incision into fine-grained sediment.

Bayfield Peninsula

Three miles west of Ashland, at the junction of Wisconsin 13 and U.S. 2, is the Northern Great Lakes Visitor Center with interpretive materials about the natural, geologic, and cultural history as well as the recreational opportunities of the entire Lake Superior region. From Ashland north, Wisconsin 13 follows the west shore of Chequamegon Bay for 26 miles to Bayfield and beyond to the Red Cliff Indian Reservation. The Bayfield Peninsula was named for Captain Bayfield of Britain's Royal Navy, who first charted much of the Great Lakes coastlines in the 1800s.

The bedrock at the surface of the peninsula and the twenty-two Apostle Islands is the reddish brown, youngest Keweenaw strata, collectively known here as the Bayfield sandstones, which were deposited by rivers 500 or more million years ago. These strata are flat lying in this area, which is the axis of the synclinal structure of the Lake Superior rift valley. Some of the youngest Keweenaw sandstones preserved along the axis of the syncline are almost pure quartz and are indistinguishable from Cambrian sandstones farther south. Indeed, some of them may actually be of Cambrian age, but without fossils, it is impossible to say. The Keweenaw basalts exposed along the Minnesota shoreline and younger Keweenaw strata on Isle Royale near the northern Minnesota shore dip beneath the lake and lie thousands of feet below the Bayfield Peninsula; they rise again to the surface on the southeastern side of the syncline on the Keweenaw Peninsula of northern Michigan and in northern Wisconsin from Mellen northeast to Hurley.

The reddish brown Bayfield sandstones were quarried extensively along Wisconsin 13 and on some of the islands during the brownstone era of architecture in the late 1800s. The great Chicago fire of 1871 stimulated quarrying for rebuilding that city. In the long run, however, railroad construction provided the most important stimulus, for much stone was needed for bridges and culverts. When the tracks were all laid by the early 1900s, the industry collapsed. Washburn was a major center of quarrying and shipping of the stone. The historical museum there has a good summary of that important industry and is itself housed in one of the finest examples anywhere of a brownstone building, which was built in 1890 as a bank. The long-abandoned quarries at Washburn are inaccessible today, but you can see the old Pike Quarry 5.5 miles north of Washburn on the west side of Wisconsin 13 just beyond the junction with Whitting Road.

To serve the booming mining and quarrying industries of Lake Superior, the DuPont Chemical Company in 1902 built an explosives manufacturing plant north of Washburn. The chemical ingredients were imported from Spain and Chile and boxes for the explosives came from Milwaukee. The two world wars greatly stimulated production, and the plant was ultimately the nation's largest producer of TNT until it closed in 1976.

Between Ashland and Washburn, Wisconsin 13 wraps around the southwestern and western parts of Chequamegon Bay. For about two and a half miles west of Ashland, the road crosses an area of peat and postglacial stream sediment deposited at the mouth of Fish Creek. Across the head of the bay, the road follows the crest of a beach ridge that was probably deposited during a slightly higher stand of Lake Superior during the last several thousand years. From the head of Chequamegon Bay to Washburn, the highway crosses an area of wave-washed, clayey till and lake sediment. Between Washburn and Bayfield, Wisconsin 13 wraps around several sandstone hills that have a thin cover of wave-washed till. A sequence of old beaches wrap around these hills. They formed as ice-marginal lakes in the western Lake Superior basin dropped from the Glacial Lake Duluth level. In map view these hills appear to be remnants of sandstone left between what may have been channels eroded beneath the ice. The Apostle Islands are the partly submerged continuation of these sandstone hills. In the middle of the southern part of the Bayfield Peninsula, more than 500 feet of glacial sediment and outwash underlie the high areas in places.

Apostle Islands National Lakeshore

The Apostle Islands National Lakeshore with headquarters at Bayfield includes all but one of the twenty-two islands, which were named by French trappers who apparently could not count. The islands are especially noted for picturesque red sandstone cliffs sculptured by Lake Superior storm waves. Caves, arches, and pillars regularly provide colorful photos for calendars. In winter, many island cliffs are beautifully adorned with huge icicles formed from wave spray. Access to the islands is only by private or chartered boat.

Madeline Island, the largest and most inhabited of the islands, is not part of the national lakeshore. It is easily reached in the summer by regular car ferry service and in winter by crossing over ice. A state historical museum provides information on brownstone quarrying as well as Ojibwa Indian traditions, fur trading, missionaries, lumbering, and fishing in the islands region. Madeline Island was one of the earliest and most important trading centers on Lake Superior, but today it is primarily a recreation site. Big Bay State Park on the south shore has splendid cliffs of the red Bayfield sandstone and a sandy beach facing Big Bay. In cliffs, you can see crossbedding and rare thin pebbly layers, which were formed by ancient sprawling sandy rivers with broad, multichanneled floodplains. Behind the modern mile-long sandy barrier beach is a large wetland, which must have been the upper end of a much longer bay immediately after glaciation. The encroachment of sediment and vegetation have largely filled the former upper bay.

Wisconsin 29
Thorp—Ringle
70 miles (112 km)

The Cambrian strata exposed around the Chippewa Falls–Eau Claire area in the Western Uplands extend eastward as far as Thorp with underlying Precambrian rocks exposed along the rivers. Bedrock is poorly exposed along most of Wisconsin 29 between Thorp and Ringle, so geologists have inferred the older geology from scattered exposures along roads and rivers as well as from water wells and geophysical measurements.

The Precambrian basement of the Northern Highlands–Western Uplands boundary region here is approximately at the northern boundary of the Marshfield continent along the extension of the Eau Pleine fault zone. A variety of Penokean granites and other igneous rocks have intruded Archean gneisses. From Thorp eastward all the way to Ringle, the Precambrian bedrock is part of the Penokean volcanic belt. Large patches of the oldest Cambrian strata, which directly overlie the Precambrian rocks, extend for 20 miles east from Thorp to Abbotsford.

The shape of the surface of the underlying bedrock controls the general shape of the landscape between Thorp and Abbotsford. Patchy remnants of reddish brown sandy glacial sediment and older brown, silty glacial sediment—both deposited much earlier than about 26,000 years ago when the Laurentide Ice Sheet advanced into Wisconsin—occur throughout the area. Glacial landforms are not preserved in this area of older glaciation.

East of Abbotsford, Cambrian strata have been entirely eroded. Sixteen miles east, a geographic marker designates Wisconsin 29's crossing of the ninetieth meridian of longitude, which is one-quarter of the way around the globe from the zero meridian at Greenwich, England. Shaded ginseng fields become common as the route approaches Wausau. Most of the local crop of this herb is exported to Asia, where it is especially prized for enhancing good health.

Between Abbotsford and Edgar, Wisconsin 29 crosses a low-relief, gently rolling landscape blanketed by up to several tens of feet of brown silty glacial sediment deposited by glaciers advancing into the area from the northwest, probably hundreds of thousands of years ago. Generally, these old glacial sediments are best preserved on the uplands between stream valleys. East of Edgar, the cover of glacial sediment over bedrock becomes very patchy and is absent in most places. Presumably the glacial sediment has been eroded from the somewhat steeper topography closer to the Wisconsin River. Between Edgar and Wausau, bedrock is covered with material derived from the weathering of the underlying rock mixed with windblown loess and possible weathering products from the glacial sediment, which may have covered much of this area. Eastward dispersal by glaciers of rock from places like Rib Mountain indicate that ice from the northwest advanced into the Wausau area and extended beyond the present Wisconsin River. How far beyond is unknown. About 3 miles east of Marathon City, Wisconsin 29 descends from the bedrock uplands onto the outwash plain along the Rib River. The Rib River carried meltwater draining from the late Wisconsin margin of the Laurentide Ice Sheet when it was standing at or near its maximum extent about 20 miles to the northwest. Rib Mountain looms south of the highway for the 2 miles west of Wausau. For the geology of the Wausau area and Rib Mountain, including the origin of the broad wetland near the confluence of the Rib and Wisconsin Rivers, see **I-39/U.S. 51: Stevens Point—Hurley.**

East of I-39, Wisconsin 29 crosses an outwash plain along the west side of the Wisconsin River. The river carried meltwater and sediment from the Laurentide Ice Sheet as long as its margin was south of the Lake Superior drainage divide along the Wisconsin-Michigan border to the north. In places the sandy outwash in this part of the valley is hundreds of feet thick. East of the Wisconsin River, Wisconsin 29 continues for about 9 miles across the outwash plain parallel to the Eau Claire River, which carried meltwater from the Langlade and Green Bay Lobes. About 1.5 miles east of Ringle, the route crosses the late Wisconsin terminal moraine of the Green Bay Lobe. The moraine, which is quite hummocky in marked contrast with the landscape to the west, can be traced continuously for tens of miles both north and south. At Ringle, clay-rich material derived from the weathering of the underlying rock has been used to make brick. A brickyard opened here in 1893 and made more than one million bricks per year.

The bedrock at Ringle is the western margin of the Precambrian Wolf River igneous complex, which is discussed in **Wisconsin 29: Ringle—Green Bay** in the Eastern Uplands.

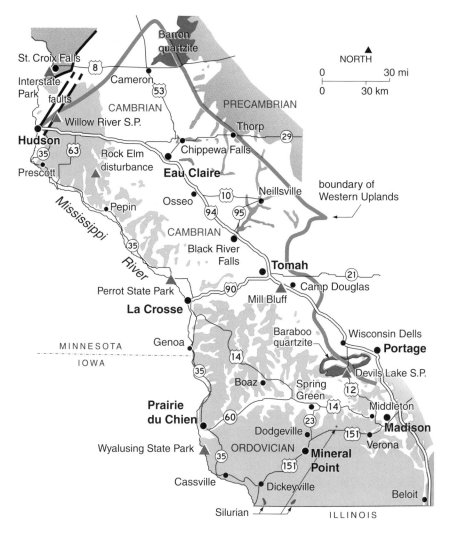

Roads and points of interest in the Western Uplands. Ordovician, Cambrian, and Precambrian rocks are differentiated.

Western Uplands

The lead mining region of southwestern Wisconsin drew the first Anglo-American settlers to the state in the 1820s. Except for stone quarrying, the chief natural resource of the Western Uplands today is its scenery. Most of the region is known as the Driftless Area because glacial deposits, which in the past were collectively called "drift," are lacking except for along the edges of the region. The northern one-fourth of the Western Uplands, however, differs from the Driftless portion because it was glaciated during earlier ice advances, some probably many hundreds of thousands of years ago. Weathering and erosion have since blurred the typical features of glaciated landscapes there, so the evidence is more subtle than in northern and eastern Wisconsin, which were glaciated 26,000 to 10,000 years ago during the last part of the Wisconsin Glaciation. The line marking the maximum extent of the late Wisconsin Glaciation is the boundary between the Western Uplands and the Northern Highlands.

Prior to agricultural development by European immigrants, the Driftless Area was covered by a mixture of native prairie and oak savanna vegetation on the uplands and riparian forests along the larger stream bottoms. The total area of woodland was less than today because frequent fires impeded the spread of trees. After European settlers began to suppress fires, many more young trees survived. The northern part of the Driftless Area included large stands of pine forest, which were logged extensively during the famous days of Paul Bunyan around the early 1900s. Sawmills dotted that region and huge rafts of logs were floated down the tributary streams and into the Mississippi River to those mills.

Driftless Area

Having escaped the footprint of ice, the Driftless Area has undergone millions of years of landscape evolution by running water, which has given it a very different face from the rest of the state. Natural lakes and wetlands so common in glaciated regions are absent from the Driftless Area except locally on river floodplains. Instead, systems of connected tributaries and larger streams have produced a well-drained, deeply dissected terrain. Outcrops of Paleozoic bedrock are especially abundant and continuous in the bluffs along the Wisconsin and Mississippi Rivers. During the last glaciation, these rivers carried large volumes of meltwater that undercut the bluffs and removed slope deposits.

119

At various times throughout the last several million years, continental ice sheets have advanced to all sides of the Driftless Area, but never covered it. Why was this area spared? The broad lowlands containing Lake Superior and Lake Michigan deflected the generally southerly flow of ice either toward the east or west of the Driftless Area. In addition, the area is near the southernmost extent of the ice sheets so that the ice was thin enough that even the modestly higher topography of the Driftless Area was enough to limit the ice's further expansion.

The bedrock exposed in the Driftless Area consists primarily of 500- to 440-million-year-old sedimentary strata of late Cambrian and Ordovician time. Small areas of Precambrian rocks appear along several river valleys in the northeastern part of the Western Uplands. At the other extreme, several hills in southwestern Wisconsin have small caps of Silurian strata thought to be as young as 425 million years. These are but small remnants left from the erosion of what must have been a blanket of Silurian and even younger Paleozoic marine strata, which formerly covered the state. At widely scattered localities on ridges in the Driftless Area, there are patches of still-younger gravels believed to be of Cretaceous age, or roughly 100 million years old, but they could be much younger. They are probably remnants of widespread river deposits formed over a long span of time before the present river valleys became established.

The Paleozoic strata appear perfectly flat to the human eye, but in fact they are tilted westward very slightly. Although this tilt is only about one-tenth of a degree, it is enough to cause each stratum to decline in elevation 10 to 12 feet for every mile traveled in a westward direction. The base of the Cambrian rock exposed at an elevation of 800 feet above sea level at Black River Falls on I-94 is about 600 feet lower at the Mississippi River, 50 miles to the west, where it is only 200 feet above sea level. This means that it lies about 500 feet beneath the land surface, for the river is at an elevation of about 700 feet here. As you travel up and down over the ridges and valleys of the Driftless Area, imagine you are on a roller coaster traveling back and forth through geologic time; going uphill you move through younger strata, but going downhill you cross older ones.

Precambrian Record

The oldest rocks exposed in the Western Uplands are of early Precambrian (Archean) age. They are exposed beneath Cambrian or younger material only along rivers and in a few quarries near the boundary with the Northern Highlands. They are best seen along the Black River at and northeast from Black River Falls for about 15 miles upriver. Most of these old rocks are metamorphic banded gneisses formed originally as volcanic and intrusive igneous rocks approximately 2,800 million years ago. They were

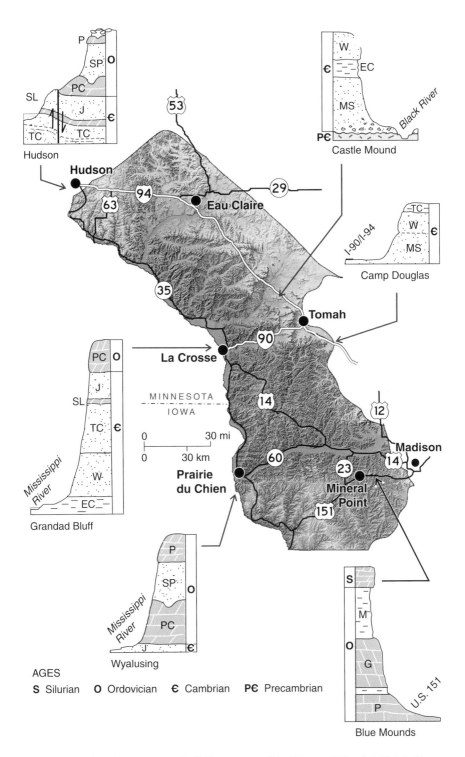

Cambrian and Ordovician strata in different parts of the Western Uplands. MS, *Mt. Simon sandstone;* EC, *Eau Claire formation;* W, *Wonewoc formation;* TC, *Tunnel City formation;* SL, *St. Lawrence formation;* J, *Jordan sandstone;* PC, *Prairie du Chien dolomite;* SP, *St. Peter sandstone;* P, *Platteville dolomite;* G, *Galena dolomite;* M, *Maquoketa shale.*

deformed and metamorphosed about 1,850 million years ago when younger granites were intruded during the Penokean mountain making episode, which affected practically all of Wisconsin as well as large parts of Minnesota and Michigan. During late Precambrian time, the north-central part of Wisconsin was warped upward to form the Wisconsin dome, which was above sea level at times during Paleozoic time, creating shoreline and shallow-sea depositional environments. Paleozoic strata thicken to the west, south, and east of the dome.

Cambrian Sandstones

After several hundred million years of weathering and erosion, quartz-rich sandstones were deposited in a late Cambrian sea beginning about 500 million years ago. The Cambrian sandstones are poorly cemented and so they tend to form hillslopes rather than cliffs throughout the region. In places they have been quarried for various uses.

The boundary between these flat-lying strata and underlying, deeply eroded Precambrian rocks is an unconformity. It is exposed along the Black River and along the Chippewa River in and near Eau Claire north of the Driftless Area. Cambrian sandstones appear monotonously similar at first, suggesting that they all formed in the same manner. Closer examination of their stratification and fossils, however, reveals important differences. Most

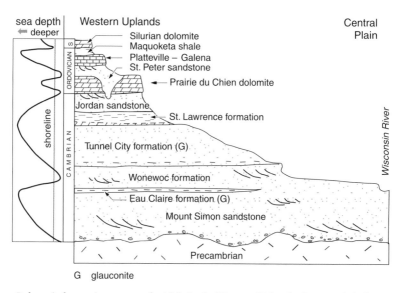

Paleozoic formations exposed widely in the Western Uplands. Curve at left shows relative position of sea level when the different formations were deposited.

of the sandstones have inclined internal lamination called *crossbedding*, which was formed by migrating dunes. We can tell whether wind or water currents moved the dunes by inspecting the associated ripples, which tend to be larger if formed by water than wind. Furthermore, water ripples formed by waves differ in shape from those formed by currents. Even better clues for ancient environments of deposition are provided by fossils, including the tracks and burrows of soft-bodied animals. Because animals had not yet learned how to live permanently on land, the mere presence of fossils in Cambrian strata suggests a marine environment.

Typical crossbedding in Cambrian sandstone at Ferry Bluff on the Wisconsin River. —R. H. Dott, Jr., photo

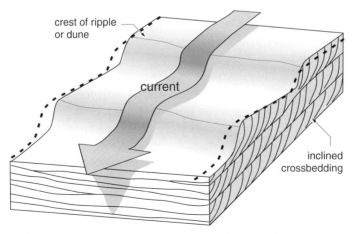

Crossbedding formed by the migration of either wind- or water-formed dunes. Grains eroded from the dune crests are deposited downcurrent. Each lamination represents the downcurrent face of a dune. —From Dott and Batten, 1988

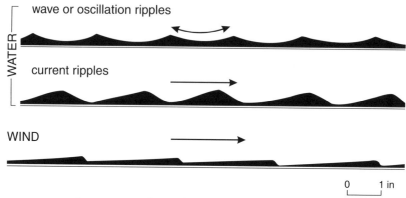

Symmetry, spacing, and relative heights of ripple marks.

The first Cambrian sediments were pebbly, coarse sands deposited along the shoreline of the advancing sea by strong tidal currents. These contain the tracks of crawling animals and burrows of animals that lived in very shallow, agitated water. Deposition of these crossbedded sandstones was followed by the accumulation of finer, sandy and shaly sediments having more diverse marine fossil shells and tracks, including those of trilobites. Some of these finer strata also contain the green mineral glauconite, which forms on the seafloor where deposition is very slow. Although the fine-grained sediments formed offshore in relatively deeper water, their stratification reveals the effects of episodic storm waves, which on rare occasions could stir the sea bottom even where it was 80 feet deep or so. A subtle type of undulatory or hummocky lamination formed by storm waves is common in these sandstones. Because Wisconsin then lay at tropical latitudes, we believe that the storms were like modern tropical hurricanes. The shoreline was by now farther eastward, lapping onto the Wisconsin dome.

The sea oscillated over Wisconsin at least twice during late Cambrian time. The next strata include wind and river sandstones lacking fossils and are best displayed in the Baraboo, Dells, and Central Plain region just east of the Western Uplands. After they were deposited, the sea again flooded widely, probably completely drowning the Wisconsin dome to produce a second interval of more fossiliferous, fine sandstones and minor limestone or dolomite in the Western Uplands. These again show evidence of stormy episodes separated by longer intervals of normal or fair weather, during which were deposited thin, fine silts and muds containing glauconitic greensands. The youngest Cambrian strata are sparsely fossiliferous sandstones, which reflect another shallowing trend that culminated with emergence of Wisconsin as a very low land at the end of the period.

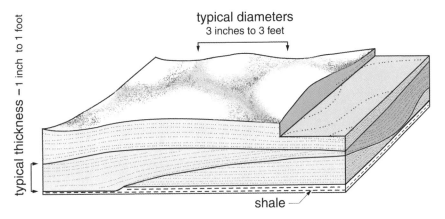

typical diameters
3 inches to 3 feet

typical thickness – 1 inch to 1 foot

shale

Undulatory or hummocky lamination formed by large storm waves in water depths generally a few tens of feet deep. The low hummocks are roughly circular.

Straight, vertical dwelling tubes (Skolithos) of ancient wormlike animals that are characteristic of shallow, sandy sea bottoms. These tubes are in the St. Peter sandstone. —R. H. Dott, Jr., photo

Ordovician Strata

In contrast with Cambrian strata, gray limestone and dolomite are the dominant Ordovician rock types. The early Ordovician Prairie du Chien dolomite is the single most conspicuous formation in the Western Uplands because it is more resistant to erosion than underlying sandstones. Look for its trademark caps on the cliffs overlooking the Mississippi River and on many ridges elsewhere. Oolite and chert nodules are common in this dolomite, but stromatolites and animal burrows are the only common fossils. The early Ordovician sea covered all of Wisconsin, but it was probably no more than 10 to 20 feet deep. High rates of tropical evaporation and restricted influx of normal seawater from distant, deeper parts of the sea made the waters over Wisconsin too salty for most animals.

You can see the middle Ordovician St. Peter sandstone, which is pure quartz like the Cambrian sandstones from which it was derived, overlying the Prairie du Chien dolomite on hillslopes in the southern part of the Driftless Area and also near the confluence of the St. Croix and Mississippi Rivers. It reflects another lowering of sea level during which caves began to form in the underlying dolomite, and Cambrian sandstones were eroded to provide sand for redeposition. Much of the St. Peter sandstone in southern Wisconsin was deposited by wind and rivers, whereas it is mostly marine in the adjacent states.

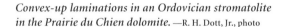

Convex-up laminations in an Ordovician stromatolite in the Prairie du Chien dolomite. —R. H. Dott, Jr., photo

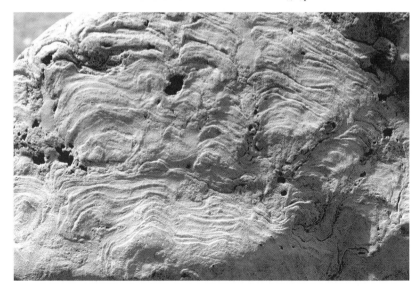

An Ordovician trilobite (Isotelus) *from Wisconsin.*
—Photo courtesy of Milwaukee Public Museum

Fossiliferous, tan dolomite and gray limestone from late Ordovician time occur chiefly in the southernmost Driftless Area south of the Wisconsin River. These are more resistant to erosion than the underlying St. Peter sandstone, so they cap most ridges. Limestone and dolomite are soluble in slightly acidic water, so they are susceptible to leaching by groundwater. When decay products from plant material as well as carbon dioxide are dissolved in groundwater, it can eat such rocks away wholesale along fractures, creating caves. The Driftless Area has more than sixty known caves, most of which are small; only four are open to the public. Some of these caves began forming about 450 million years ago during Ordovician time, when the sea retreated from Wisconsin, and they have continued to form ever since.

The late Ordovician Platteville and Galena strata are the most fossiliferous rocks in Wisconsin. Storm waves, which tore up the limy seafloor, concentrated the fossils in shell-rich layers.

Rude awakening

bliss

terror

R.I.P.

Fossil-rich shell layers form when storm waves wreak havoc on seafloor communities.

Silurian Remnants

Small, isolated patches of chert and dolomite containing rare Silurian marine fossils cap several high hills in southwestern Wisconsin. These include Blue Mound west of Madison and several other mounds farther southwest. Silurian strata are widespread in Illinois and Iowa, so these now-isolated patches, together with the extensive Silurian dolomites of eastern Wisconsin, are clues that all of Wisconsin was inundated by a sea that covered the entire continent. The patches of Silurian strata illustrate again the very slight westward inclination of the strata in western Wisconsin. The base of the Silurian caprock on Blue Mound near Madison is at an elevation of about 1,650 feet but descends to about 1,300 feet at Platteville and 1,050 feet west of Dubuque, Iowa, 65 miles southwest of Blue Mound.

Lead and Zinc Mining

Southwestern Wisconsin lies in the heart of the Tri-State Mining District, which, because of its lead and zinc ores, was one of the earliest regions in the upper Mississippi Valley to be settled by Europeans. The presence of the minerals was well known to Native Americans, who collected crystals for amulets. French explorers and trappers learned of the ores from Indians during the 1700s. Julian Dubuque, for whom the city in northeastern Iowa was named, made an agreement with the natives to mine lead. After the American Revolution, the settlement frontier moved rapidly westward to the Mississippi Valley. Lead mining began first in Missouri and then around 1820 in northwestern Illinois and at New Diggings, Wisconsin. Soon at least six steamboats were kept busy serving the bustling river towns of

Crystals of the lead mineral galena, Wisconsin's state mineral, from a mine in Shullsburg.
—G. Robinson and W. Cordua photo

Lead—as well as miners—were hauled in buckets from underground mines in southwest Wisconsin in the early 1800s. —From D. D. Owen, 1840

this northern district. In the 1830s and 1840s, miners from Cornwall brought important know-how to the district. Shallow lead production peaked quickly in the 1840s. About 1860, zinc ore was found at depths greater than 100 feet, giving a welcome boost to the industry but causing new problems with groundwater inflow. Zinc production peaked around 1915, and by the late 1970s, all mining ceased. Piles of waste rock, rusting buildings, and abandoned hillside "badger holes" still give testimony of that bygone era. Today, former mines at Platteville, Shullsburg, and Potosi remain open to tourists, and there are mining museums at Platteville and Shullsburg.

The ore minerals were deposited within limestones and dolomites from solutions of hot water rich in dissolved lead, zinc, copper, and sulfur as the fluids percolated through the rocks sometime after they were buried. Theories explaining the source of fluids that produced the Mississippi Valley–type lead and zinc deposits, examples of which occur widely around the world, have changed dramatically over the years. Prior to 1960, it was assumed that the solutions were derived from hot, igneous masses located somewhere beneath the strata in which the ores occur. But igneous rocks were never found in association with Mississippi Valley–type ores. This nagging problem finally led to the conclusion that igneous processes had nothing to do with the lead and zinc ores. Instead, geologists now believe the ores precipitated from salt-rich groundwater or brine, which migrated hundreds of miles. The brine was heated as it passed through deeply buried strata and dissolved metallic elements from them. As it migrated to shallower, cooler depths, it became oversaturated in metals and precipitated the ores. The Wisconsin ore minerals are thought to have been derived from fluids that migrated from 500 miles south in Arkansas and Tennessee through a gigantic plumbing system as much as 13,000 feet deep beneath Illinois. At cooler depths of 1,000 feet or less, the ore minerals were precipitated at temperatures of 200 to 300 degrees Fahrenheit (95 to 150 degrees Celsius) along fractures and in cavities, including small caves within Ordovician limestones and dolomites. The late Ordovician Maquoketa shale was an impermeable seal that inhibited the upward migration of the ore fluid, causing most of the metals to precipitate in the underlying Galena and Platteville formations. Geologists believe the mineralization occurred about 245 million years ago in early Triassic or late Permian time, when mountain building lifted up the Tennessee-Arkansas region. Gravity then caused the brine solution to migrate northward through the deep Illinois basin and up the southwestern flank of the Wisconsin dome.

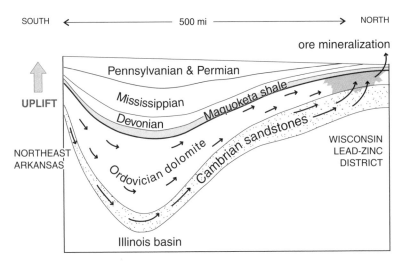

Hot mineral solutions flowed through the Illinois basin to Wisconsin and precipitated lead and zinc ores.

The Wisconsin flag and seal show a miner with his tools and thirteen lead ingots. Mining's importance to the state's early history is also reflected by town names such as Lead Mine, Mineral Point, New Diggings, and Potosi—named after a lead-mining town in Missouri that, in turn, is named for a rich district in Bolivia discovered in 1545. Wisconsin's first territorial capital was established in 1836 within the lead district at Belmont, 25 miles northeast of Dubuque, through the successful persuasion of a land promoter. In 1837, however, the Territorial Legislature, unhappy about the lack of amenities at Belmont, voted to move the capital to Madison, the choice of which was engineered by an even craftier promoter. The nickname Badger State derived from the name farmers gave to miners, who kept poking holes in their fields; tension eventually led to a bitter land-use clash between pick and plow.

In the 1830s, the federal government began sponsoring geological surveys of what was then called the Northwest Territories, which were under its jurisdiction until they gained statehood (Wisconsin in 1848). D. D. Owen made the first detailed geological observations of the upper Mississippi River country in 1840 and again in 1847–1849. The lead-zinc district was the major subject of study for obvious economic reasons but also because of the politically sensitive land-use conflict between mining and farming. This survey named several of the Cambrian and Ordovician formations exposed in the Driftless Area, and its reports contain many handsome drawings showing those formations in the scenic bluffs along the Mississippi.

Quaternary Glaciation

In contrast to the southern two-thirds of the Western Uplands (the Driftless Area), the northern part of the region has been glaciated a number of times. These glaciations were long ago—prior to the main late Wisconsin advance of the Superior and Chippewa Lobes into northwestern Wisconsin—but the landscape still bears clear indication of their impact. The shape of the underlying bedrock controls the general topography in the northern part of the Western Uplands, but the bedrock surface is not so irregular as it is in the Driftless Area. This is in part because dolomite does not cap the hills as it does farther south, but also in part because the area has been glaciated a number of times.

The earliest known glaciation of the area was by ice flowing from the northwest. Gray, silty till preserved in places in west-central Wisconsin is very similar in color and grain size to that found far to the east in the southern part of the Northern Highlands. This till is not common in northern Wisconsin, where ice advances from the Lake Superior basin typically deposited reddish brown, sandy till. The gray, silty till to the east must have come from a northwestern source, suggesting early advances from

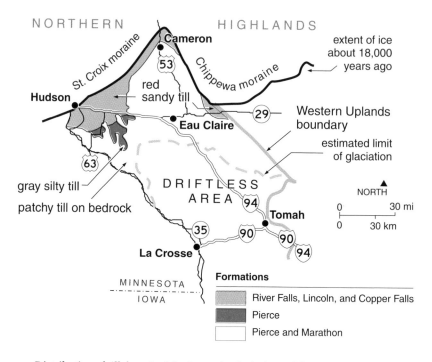

Distribution of till deposited during early glaciations of the Western Uplands.

Minnesota that extended far to the east. It is not possible to trace the till units continuously across the intervening area because it has been eroded away in most places. The southern and eastern extent of these early glaciations therefore remains obscure.

We do not know precisely when these early glaciations came from the northwest, but the extent to which erosion has removed the glacial deposits indicates the glaciations occurred long ago, perhaps several hundred thousand years ago. Another line of evidence comes from ice-marginal lake sediments. When the ice crossed the St. Croix River, it flowed into the mouths of a number of west-flowing rivers. The ice dammed the rivers and the valleys filled with water, forming extensive ice-marginal lakes. Thick sequences of clayey lake sediment are present in the valleys of the Chippewa, Trimbelle, Kinnickinnic, and other rivers in the area. Mineral grains in this fine-grained sediment record the earth's magnetic field at the time of deposition. These grains show that, when these sediments were deposited, the magnetic field was reversed in polarity relative to its present polarity. We know that a global magnetic reversal occurred 790,000 years ago, which suggests that the earliest ice advances occurred prior to that.

A later advance into the northern Western Uplands was from a more northerly source. The till deposited by this advance is reddish brown and sandy, typical of most till in northern Wisconsin derived from the Lake Superior basin. It also contains many rocks that could only have been derived from that basin. This till is much more deeply weathered than that deposited during the advances farther north in the Northern Highlands near the end of the Wisconsin Glaciation, suggesting that it was deposited earlier, perhaps more than a hundred thousand years ago. Younger reddish brown till in the northernmost and northeasternmost part of the region was probably deposited just prior to the late Wisconsin advance of about 18,000 years ago.

The advances from the northwest that deposited the silty gray till seem to have reached the farthest south and east of any of the early glacial advances, but their exact extent is unknown. We think they reached as far east as the Wisconsin River in the Northern Highlands. All that remains of these early glaciations are scattered patches of till, typically much weathered and mixed with other types of sediment by erosion, and a few erratic boulders. The till deposited by these advances must have been much more extensive prior to removal by erosion.

There is no evidence of glaciation in the southern two-thirds of the Western Uplands except for some till and a moraine on the north side of the Wisconsin River just east of its confluence with the Mississippi River. These very old glacial deposits and related outwash were not eroded by the Wisconsin River because they are on top of a bedrock terrace. Ice advancing from the west flowed a short distance into the mouth of the Wisconsin River to near Bridgeport. This blocked the mouth of the valley, and the meltwater from the glacier flowed eastward, opposite to the modern flow direction. Remnants of the ancient outwash deposits have been found in several places in the lower Wisconsin River valley. Their very weathered nature indicates that they were deposited many hundreds of thousands of years ago. These glacial deposits resemble those left by the advances from the northwest in the northern part of the Western Uplands. Perhaps they were deposited by the same early glaciations.

Although the glaciers did not reach the Driftless Area, they did have a number of widespread impacts there. The cold climate that allowed glaciers to expand into the Midwest also led to perennially frozen ground. The permafrost was probably as much as hundreds of feet thick and extended through all of the Western Uplands at times during the Quaternary. Casts of ice wedges and tundra polygons are abundant in the northern part of the region and have been found in many places farther south. Most of these features probably formed when, for a time, permafrost extended far beyond the glaciers that covered northern and eastern Wisconsin 26,000 to

10,000 years ago, but some may have formed during earlier permafrost episodes. Our best estimate is that the most recent episode of permafrost lasted from about 26,000 to about 13,000 years ago.

In permafrost areas today, the ground thaws to depths of a few feet during the summer, but below that, the ground remains frozen and prevents downward drainage of water. Therefore, the thawed ground becomes very wet and easily slides down even modest slopes, which causes very high rates of erosion of the uplands and hillslopes. The periods of permafrost likely account for much of the erosion of the deposits from early glaciations.

Another widespread impact of the Quaternary glaciations was loess accumulation on the landscape. The great meltwater rivers, such as the Wisconsin, the Mississippi, and the Missouri, drained the Quaternary glaciers and carried water heavily laden with silt. These were braided rivers with complex channel and bar patterns, whose water levels tended to change frequently. On warm sunny days, melting of glacier ice led to higher river levels. At night, or on cool cloudy days, river levels fell and exposed sand and gravel bars. A layer of silt deposited on the exposed surface dried and blew eastward with the prevailing wind. The loess settled out of the air and accumulated widely across the landscape. In some places near the Mississippi River, it is tens of feet thick, but it thins to only a few feet in the eastern part of the Driftless Area. In places in the Western Uplands, geologists have identified loess from a number of different glaciations.

The braided meltwater rivers also shaped the major valleys; they cut the steep bluffs that flank the Wisconsin and Mississippi Valleys, undercut the bedrock, and carried rock debris away. The Wisconsin and Mississippi Rivers, as well as the Black and the Chippewa, flow within broad, sandy outwash plains deposited by the braided meltwater streams.

Interstate 90/Interstate 94
Camp Douglas—Tomah
10 miles (16 km)

Cambrian sandstones are well exposed along the highway at Camp Douglas and nearby Mill Bluff State Park, a unit of the Ice Age National Scientific Reserve. Castle Rock Wayside at Camp Douglas and adjacent higher cliffs expose spectacular pinnacles of sandstone of the oldest Cambrian formations. Together with Mill Bluff, these picturesque buttelike hills are simply remnants of a former, blanketlike covering of Cambrian strata. The sandstone displays prominent crossbedding; the inclined stratification here formed within constantly shifting sandbars in braided river channels.

Hills such as these provide outstanding views of the nearly flat Central Plain to the east, which was the former floor of Glacial Lake Wisconsin. West of Mill Bluff, the route again passes onto the edge of the Central Plain, but you can see more sandstone hills and roadcuts through sandstone. The erosion of poorly cemented Cambrian strata from such hills provided sand to the Central Plain. Some of them were islands in Glacial Lake Wisconsin, which flooded much of the area from about 18,000 to 14,000 years ago.

Erosion formed these picturesque buttes in Cambrian sandstone at Camp Douglas on I-90/I-94. Rivers deposited most of these sandstones.
—Photo courtesy of Milwaukee Public Museum

View from Mill Bluff State Park eastward toward the flat bed of Glacial Lake Wisconsin. The hills in the distance were islands in the lake.
—Photo courtesy of the Wisconsin Department of Natural Resources

Interstate 90
Tomah—La Crosse
46 miles (75 km)

Interstate 90 from the junction with I-94 on the edge of the Central Plain at Tomah to La Crosse on the Mississippi River follows the La Crosse River most of the way. Although I-90 crosses the middle of the Driftless Area, the La Crosse Valley is so broad and the topography so subdued that few outcrops are visible near the highway. Practically all of the route is at the level of the Cambrian Wonewoc formation, but at the high point of the route halfway between Tomah and Sparta, the next-younger formation, the Tunnel City, appears in a few roadcuts. The brown, silty material overlying the bedrock is loess. This windblown sediment is well over 10 feet thick in many places here but thins rapidly eastward away from the Mississippi River, which was its major source.

Sparta is the northwest terminus of the Elroy-Sparta State Trail, the nation's first of many rail-to-trail conversions for bicycling and hiking. The novelty of three tunnels through Cambrian sandstones makes the trail especially popular. The tunnels provided easier grades where the railroad crossed the drainage divide between the Central Plain and the Mississippi Valley.

West Salem, 10 miles east of La Crosse, was the boyhood home of writer Hamlin Garlin, who promoted the nickname "Coulee Country" for this region near the Mississippi River. Many small tributaries to the Mississippi qualify as *coulees,* a French word for steep-sided valleys with only intermittently flowing water.

Interstate 94
Tomah—Hudson
144 miles (235 km)

Just east of Tomah is a series of cranberry bogs, many more of which dot the plain farther east. A little north of Tomah, the road leaves the Central Plain behind. On the west side of the highway is Fort McCoy, a large military reservation. The sandstone hills here lack the cap of resistant Ordovician dolomite that is present in the southern and western parts of the Driftless Area. Because erosion has removed the dolomite, the hills tend to have more rounded crests. Prior to logging in the late 1800s, this region was covered with majestic white and red pine trees; today the forest is composed mainly of jack pine and oak trees with some white birch. Much of this forested area is part of the Black River State Forest.

At milepost 122 on the westbound side is a rest area with a scenic view to the east of sandstone mounds or buttes. The flat, sandy bed of Glacial Lake Wisconsin lies about 15 miles to the east. One hill visible to the north from the viewpoint is Iron Mound, 4 miles east of Black River Falls, which was the site of the former Jackson County Iron Mine. The ore was a typical Precambrian banded iron formation. Attempts to mine and smelt it in the 1800s proved uneconomical, but a modern process for smelting low-grade ore, or taconite, finally made this ore minable from 1969 to 1982.

At the south edge of Black River Falls along U.S. 12 is Castle Mound in the Black River State Forest. This ridge, visible just west of the interstate, exposes a succession of Cambrian sandstones and provides a superb view from the top. At Black River Falls, the Black River has cut through the lowest Cambrian sandstone into underlying Precambrian metamorphic rocks, forming the westernmost exposure of these very old rocks in Wisconsin. Here, a granite intruded into older gneiss and iron deposits about 1,850 million years ago during the major Penokean mountain building event, which affected much of the Lake Superior region.

Settlers built a dam at the waterfalls on the Black River, as they did at many other waterfalls in Wisconsin, to power mills. Later these dams provided electricity to light the towns and run small manufacturing enterprises. The still-functioning local hydroelectric stations have long since been integrated into modern, regional power transmission networks.

The Black River was the outlet from Glacial Lake Wisconsin to the Mississippi River from about 18,000 years ago until about 14,000 years ago. During that time, the western edge of the Green Bay Lobe of the Laurentide Ice Sheet dammed the Wisconsin River at the Baraboo Hills, resulting in the formation of Glacial Lake Wisconsin. The water in the lake rose until it reached the level of the next lowest outlet, the Black River, into which the lake spilled. At the peak of the last glaciation, the Black River carried meltwater derived from a large part of the ice sheet then covering eastern and northern Wisconsin. The broad sandy outwash plains, which extend far beyond the modern floodplain, were deposited by braided meltwater rivers. The Black River now drains part of central and west-central Wisconsin.

Three miles northeast of I-94 from Hixton is Silver Mound, which is an important archaeological site. At least 10,000 years ago, humans visited and lived temporarily in rock cave shelters in Wisconsin. An unusually hard pocket of Cambrian Wonewoc sandstone attracted them to Silver Mound. Cemented by silica, the hard sandstone is ideal for making projectile points, knives, and other tools. Besides human-made tools and pottery, a rare fossil animal related to primitive snails has also been found at Silver Mound.

Why the sandstone should be so well cemented in this small area is a mystery. The mound is private property, therefore permission is required for visits.

Six miles west of Hixton, poorly cemented Wonewoc sandstone is quarried for a very different use in a process for enhancing the flow of oil wells in the Gulf of Mexico region. Fluids under very high pressure are pumped into a well to force open small fractures. Millimeter-size sand grains carried by the fluid then prevent the fractures from closing, thus increasing the overall permeability of a rock. Quartz grains from the Wonewoc and Jordan sandstones of Wisconsin and Minnesota are the favorites for this purpose. Wisconsin may not have any oil, but it surely has a lot of quartz sandstone!

Precambrian Gneiss at Hatfield and Neillsville

Those who like very old things may enjoy an optional side trip of about 50 miles to see some of Wisconsin's oldest rocks. You can take this trip either northeast from Black River Falls or east from Osseo by following the directions in reverse.

From Black River Falls, exit onto Wisconsin 27 for 2.5 miles, then turn right on County E, and proceed 9 miles to Hatfield. At the southeast edge of town, below the Lake Arbutus Dam, you can see Archean gneiss overlain by Cambrian sandstone. This gneiss is one of the oldest rocks in Wisconsin, which formed originally as volcanic rocks about 2,815 million years ago and was then metamorphosed 1,850 million years ago. Younger dikes cut across the gneiss. Continuing north about 15 more miles via County J, Wisconsin 95, and Wisconsin 73 brings you to Neillsville, where a large quarry exposes a different gneiss, which formed about 2,535 million years ago as an igneous intrusion into the older metamorphosed volcanic rocks that you can see at Lake Arbutus. This rock was also metamorphosed about 1,850 million years ago during Penokean mountain building. Cambrian sandstone overlies the gneiss at the top of the quarry wall. From Neillsville you can return to I-94 either by driving west on U.S. 10 to Osseo or southwest on Wisconsin 95 through Merrillan to Hixton. At Merrillan, the Mt. Simon sandstone is well exposed just below a dam on Halls Creek; stratification features indicate deposition by tidal currents.

Osseo to Hudson

There are no notable bedrock exposures along the interstate between Osseo and Hudson, but bedrock does appear along the principal rivers and in roadcuts and quarries. For example, the best exposures of the oldest Cambrian formation, the Mt. Simon sandstone, occur along the Chippewa River within Eau Claire and at Chippewa Falls. Both the Mt. Simon and

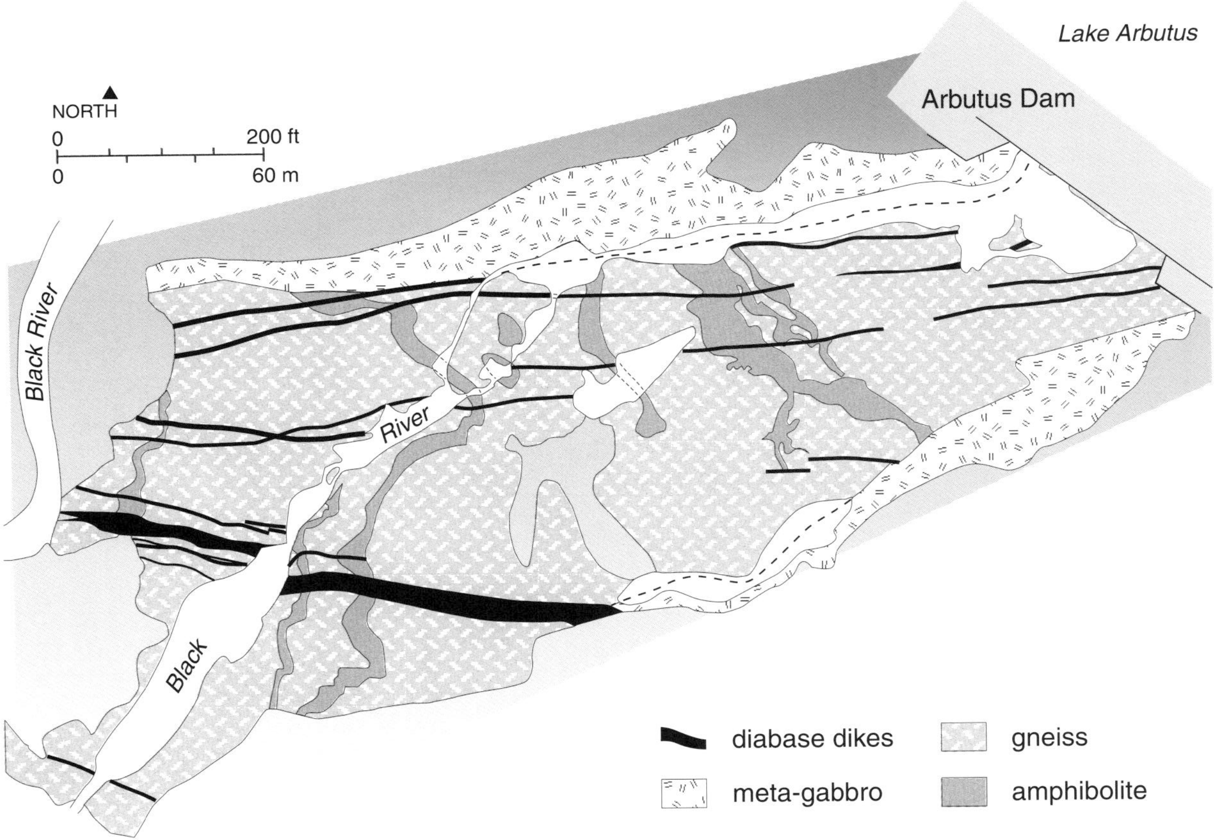

Archean bedrock exposed south of Arbutus Dam at Hatfield. This gneiss is 2,815 million years old but was metamorphosed 1,850 million years ago and intruded by various igneous rocks. — After Brown, Clayton, Madison, and Evans, 1983

Lake Arbutus

Arbutus Dam

Black River

River

Black

NORTH

200 ft

60 m

0

0

diabase dikes

gneiss

meta-gabbro

amphibolite

Eau Claire formations were named at Eau Claire, which means "clear wa-ter" in French. The base of the Mt. Simon sandstone is exposed at Big Falls and Little Falls on the Eau Claire River, 9 miles east of the city. There it overlies Precambrian metamorphic rocks dated as 1,900 to 1,850 million years old, making them at least 1,300 million years older than the sand-stone—plenty of time for the profound erosion of those older rocks, which were formed at depths of many miles within the earth.

West of Eau Claire, younger Cambrian and early Ordovician formations are exposed in places along some of the tributary valleys near the Missis-sippi and St. Croix Rivers. You can visit Crystal Cave in Ordovician dolomite about 8 miles south of the interstate by leaving I-94 at exit 28 to Wisconsin 128 and Wisconsin 29. One of Wisconsin's four commercial caves, Crystal Cave is 70 feet deep and about 4,000 feet long with 1,300 feet open to the public. It was first opened in 1942 and few improvements were made until 1985, when it was purchased by a geologist couple, who cater to grade school children.

Osseo marks the southern boundary of the west-central glaciated up-lands, which lie north of the Driftless Area. This region has remnants of glacial deposits that pre-date the glaciation that covered much of northern and eastern Wisconsin between 26,000 and 10,000 years ago. In contrast with the more recently glaciated areas, erosion has destroyed the glacial landforms and much of the sediment here, obscuring the history of the earlier glaciations that occurred hundreds of thousands of years ago. Fea-tures such as ice wedge casts characteristic of permafrost, permanently frozen ground near the periphery of glaciers, have been recognized widely in west-central Wisconsin, including sites near Fairchild and Eau Claire. Fossil tundra polygons have also been recorded at a few sites. These perma-frost features, which still form today in regions of Arctic tundra, indicate that the ground was frozen deeply for extended periods on the order of tens of thousands of years. During the summer thaw, the upper few feet of soil became water saturated and moved downslope, obliterating features formed by earlier ice advances.

Between Osseo and Eau Claire, I-94 crosses an area of thin and patchy glacial deposits that do not disguise the shape of the underlying bedrock. At Eau Claire, the highway crosses the Chippewa River and its broad outwash plains that were deposited by meltwater from the late Wisconsin Chippewa Lobe, which reached its maximum extent about 18,000 years ago about 20 miles north of Eau Claire. Near the Dunn–St. Croix County line, the route crosses into an area where red, sandy till mantles much of the landscape. This till is very weathered and glacial landforms are subtle at best. Clearly this area was glaciated long before the late Wisconsin advance of the Supe-rior Lobe into the Hudson area about 18,000 years ago.

Near the Menomonie exit, a rest area for westbound traffic has a fine garden of prairie plants, which gives an impression of the lush grassland vegetation that covered large parts of western Wisconsin before settlement. Between Baldwin (at the U.S. 63 intersection) and Hudson, I-94 passes through the Northern Highlands for the last 20 miles to the St. Croix River. It crosses outwash plains and somewhat hummocky uplands covered with red sandy till deposited by a late Wisconsin advance of the Superior Lobe. Here, the ice was flowing southeastward.

Like many of the towns in the northern half of Wisconsin, Hudson was founded as a lumber milling center. At Hudson, the St. Croix River widens to form Lake St. Croix, thanks to damming 10 miles south by the delta of a tributary, the Kinnickinnic River. In the bluffs along the St. Croix River, as well as within Hudson, Cambrian sandstones are exposed. At least two faults have offset the Cambrian and Ordovician strata in the vicinity of Hudson. They are visible in river bluffs to the south on both sides of the river, but trend northeast past Hudson for at least 10 to 20 miles; Paleozoic strata

Landscape image of the northern part of the Western Uplands shows the outwash plains along the Chippewa River. The uplands are Paleozoic rock with a patchy cover of till from early glaciations.

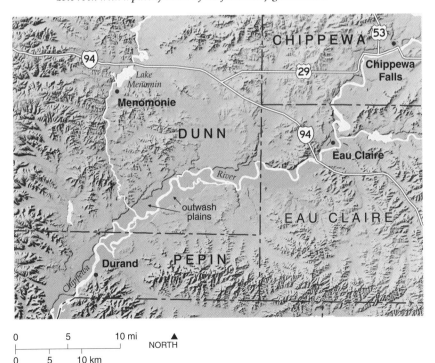

0	5	10 mi

NORTH ▲

0	5	10 km

have been offset vertically as much as 400 feet. These faults parallel others farther north, which have offset late Precambrian rocks exposed near Lake Superior. Some of these old faults were reactivated after Ordovician time.

Willow River State Park

You can reach Willow River State Park, only 6 miles northeast of Hudson, in a few minutes from the interstate. Exit 3 miles east of Hudson north from I-94 at U.S. 12 and follow County U and County A to the park, or take County A northeast from Hudson. The park once contained three dams that were erected many years ago on the Willow River, first for milling grains harvested from the adjacent farmland, but later for hydroelectric power. Today, only one dam survives, forming picturesque Little Falls Lake, which is popular for fishing and swimming. Cambrian sandstones containing marine fossils are exposed below the dam, and scenic Willow Falls above the lake cascades over ledges of the Ordovician Prairie du Chien dolomite. The sandstones at the dam belong far below the Prairie du Chien dolomite, but they are now at about the same elevation. An unusual 10-degree eastward tilt of the sandstones confirms that something is strange here. The sandstones have been raised 300 or 400 feet along the Hudson fault, which must extend northeast through the park.

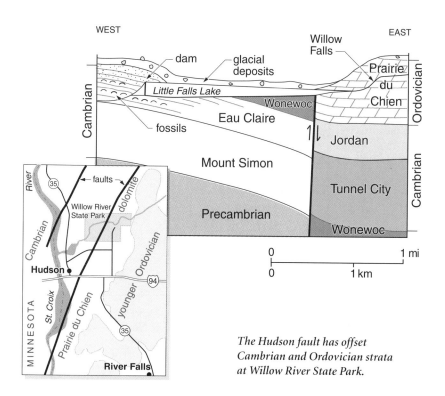

The Hudson fault has offset Cambrian and Ordovician strata at Willow River State Park.

U.S. 14
La Crosse—Madison
136 miles (218 km)

U.S. 14 provides a beautifully scenic route through the heart of the Driftless Area away from frenetic interstate traffic. It provides a geological roller-coaster ride up and down through the Cambrian and Ordovician rocks, past beautiful farm fields and woodlots. At La Crosse, the route is low in the Cambrian strata. At the junction where U.S. 14 leaves Wisconsin 35 (The Great River Road) a high cliff exposes the Wonewoc formation, as do cliffs 3 miles farther east. From the Mississippi Valley, U.S. 14 climbs for 6 miles up through younger Cambrian sandstones to the first ridgetop, which is capped by the lower part of the Prairie du Chien dolomite of Ordovician age. The roller-coaster descent from this ridge takes one back down through the sequence of rocks into Coon Valley on the uppermost part of the Jordan sandstone of Cambrian age.

Coon Valley was the site of the first federal experiment in watershed conservation during the 1930s. The University of Wisconsin and what was to become the U.S. Soil Conservation Service tested potential solutions to the problem of soil erosion caused by the cultivation of steep slopes using horse-drawn plows. This plowman's folly caused flash floods and severe gullying in the region for fifty years. The effects of a storm in 1922 were described as follows: "The team had to swim the new gully with the wagon floating where the field was only minutes earlier" (Sartz 1977). Debris piled at the outlet of one such gully buried a road 14 feet deep and was spread an average of 6 feet deep over a 40-acre area. The 1930s experiments produced effective solutions: contour plowing and alternate strips of different crops. The advent of tractors also helped, for they are not safe on steep slopes; today, farming in the Driftless Area is confined to the broader uplands and the valley bottoms, leaving the easily eroded steep slopes in forest.

From Coon Valley, you can take a short side trip to visit Norskedalen, meaning "Norwegian Valley," a heritage center depicting farm buildings built a century ago by Norwegian immigrants who settled this part of Wisconsin. It is 3 miles northeast via County P and PI. The Jordan sandstone is well exposed along the way.

From Coon Valley, U.S. 14 climbs southeastward again up through the Jordan sandstone to the Prairie du Chien dolomite, in which there is a large quarry on the east side of the highway near the summit. The road then traverses a fertile upland for about 20 miles through Westby and Viroqua. This upland is 5 to 6 miles wide and drops off steeply to both the east and west; the village of Avalanche 6 miles to the east in the Kickapoo Valley seems aptly named.

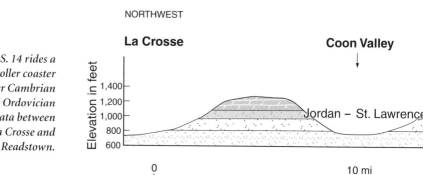

NORTHWEST

La Crosse   **Coon Valley**

U.S. 14 rides a roller coaster over Cambrian and Ordovician strata between La Crosse and Readstown.

Jordan – St. Lawrence

0   10 mi
0   15 km

You can see the Ordovician St. Peter sandstone in several roadcuts capping the high country, for example 2 mile south of Viroqua at the junction with Wisconsin 27 and Wisconsin 82. Two miles farther southeast is a quarry on the east side of the highway in the Prairie du Chien dolomite, which underlies the St. Peter sandstone. In places the sandstone occupies ancient channels eroded into the dolomite. The highway continues to descend a long valley through Cambrian sandstones for 4 more miles to Readstown, where it crosses the Kickapoo River.

In the 25 miles downstream from here to the Wisconsin River, the Kickapoo has long been notorious for disastrous floods. The steep slopes of the region and disturbance of the native forest cover by agriculture aggravated the runoff of water. In the 1970s, the Corps of Engineers began to construct an earthen dam near LaFarge, 15 miles upstream from Readstown, in an attempt to control the annual flooding. The planned lake was touted as a recreational boon, but ecologists argued that it would quickly become stagnant and cause serious ecologic disturbances to the area. Economists also argued that it would be cheaper to move whole towns out of the valley bottom than to complete the proposed flood control project. The town of Soldiers Grove, 4 miles south of Readstown, was moved about half a mile from the riverside to higher ground, but the dam was not completed.

From Readstown, which lies near the middle of the Cambrian strata, U.S. 14 climbs again to the Prairie du Chien dolomite on a rolling upland around Sugar Grove, then roller coasters down to Bosstown where sandstone reappears. Six miles southeast of Bosstown is a junction with Wisconsin 171. One mile south is the hamlet of Boaz. A historical sign at the junction commemorates the founding of the Rural Electrification Authority in the 1930s. Just east of the sign, Wisconsin's first recorded discovery of a mastodon skeleton was made in 1897 by four farm boys. The Dorsch

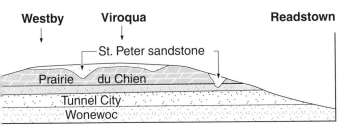

SOUTHEAST

Westby   Viroqua   Readstown

St. Peter sandstone

Prairie   du Chien

Tunnel City
Wonewoc

family excavated it and in 1915 sold it for display in the University of Wisconsin's geology museum at Madison, where it can be seen today. Many other less-complete mastodon skeletons have been found subsequently over the state, generally in old bog deposits. The Boaz specimen is particularly interesting not only because it was a first, but also because an Indian spear point was reported with it. This artifact became separated from the skeleton, however, and it took nearly a century of archaeological detective work to reunite the two. The point was crafted from gray quartzite, which possibly came from the well-known Silver Mound Indian quarry site northeast of Hixton. The point is of the distinctive fluted Clovis style, which archaeologists date back to about 12,000 years ago. On U.S. 14 just east of the Boaz junction, a historical marker records the mastodon discovery.

Three miles east of the Boaz junction, the road divides and passes over another ridge; the Cambrian Jordan sandstone is well exposed here. Five miles beyond lies Richland Center on the Pine River, which has cut deeply enough to expose the same older Cambrian formations that are exposed at La Crosse. At the south edge of Richland Center, a quarry on the north side of the road exposes the Tunnel City and overlying Jordan formations. Tunnel City strata here are rich in glauconitic greensands and storm deposits. Storm waves first eroded the sea bottom, concentrating flat sandstone pebbles, which were then covered with undulatory, laminated deposits. After each storm, long intervals of intense burrowing by animals blurred the stratification. A side trip 8 miles north of Richland Center on Wisconsin 80 takes you to Pine Natural Bridge, a keyhole cut through Cambrian sandstones.

Famous American architectural pioneer Frank Lloyd Wright was born in Richland Center in 1869. The A. D. German Warehouse, now a local museum near the center of town, was designed by Wright for a local friend

*Hummocky lamination in Cambrian greensand formed by storm waves.
Tunnel City formation, southwestern Wisconsin.* —J. L. Sutherland photo

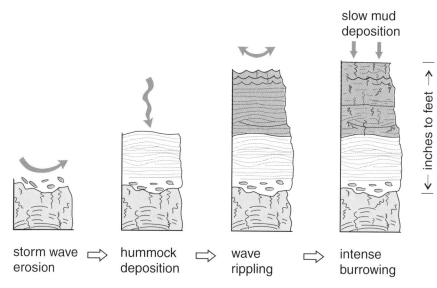

slow mud
deposition

inches to feet →

storm wave ⇨ hummock ⇨ wave ⇨ intense
erosion   deposition   rippling   burrowing

*Typical storm deposits in Cambrian sandstones in Wisconsin. First, storm waves
scoured the sea bottom, producing some flat pebbles of previously deposited sands.
Then, hummocky laminations buried these pebbles as the storm waves diminished
in intensity, and finally wave ripples formed. As fair-weather calm was restored, animals burrowed into the storm deposits. Glauconite grains are scattered throughout.*

and built at the end of World War I. It shows some of the same designs that distinguished Tokyo's famous Imperial Hotel, which he designed about the same time and which survived the devastating earthquake of 1923, to Wright's great delight. Between Richland Center and Madison, U.S. 14 is dedicated to Wright.

Continuing south from Richland Center on U.S. 14, white sandstones of the older Cambrian Wonewoc formation appear in roadcuts. East of Gotham, U.S. 14 passes over the broad outwash plains of the Wisconsin River valley. Low hills on these plains are wind-formed sand dunes up to 10 to 15 feet high. At Spring Green, U.S. 14 crosses to the south bank of the river and continues eastward to Mazomanie. Tower Hill State Park and Governor Dodge State Park, both south of Spring Green, are discussed in **Wisconsin 23: Dodgeville—Tower Hill State Park**.

Wisconsin River Valley

The Wisconsin River from Sauk City, 20 miles upriver from Spring Green, to its mouth at Prairie du Chien flows through a wide floodplain between broad, sandy outwash plains. Its channel averages an eighth to a quarter of a mile wide, meandering irregularly from one side of the valley to the other. The channel splits and rejoins at many points to form semipermanent wooded islands; backwater sloughs are also common along the margins of the channel. At low-water stages, many sandbars are visible within the main channel as temporary islands and shallow shoals. These are favorite sites for boaters to stop for picnics, swimming, fishing, and overnight camping, especially in this stretch of the valley. The unwary should be warned that the margins of these sand bodies drop off abruptly into deep water and the sand may collapse without warning. The current in this river is faster than it appears, averaging more than 5 miles per hour. Thanks to an unplanned experiment some years ago, we can attest to the fact that it is very difficult to paddle a canoe upriver even at low water. The river sediment is dominated by medium to coarse sand and small pebbles, which have been derived chiefly from the erosion of glacial deposits that cover the upper three-fourths of the river's drainage basin above Sauk City. The twin towns, Sauk City and Prairie du Sac, are on broad outwash plains deposited by meltwater from the Green Bay Lobe. The Johnstown moraine is opposite on the east side of the Wisconsin River.

Cliffs along the Wisconsin River all the way up to Sauk City expose Cambrian formations. At river level is the Wonewoc formation with the overlying Tunnel City strata containing green glauconite grains exposed at Tower Hill and in Ferry Bluff about 15 miles farther upriver on the north bank. The Jordan sandstone and Prairie du Chien dolomite cap all of the higher ridges on either side of the valley, but the forest generally obscures the rocks. Ferry Bluff, accessible from Wisconsin 60 or by boat, provides a spectacular

*Islands and sandbars on the Wisconsin River near Spring
Green. The sandbars are constantly changing.* —L. J. Maher photo

view of the river valley, and has good outcrops of the upper half of the
Cambrian sandstones and the dolomite. Here, the greensand interval is
replaced by only slightly glauconitic crossbedded sandstones exposed along
the trail just below the top of the bluff. The top has a remnant patch of
native prairie vegetation.

At the east edge of Mazomanie on U.S. 14, the Tunnel City formation
with green glauconite is exposed at road level with the younger formations
present uphill, including the lowest part of the Prairie du Chien on top.

Mazomanie to Madison

At Mazomanie, U.S. 14 leaves the Wisconsin River valley and its broad
outwash plains to follow a tributary, Black Earth Creek, which was a major
path for glacial meltwater at the end of glaciation around 15,000 years ago.
Today, this stream receives its water from smaller tributaries fed by cold,
clear spring water seeping from hillsides at the base of the Prairie du Chien
dolomite. Thanks to the high quality of its water, Black Earth Creek has
long been a fine trout stream, but increasingly dense settlement of its drainage basin threatens the water quality. Roadcuts between Mazomanie and
Madison expose chiefly the upper half of the Cambrian sandstone strata.
At Black Earth, 3 miles east of Mazomanie, a dolomite stratum named for

this town is well developed. Four miles east at Festge County Park, a resistant cliff of Prairie du Chien dolomite provides an overlook of Black Earth Creek valley. The last exposure of Paleozoic rocks on U.S. 14 before Madison is a roadcut on the north side 3.5 miles east of Cross Plains, which exposes the boundary between the Prairie du Chien and the underlying Jordan sandstone.

Just east of Cross Plains, a big gravel pit on the south side of the valley is exploiting a large volume of glacial outwash gravel deposited just west of the Johnstown moraine, which crosses the highway 1 mile east of the pit but is not obvious. This moraine marks the maximum advance of the Green Bay Lobe of about 18,000 years ago and also marks the eastern edge of the Driftless Area. Just beyond the gravel pit and south of U.S. 14 is the Cross

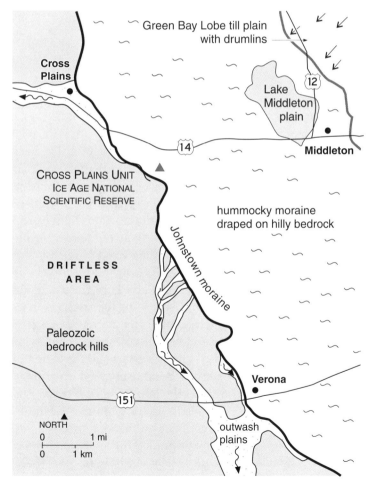

The Johnstown moraine marks the western edge of the Eastern Uplands.

Plains Unit of the Ice Age National Scientific Reserve, which features several lake basins and a meltwater channel that formed right at the outer edge of the late Wisconsin Green Bay Lobe. To reach the Cross Plains Unit, take Cleveland Road south 1 mile to the intersection with Timber Lane. The low ridge just before the intersection is the Johnstown moraine. Just to the right on Timber Lane is a small pulloff area and a trail leading into the woods on the north side of the road to a meltwater channel called Wilkie Gorge. You can see the lake basins that formed along the ice margin by driving east and south for 2 miles. The road parallels the moraine, which is a prominent wooded ridge on the east side of the road.

U.S. 53
Eau Claire—Haugen
65 miles (100 km)

Within Eau Claire, Cambrian formations are exposed along the winding Chippewa River, especially when the water level is low. Mt. Simon, a bluff overlooking the river in a park in the north part of the city, is the namesake for the Mt. Simon sandstone, but most of the formation has been submerged here by a nearby dam. The next-younger formation was named for the city of Eau Claire. In this north country of widespread glacial deposits and dense woods, bedrock exposures are few. Streams and rivers provide the best outcrops, especially at waterfalls, but mill dams built by early settlers at such falls now obscure the bedrock. Many of the first towns in the region were located at the mill sites, including Eau Claire and Chippewa Falls.

In Chippewa Falls, 9 miles northeast of Eau Claire, the lower 60 feet of Mt. Simon sandstone appears in Irvine Park along the east bank of Duncan Creek upstream from the Bear Den Road bridge across the creek. Here, a few feet of pebbly conglomerate and coarse sandstone rest upon eroded and weathered Precambrian gneiss. This lowest part of the formation was deposited by a sprawling, braided river, but most of the formation was deposited by vigorous tidal currents as the late Cambrian ocean gradually flooded most of Wisconsin. Fossil shells are rare in the Mt. Simon sandstone, but the traces left by fossil animals are more common—variously shaped burrows formed by wormlike animals and tracks and trails made by animals that crawled across sand. The large *Climactichnites* trail, which resembles a tire track, is particularly impressive, but trilobite resting depressions and various worm trails are also present.

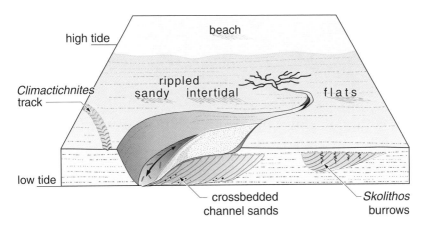

Deposition of sediments characteristic of a sandy tidal environment.

The Eau Claire formation is finer grained than the Mt. Simon, even containing considerable shale, and has many wave-formed ripple marks and larger, undulating or hummocky laminations formed by storm waves. Whereas the Mt. Simon sandstone was deposited in a shallow marine environment dominated by vigorous tidal currents, the Eau Claire formation accumulated in a somewhat deeper environment as the ocean continued to advance over Wisconsin, moving the shoreline farther northeast. The presence of grains of the green mineral glauconite, which forms by sluggish chemical reactions between seawater and clay particles, especially clayey animal fecal pellets, indicates that the Eau Claire deposition was slower on average. The more dramatic effects of tropical storm waves interrupted long, boring spells of slow deposition of clay and fine sand with glauconite. The Eau Claire formation contains many fossil skeletons as well as many trails and burrows. It is exposed best today in quarries and cuts along county roads west of Chippewa Falls and around Colfax.

Along U.S. 53, the landscape reveals only the effects of glaciation; there is a roadcut of Cambrian sandstone 10 miles north of Chippewa Falls and the next outcrops of pre-Quaternary rocks are near Cameron, 35 miles farther north. Between Eau Claire and Chippewa Falls, the highway crosses the Chippewa River, which was a major drainage for meltwater from the Chippewa Lobe. The maximum late Wisconsin extent of that lobe is marked by the Chippewa moraine, which is roughly parallel to U.S. 53 about 4 miles to the east. Broad outwash terraces flank the Chippewa River. The uplands on either side of the valley are bedrock with patchy glacial deposits from earlier glaciations.

Impressions of abundant skeletal material of trilobites in the Eau Claire formation near Chippewa Falls.
—C. W. Byers photo

A side trip from Bloomer, which is 8 miles north of Chippewa Falls, provides access to the Chippewa Moraine Unit of the Ice Age National Scientific Reserve, where an interpretive center and trails introduce visitors to a spectacular hummocky glacial landscape. Take Wisconsin 40 north from Bloomer for about 10 miles, then follow County M east for about 4 miles, then turn south on Ice Age Drive.

Between Bloomer and Cameron, U.S. 53 crosses nearly flat but pitted outwash plains deposited beyond the western margin of the Chippewa Lobe and a bedrock upland with thin deposits from early glaciations. South of Cameron, the road descends onto the extensively pitted outwash plain flanking the Red Cedar River. Streams carrying meltwater southward between the Superior Lobe to the west and the Chippewa Lobe to the east deposited the outwash plain. About 3.5 miles north of Cameron U.S. 53 crosses the Red Cedar River and then rises onto an upland area west of Rice Lake, which is covered with till deposited beneath the Superior Lobe. Here, along the southeastern margin of the lobe, ice was flowing to the southeast. About 3 miles north of Rice Lake, the highway descends back onto the pitted outwash plain, which it crosses all the way to Haugen. The Tuscobia State

Trail, a segment of the Ice Age National Scenic Trail, crosses the highway about 4 miles north of Rice Lake. At Haugen, U.S. 53 rises onto the hummocky, lake-dotted St. Croix moraine of the Superior Lobe and enters the Northern Highlands.

The Precambrian red Barron quartzite, which is identical with the Baraboo quartzite farther south, forms the Blue, or Barron, Hills northeast of Cameron and east of Rice Lake. Within the Barron quartzite are soft, fine-grained, red claystones, which were quarried 5 miles east of Rice Lake by Native Americans for carving ceremonial pipes, or calumets. The best-known pipestone quarry is at Pipestone National Monument in southwestern Minnesota. Native Americans traded raw pipestone and finished pipes far and wide, presenting a challenge for archaeologists to trace individual artifacts to a particular quarry source, but geologists who specialize in geoarchaeology can often identify, or "fingerprint," clay minerals from specific sites. The red quartzite also appears 6 miles east of Cameron on U.S. 8, where Cambrian sandstone and conglomerate of the Eau Claire formation were deposited upon the quartzite. The Barron, like the Baraboo quartzite, formed islands in the Cambrian sea.

The south- to southwest-flowing ice of the Chippewa Lobe covered the Blue Hills and transported boulders of the quartzite to the south and west. Look for them scattered in farm fields. A notable feature of the Blue Hills is the extensive cover of countless angular fragments of quartzite on slopes and upland areas. Individual fragments are typically about a foot or two in size, similar to the spacing between fractures in the quartzite. Permafrost probably accelerated the fracturing and downslope movement of the fragments.

U.S. 151
Dubuque (Iowa)—Madison
85 miles (138 km)

U.S. 151 enters the southwestern corner of Wisconsin, crossing the Mississippi River at Dubuque, Iowa. Silurian dolomite is exposed in the hills just west of Dubuque. The highway bridge crosses the Mississippi next to Lock and Dam No. 11, one of nine such combinations along the Wisconsin reach of the river. Constructed in the 1930s, the locks and dams enhance navigation of the upper river as far as Minneapolis, especially for freight barges.

Roadcuts along the highway just east of the bridge expose the Ordovician Galena dolomite, which underlies much of the uplands along the route to Madison. U.S. 151 immediately joins Wisconsin 35, the Great River Road, which enters from the south through historic Galena, Illinois, the pre–Civil War home of Ulysses S. Grant. From the junction of the two highways, Sinsinawa Mound is visible on the southeastern skyline; the Native American name means "home of the young eagle." This is one of several hills along the Illinois border capped by Silurian dolomite, which is more extensive to the south in Illinois and west in Iowa and originally must have covered all of Wisconsin. The roads divide at Dickeyville, where a grotto of the same name constructed by a German-Catholic priest in the late 1920s is studded with specimens of fossils and rocks as well as modern shells and millions of pieces of colored glass.

Northeast of Dickeyville, Ordovician fossiliferous dolomites of the Platteville and Galena formations cap most ridges and the St. Peter sandstone forms slopes; these appear in several roadcuts. Just north of Dickeyville, U.S. 151 descends into the valley of the Little Platte River. This valley has a conspicuous meandering pattern. Along the margins of the valley are remnants of an older, higher floodplain that formed during the most recent glaciation, about 26,000 to 12,000 years ago. At that time, the river built up its floodplain in response to the rapid buildup of the Mississippi River valley into which it flows. The Little Platte has since eroded down to its present level.

Platteville, 11 miles northeast of Dickeyville, is named for "plattes," bowl-shaped plates of smelted lead made by Native Americans using a technique taught to them by French traders. A former school of mines established here in 1907 is today a division of the University of Wisconsin. A mining museum offers a tour of the former Bevans lead mine, which dates back to 1845. For the incurable mining or spelunking enthusiast, a side trip to

Platte Mound from U.S. 151 near Platteville. Typical of Wisconsin mounds, it is simply an erosional remnant of widespread strata. M stands for the former Platteville School of Mines. —R. H. Dott, Jr., photo

Shullsburg, 20 miles southeast of Platteville, provides an opportunity to tour the Badger Museum and Mine. For those who want still more, a 15-mile drive west and south from Shullsburg via New Diggings just into Illinois on Illinois 84 takes you to the small Vinegar Hill lead mine. En route is the Point of Beginning from which the first survey of Wisconsin Territory was begun in 1831. A low mound just east of Wisconsin 80, 1.5 miles south of Hazel Green, marks this point on the Wisconsin-Illinois border.

A few miles east of Platteville, U.S. 151 passes just south of Platte and Belmont Mounds, two high hills capped by Silurian chert and dolomite. First Capitol State Park commemorates the first territorial capitol, which stands at the foot of Belmont Mound about 3 miles north of U.S. 151.

Lead was struck in 1827 in Mineral Point. Shake Rag Street is a living museum of Cornish miners' houses. "Shake rag" refers to a signal given by miners' wives that it was time for those "badgers" working in mines just across the valley to come home for dinner. Wisconsin has long been famous for beer making as well as lead mining, and the territory's first brewery was established here in Mineral Point in 1835; others soon followed in practically every new town.

Brachiopods, snails, cephalopods, and a trilobite, all from Ordovician time. The central circular fossil is thought to be either sponge or algae. —From D. D. Owen, 1840

Traveling through the fine farmland of this part of Wisconsin, which was once lush prairie with fertile loess soil developed upon Ordovician limestone and dolomite, one can understand why the land-use conflict developed between the early farmers and miners. Dodgeville, the county seat, has a classic-style courthouse dating from 1859. A slag furnace was built here in 1868 to remove lead from waste rock. Four miles north via Wisconsin 23 is Governor Dodge State Park with outcrops of Ordovician strata. It is described in **Wisconsin 23: Dodgeville—Tower Hill State Park**.

Much of U.S. 151 is a four-lane divided highway with many deep cuts in the Platteville and Galena dolomites. The Galena is noteworthy for its 150 or more subtle stratification surfaces with thin crusts of iron and manganese, which were precipitated from seawater during many intervals when no new sediment was accumulating. Together with concentrations of fossils in rich layers, the thin crusts indicate that deposition of the dolomite was very spasmodic. It is estimated that the pauses in deposition may account for 30 percent of the total time span represented by the formation. The environment of deposition must have been at least 50 or 60 feet deep; only the most violent tropical storm waves disturbed the sea bottom.

Weathering has taken advantage of variable textures in the Galena dolomite, producing a very porous character resembling termite-infested wood. Most of the mottled appearance reflects an intricate network of large animal burrows highlighted by the leaching of the slightly more soluble burrow fillings. Larger cavities in the roadcuts are small caves intersected by the highway; some contain red clay that accumulated after the caves formed. Most of the cavities and fissures were zones of lead and zinc mineralization that have been dissolved. Together with old mine workings, these zones have created problems for highway engineers.

Deep roadcuts in Ordovician dolomite on U.S. 151 near Dodgeville. —R. H. Dott, Jr., photo

Porous, termite-eaten appearance of Ordovician Galena dolomite is common in roadcuts from Dodgeville to Verona. Weathering has etched out the countless animal burrows that characterize this formation. —R. H. Dott, Jr., photo

In some places sediment fills fractures or solution openings in the rock, as in the roadcuts, but it also forms a cover of variable thickness all across the broad uplands of southwestern Wisconsin. This material contains both loess, windblown silt derived from silt-covered gravel bars along major glacial meltwater streams, and material formed by the weathering of underlying bedrock. In most places, gradual downslope movement has mixed the loess and weathering material. The loess near the Mississippi River, its major source, is tens of feet thick in places, whereas in the Madison area, it is rarely more than 2 feet thick.

U.S. 151 between Dodgeville and Verona follows closely an old military road that connected forts at Prairie du Chien on the Mississippi River with Portage, 100 miles northeast, and Green Bay, another 100 miles farther northeast. The route lies along a cuesta, a north-facing escarpment eroded from late Ordovician dolomite. This escarpment is a major drainage divide, with streams on the north side flowing to the Wisconsin River, while those to the south flow to the Mississippi. The St. Peter sandstone and older strata form the steep slopes of the valleys leading northward.

NORTHWEST

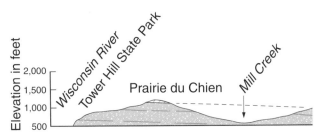

Cross section from Wisconsin River to Blue Mound State Park.

Blue Mound State Park

Just north of the highway almost halfway between Dodgeville and Madison, you can see Blue Mounds, two of the several hills in the region capped by Silurian chert and dolomite. West Mound in Blue Mound State Park is the highest point in southern Wisconsin, at 1,719 feet above sea level. You can see scattered blocks of silicified dolomite with a few rare fossil molds and large pores on the slopes of the mound. The state park observation tower offers a superb view of the Driftless Area, including the Wisconsin River valley and the Baraboo Hills 35 miles to the north. Nearby East Mound has Brigham County Park in a maple forest on its summit, which also offers a fine view.

Cave of the Mounds

A few miles to the east of Blue Mound State Park is Cave of the Mounds, one of Wisconsin's commercial caverns. This small, beautiful cave in the Galena dolomite was designated a National Natural Landmark in 1988. It was discovered in an interesting way. There had long been a quarry on the site, and in 1939 the operator set off a large explosive charge. When the dust settled, he was peering into a cave, which proved to be 70 feet deep and about half a mile long, and possessed handsome stalactites, stalagmites, and other dripstone features. The owner quickly recognized that his newly discovered asset held far more commercial value than the quarry operation. The cave opened in 1940 and immediately attracted large crowds. The Chicago & Northwestern Railroad even offered special train tours from Chicago to southwestern Wisconsin with a stop at Cave of the Mounds as a featured attraction. The train left Chicago at 7 A.M. and returned the same day at 10 P.M. The fare was $4.90 and dinner on the train cost only $1.00; cave admission was $0.28. Ah, for those good old days!

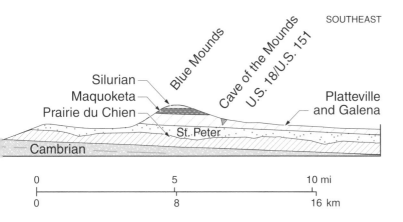

SOUTHEAST

Silurian
Maquoketa
Prairie du Chien

Blue Mounds

Cave of the Mounds
U.S. 18/U.S. 151

Platteville
and Galena

St. Peter

Cambrian

0	5	10 mi
0	8	16 km

Stalactites and stalagmites in Cave of the Mounds near U.S. 151 and Blue Mound State Park.
—Photo courtesy of Cave of the Mounds

Cave of the Mounds probably began to form a few million years ago when the dolomite lay below the local water table. Runoff water from rain and melting snow absorbed carbon dioxide from the air, which combined with hydrogen to make carbonic acid. The result was weakly acidic ground-water, which dissolved the dolomite along fractures in the bedrock, form-ing the cave. As surface erosion of the area proceeded over hundreds of thousands of years, the water table gradually sank below the cave level. A stream flowed through the cave, and water dripping from the ceiling slowly deposited various dripstone forms. Most familiar are stalactites growing down from the ceiling and stalagmites growing up from the cave floor; eventually the two may join to form a pillar. It is the great variety of forms and colors of dripstones that give caves their beauty and romance.

Verona Area

At Verona, just 5 miles from Madison, U.S. 151 leaves the Driftless Area and crosses into an area of recent glaciation at the edge of the Eastern Up-lands. Here, the broad, slightly hummocky Johnstown moraine was depos-ited by the Green Bay Lobe between about 18,000 and 15,000 years ago. About 1 mile south of U.S. 151, along Wisconsin 69 and County M, and also north of Verona, a number of large gravel mines operate in the outwash plain immediately west of the moraine. The coarse gravel deposited very near the ice margin provides a high-quality aggregate resource. Prairie Moraine County Park at Verona has several hiking trails on the crest of the Johnstown moraine, including a segment of the Ice Age National Scenic Trail. Take County PB south about 2 miles; the park is on the east side of the road. The hummocky moraine deposits are draped over deeply dis-sected bedrock not very different from that of the Driftless Area. Near its outermost margin, the ice sheet was so thin that it was not very effective in eroding the landscape, making it difficult to distinguish the glaciated area from the Driftless Area. Only a few miles farther east, between Verona and Madison, however, the landscape stands in sharp contrast to the Driftless Area. There, the glaciers effectively smoothed prominent bluffs and hills and filled deep valleys with sediment. The high points on the landscape between Verona and Madison are till-mantled bedrock hills.

Dodgeville—Tower Hill State Park
20 miles (32 km)

Wisconsin 23 takes you through typical Driftless Area terrain. Broad uplands had native prairie before European settlement and the deep valleys were forested, as most are still today.

Governor Dodge State Park
Four miles north of Dodgeville via Wisconsin 23, Governor Dodge State Park is a fine example of the Driftless Area. The Ordovician St. Peter sandstone is exposed in steep bluffs and the overlying Platteville formation extends across the uplands. Prairie vegetation is being restored on the park uplands. The Platteville formation is exposed along the road to Cox Hollow Lake about 1 mile southeast from the park entrance, where the road begins to descend to the lake. The underlying St. Peter sandstone is exposed farther down this grade and especially in the cliff at Enee Point opposite Enee Picnic Area. The lower half of the St. Peter sandstone in the park displays stratification characteristic of wind deposition, but the upper part has worm burrows indicative of shallow marine deposition. You

The rock sequence exposed in Governor Dodge State Park shows the transition from lower wind-blown to upper marine portions of the St. Peter sandstone.

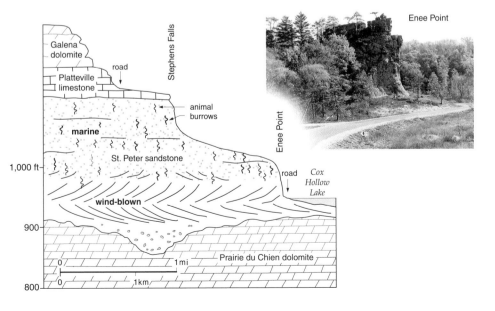

can see this in the rock shelter used by early Native Americans, which is accessible by a short walk from Deer Cove Picnic Area on the north shore of the lake. Wind dunes formed the large inclined strata in the shelter, whereas an advancing sea formed the overlying flat stratification, which extends upward from the roof of the shelter. A zone 2 or 3 feet thick in the roof of the shelter shows subtle burrows formed by marine worms, who lived in very shallow water as that sea drowned the wind dunes. Continue on the trail beyond the center of the shelter to see the best exposure of this burrowed zone. At the top of the steep, rocky stretch, the weathered burrowed zone appears in the cliff as vertical, small ribs. The nearby Pine Cliff Nature Trail from Enee Picnic Area provides additional views of the sandstone.

To see Stephens Falls, take a short walk from a parking area located three-quarters of a mile northeast from the park entrance. Here, a stream fed partially by a nearby spring at the Platteville–St. Peter contact spills over a cliff of St. Peter sandstone. About one-eighth of a mile downstream from the falls, the trail passes through a narrow stretch with cliffs on either side, which display large wind-formed crossbedding in the sandstone like that under the rock shelter.

Frank Lloyd Wright Country

North of Governor Dodge State Park on Wisconsin 23, you can see prominent Blue Mound on the eastern horizon; it is capped by Silurian strata. For the first 5 miles north, the highway is on the Platteville and Galena formations, some zones of which are richly fossiliferous; brachiopods and bryozoans are the most abundant fossils. The road soon passes the entrance to the House on the Rock, a unique tourist attraction about which it is said that mere words cannot adequately describe it. The house was built upon a prominent cliff of St. Peter sandstone. Besides the house and spectacular view, there is room after room of bric-a-brac—nineteenth-century music-making machines, merry-go-rounds, a reconstructed 1900 main street, and much more. Just beyond the entrance to the house, on the west side of Wisconsin 23, is an exposure of St. Peter sandstone. One mile farther north and downhill is a wayside constructed on Prairie du Chien dolomite, which has fine views north to the Wisconsin River valley and southwest to the House on the Rock. This dolomite is riddled with small caves.

Next, the highway descends across uppermost Cambrian strata into the Wyoming Valley, where Frank Lloyd Wright's Welsh ancestors settled in the mid-nineteenth century. In 1932 Wright returned to the area to establish his architectural school just south of the Wisconsin River and along Wisconsin 23. His studio and home are named *Taliesin,* a Welsh word for "shining brow"—meaning the brow of the hill upon which the house was built. This lovely countryside inspired Wright's "organic architecture," in which

A quarry in Prairie du Chien dolomite near a Wisconsin 23 wayside exposes a network of caves. Some of the caves probably began forming as early as Ordovician time and have continued to be enlarged intermittently ever since. —R. H. Dott, Jr., photo

buildings are integrated with their natural surroundings. Local Cambrian sandstones and dolomites were favorite construction materials for his buildings.

Tower Hill State Park

One mile east of the Wisconsin 23 bridge over the Wisconsin River along County C is Tower Hill State Park. Here, lead gunshot was made from 1831 to 1861 by dropping molten lead from a wooden tower at the top of a cliff of Cambrian sandstone down a 180-foot shaft. During the descent, each molten mass assumed a spherical shape, which congealed into shot when it hit a pool of cool water. The lead balls were recovered, polished, and sold. Varied sizes of holes in the ladle from which the molten lead was poured determined the caliber of the shot. The lead was mined from the Mineral Point–Galena region, 40 miles southwest. The lower 120 feet of the vertical shaft, which is 4 feet in diameter, was dug by hand through Cambrian sandstone; this connects to a hand-dug horizontal tunnel 90 feet long, through which the shot was recovered. A smelter house and the upper 60 feet of the shaft were built of wood on top of the cliff. You can see the sandstone along a trail leading from the smelter house down to the horizontal tunnel. The cliff is part of the bluffs of the lower Wisconsin River that formed when

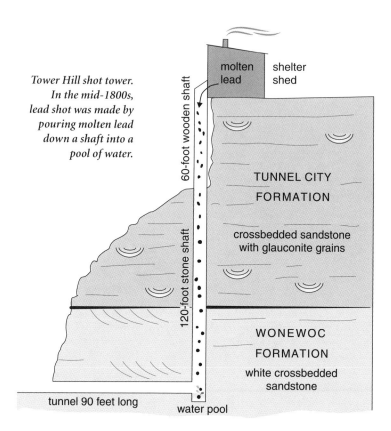

Tower Hill shot tower. In the mid-1800s, lead shot was made by pouring molten lead down a shaft into a pool of water.

60-foot wooden shaft

molten lead

shelter shed

TUNNEL CITY FORMATION

crossbedded sandstone with glauconite grains

120-foot stone shaft

WONEWOC FORMATION

white crossbedded sandstone

tunnel 90 feet long

water pool

braided outwash rivers undercut the valley walls and carried the rock debris away. There are excellent views of the floodplain, outwash plain, and bluffs from the smelter house.

Wisconsin 29
Chippewa Falls—Thorp
30 miles (48 km)

This area lies low in the Cambrian strata, so the contact with underlying Precambrian gneisses and granites is exposed along several rivers. Irvine Park in the city of Chippewa Falls and Big Falls County Park 10 miles east of Eau Claire are two accessible localities where you can see the old rocks overlain by flat Cambrian sandstones. The Precambrian gneisses are part of the ancient Marshfield continent of Archean time. Younger, Penokean granitic rocks have intruded the gneisses. Bedrock is poorly exposed along Wisconsin 29, so our knowledge of the older geology is very incomplete for this area.

Between Chippewa Falls and Thorp, brown to gray silty till, reddish brown sandy till, and some subdued drumlins attest to early glaciations. The most recent glaciation of Wisconsin reached its maximum extent about 18,000 years ago 5 miles north of Thorp, so there are no recent deposits along Wisconsin 29.

Wisconsin 35, The Great River Road
Illinois Border—Hudson
260 miles (420 km)

The Great River Road is a designated scenic route along the Mississippi River from Louisiana to Minnesota. It incorporates different numbered highways, but special green signs with a steamboat symbol help one to navigate the road. Nine lock-and-dam structures, which control the Wisconsin reach of the river, are visible from the Great River Road. Numbered southward from St. Paul, Minnesota, No. 11 at Dubuque is the southernmost one adjacent to Wisconsin. The U.S. Corps of Engineers built these locks and dams during the 1930s to facilitate navigation by countless freight barges and other craft to and from Minnesota's Twin Cities. The goal was to maintain a continuous main channel at least 9 feet deep. The dams raised the water levels and permanently drowned large areas of the floodplain, changing the behavior of the river profoundly. There are three characteristic environments within each stretch between dams: Immediately above each dam is a large, open body of water like a reservoir lake. This passes upstream into an extensive marsh area with backwaters and enclosed sloughs choked with aquatic plants. The third environment, extending up to the next-higher dam, has a maze of braided channels, sloughs, and small lakes coursing through bottomland forests. Only this last one preserves the natural, free-flowing character of the river. All three environments teem with aquatic life of many kinds, so the Wisconsin reach of the river is part of the Upper Mississippi River National Wildlife Refuge, where controlled fishing and hunting are very popular. Migratory waterfowl provide an extra dividend for the traveler, especially in the spring and fall. Modification of the river by humans has a negative side, of course. Waves created by wind and heavy boat traffic erode banks and enhance sedimentation in the quiet backwaters. In addition, pollutants from boats and runoff from adjacent agricultural lands degrade the water quality. Human modifications have upset the balance in all of the aquatic communities, threatening the survival of some species.

Picturesque bluffs on the Mississippi River near the southwest corner of Wisconsin as portrayed in an early geologic report. —From D. D. Owen, 1840

Today, the Mississippi River and its tributaries drain a large part of the north-central United States. Whenever the ice sheets advanced southward across the northern drainage divide of the Mississippi River basin, meltwater from the south-central part of the ice sheet drained into the Mississippi. At times the divide on the surface of the ice sheet was as far north as southern Hudson Bay; needless to say, the discharge of the river was much greater when it was draining such a huge ice mass. When the river was draining the great glaciers, the water would have appeared pale bluish gray and milky because of the large amount of fine, silty sediment, called *glacial flour*, released into the water from the melting ice. From bluff to bluff, the valley floor would have been a series of many complexly braided channels. A braided channel pattern is characteristic of rivers carrying large amounts of coarse sediment from glaciers, collectively termed *outwash*. These braided channels filled the valley with sand and gravel and raised the elevation of the valley floor.

The position of the ice margin contributed to the complex cut-and-fill history of the Mississippi River. In general, anytime the margin of the ice sheet was within the river basin, meltwater carried such large amounts of sediment that the river deposited sediment in the valley and raised the level of the floodplain. When the margin of the ice lay farther north, meltwater

Braided outwash river in Alaska. Note the braided pattern of channels and bars and the steep bedrock bluffs. —J. W. Attig photo

flowed first through a series of ice-margin lakes before entering the river valley. These lakes trapped sediment so that the Mississippi carried much less of it. During such times, the river tended to cut down through previously deposited outwash sediment. You can see the many remnants of sandy outwash terraces throughout the valley.

The small tributaries entering the Mississippi along the route of the Great River Road have their headwaters in the Driftless Area to the east. They did not have glaciers in their drainage basins when the Mississippi was depositing the high-level outwash surfaces. The rapid deposition of outwash in the main valley dammed the mouths of many of those tributaries, forming small lakes. The nearly flat, lower parts of many of the tributary valleys are the floors of such lakes, which have long since drained.

The braided rivers of the Quaternary Ice Age were major sources of the windblown silt called *loess*, which blankets much of the Midwest. The discharge of outwash rivers varies greatly from time to time with changes in the melting rate of the glaciers. Season as well as temperature, sunlight, and other factors affect the melting rate. When the level of the sediment-laden river falls, a layer of fine glacial flour is left draped over the sand and gravel bars between the multiple channel braids. When the flour dries, wind easily blows it away. The amount of available loess is greater when the braided river plain is broader, the changes in discharge are more frequent, and the glaciers persist longer within the drainage basin. Prevailing westerly winds deposited thick accumulations of loess east of outwash rivers such as the Mississippi and Missouri. The loess cover thins eastward with distance from its river source. Loess that accumulated during the most recent glaciation is typically tens of feet thick near the Mississippi River, but only a few feet in south-central Wisconsin. In the western part of the Western Uplands, this loess commonly overlies older loess layers deposited during earlier glaciations. The fine-grained loess contains a wide variety of mineral fragments and has provided parent material for some of the richest agricultural soils in the Midwest.

Illinois Border to La Crosse

The Great River Road enters southwestern Wisconsin from historic Galena, Illinois. It first follows Wisconsin 35 and U.S. 61 through Dickeyville, where some fossils have been incorporated with other materials into a grotto next to the Catholic church. About 3 miles west of Dickeyville, U.S. 61 crosses the Little Platte River. Just west of the river crossing and before the road climbs back to the upland, you can see a former meander of the river west of the highway and above the present river level. Such high-level, former river features, which occur widely in the Driftless Area, formed during the Quaternary Ice Age when volumes of outwash sediment raised the floor of the Mississippi River valley. This in turn raised tributary valleys. Eight miles northwest of Dickeyville, the Great River Road follows Wisconsin 133 for about 45 miles. You can rejoin Wisconsin 35 at Bloomington or continue along the river on county roads and rejoin it at Bridgeport.

The St. John Mine at Potosi is the oldest of the lead mines in Wisconsin; it was originally a cave containing ore minerals that Native Americans and then French traders exploited. Open to the public, the mine contains stalactites and other dripstone features as well as mining memorabilia. You can get a glimpse of the river at Potosi, which was a major shipping point during the heyday of lead mining when the town boasted a population of almost ten thousand.

From Potosi the Great River Road veers slightly inland until Cassville, where Nelson Dewey State Park provides splendid panoramas of the river valley from atop a cliff of the Prairie du Chien dolomite. Several channels separated by long, wooded islands characterize the river here. The state park contains the picturesque home of Wisconsin's first governor after statehood was achieved in 1848 and Stonefield Village, a reconstructed 1890s living museum village. On the top of the river bluff there are several effigy mounds, which were built widely along rivers and lakeshores in Wisconsin from approximately A.D. 650 to 1200 by Indians of the Woodland Culture.

Some mounds have recognizable shapes like birds and animals, but many are simple linear ridges. Effigy mounds have yielded a few artifacts and some were burial sites, but the purpose of most is unknown.

North of Cassville, Wisconsin 133 leaves the river and heads to Bloomington, where it rejoins Wisconsin 35. Stream valleys leading down to the Mississippi are deep and narrow, but the uplands are farmed. The loess that accumulated on the uplands during the Quaternary glaciations makes rich, easily worked soil. You can follow U.S. 18/Wisconsin 35 to Prairie du Chien, or stay closer to the river by following county roads through Bagley to Wyalusing State Park.

Wyalusing State Park

Wyalusing State Park, at the confluence of the Wisconsin and Mississippi Rivers, gains its name from a Native American word meaning "home of the warrior." To reach the park from Wisconsin 35, detour a few miles west on either County C or P before crossing the Wisconsin River at Bridgeport. The most accessible overlooks—Council Point, Signal Point, and Lookout Point—are atop a steep cliff of the Ordovician Prairie du Chien dolomite. Both rivers have large, wooded islands. The one main, open channel of the Mississippi lies near the Iowa border. Famous French explorers Louis Joliet and Father Jacques Marquette passed here in May 1673 after boating from northern Lake Michigan into Green Bay, up the Fox River in eastern Wisconsin, and then portaging to the Wisconsin River. From the river junction, they continued down the Mississippi to St. Louis and beyond. Hiking trails along the clifftop pass effigy mounds, and several trails below the cliffs have outcrops of Prairie du Chien dolomite and underlying Cambrian sandstones, in which there are several shallow caves. Roads provide access to a passenger pigeon monument and the Mississippi River below.

Prairie du Chien

The Great River Road passes through Prairie du Chien, Wisconsin's second European settlement, and the namesake for the early Ordovician dolomites that are so prominent as the caprock for the river bluffs. Broad, nearly flat, sandy terraces, such as the one crossed by Wisconsin 35 in Prairie du Chien, are remnants of the highest outwash surfaces deposited during the most recent glaciation. If you turn west on Wisconsin 27 in Prairie du Chien, notice as you go through town that you cross several lower-level outwash terrace surfaces before you reach the river. It is like descending a series of steps. The outwash beneath the highest terrace, the one crossed by Wisconsin 35, is over 200 feet thick.

For two hundred years, beginning with the French trappers of the 1600s, this was the most important trading center in the entire upper Mississippi

Valley. The French era in Wisconsin is reflected today by place names such as Prairie du Chien ("prairie of dogs"), La Crosse, Eau Claire, Trempealeau, Prairie du Sac, and Portage. During the War of 1812, the Americans built Fort Crawford here but soon lost it to British forces. After the war, it reverted to the Americans, and foreign traders were excluded from all of the region south of Lake Superior. Relations with the Indians remained stormy until 1837, by which time about 75 percent of Wisconsin had been ceded to the Americans and most tribes had been banished to more westerly territories. Villa Louis State Historical Site, a restored late-nineteenth-century grand house built by Wisconsin's first millionaire, was built upon an Indian effigy mound so it would be above the usual river flood level.

The cliffs at Prairie du Chien expose mainly the early Ordovician dolomite, but the overlying St. Peter sandstone and Platteville limestone occur on the uplands east of the river bluffs. The base of the St. Peter sandstone is exposed 1.6 miles east of Prairie du Chien in a roadcut on the north side of Wisconsin 27. Erosion shaped the surface of the Prairie du Chien dolomite before the sandstone was deposited. At one point the younger sandstone is at the same level as a nearby outcrop of older dolomite because the sand filled a channel cut into the dolomite by an Ordovician river.

Effigy Mounds National Monument

A detour across the river into Iowa of about 10 miles round-trip via U.S. 18 and Iowa 13 will take you to Effigy Mounds National Monument, where you can learn more about the early native peoples in the region. Paleo-Indians came to the upper Mississippi Valley near the end of the last glaciation. Their hunting culture was succeeded by the more advanced Woodland Culture, which is recorded in tools, pottery, and a few burial mounds. The Effigy Mounds people, who built the interesting animal-shaped mounds between A.D. 650 and 1200, represent the culmination of the Woodland Culture, which preceded the historical tribes living here when the Europeans arrived. Most effigy mound groups were constructed near bodies of water. They generally have a bird shape on the highest point with earth spirits or animal shapes at lower levels, and a water spirit with a long tail nearest the water. The animal effigies are thought to be clan symbols. Besides an excellent visitor center at the monument, vistas of the Wisconsin side of the valley are spectacular. About 5 miles south through McGregor, Iowa, is Pikes Peak State Park, which also provides an excellent view of the confluence of the Wisconsin and Mississippi Rivers.

River Bluffs

North of Prairie du Chien, the Great River Road follows Wisconsin 35 all the way to Hudson. Seven miles north of Prairie du Chien, the river valley makes an eastward bend and narrows somewhat. The cliffs here are 400 to 500 feet high, and are made up largely of Cambrian sandstones and the Prairie du Chien dolomite. Glacial meltwater rivers undercut the dolomite, which is more resistant to erosion than sandstone, and created these bold cliffs. About 12 miles north of Prairie du Chien is Lock and Dam No. 9. Whereas downstream from here, countless islands divide the channel, above the dam for about 12 miles the river resembles a long lake. Within 5 more miles, islands again divide the channel and the river is shallow enough for a causeway to connect Wisconsin and Iowa.

The area around Victory was the site of the conclusion of the most celebrated skirmish with the Indians in Wisconsin, the Black Hawk War of 1832. Black Hawk of the Sac and Fox tribes had led the U.S. Army on a chase from north-central Illinois across southwestern Wisconsin to this point, where he was forced to surrender after the massacre of hundreds of his starving followers.

At road level, there are scattered exposures of Cambrian sandstones. Notable are several such roadside outcrops between DeSoto and Victory, where the Tunnel City formation appears. It is rich in glauconite in this area, and has many bands of dark greensand. The Bad Axe River north of Victory is a typical small tributary to the Mississippi. It drains some of the deeply dissected Driftless Area extending 15 to 20 miles eastward.

At Genoa, which was settled largely by Italian immigrants, is Lock and Dam No. 8 and an electric generating plant. Next to the parking area for viewing the lock and dam at the south end of town is an exposure of glauconitic sandstones, but there is a much better exposure a few hundred yards to the north at the junction of Wisconsin 35 and Wisconsin 56. There, a high roadcut has many bands of dark greensand. The abundance of the

Flat pebbles of Cambrian sandstone in a matrix of greensand, all deposited by storm waves. Tunnel City formation, Mississippi River bluffs. —R. H. Dott, Jr., photo

green mineral glauconite tells us that the Tunnel City formation, in contrast with the other Cambrian sandstones exposed along the valley, was formed in a relatively deep marine environment where deposition was very slow. Two miles north of Genoa is one of the two best scenic viewpoints along the entire Wisconsin side of the Mississippi Valley. A half-mile drive up Ramrod Coulee will take you to a wayside in an abandoned bluff-top quarry in the Prairie du Chien dolomite. Views up and down the river are spectacular! The stone quarried here was doubtless used for building the nearby lock, dam, and power plant foundations.

La Crosse

La Crosse, named for a Native American ball game, is Wisconsin's largest community along the Mississippi River. It is at the heart of Coulee Country, a colloquial name made famous by author Hamlin Garlin, who grew up 10 miles northeast at West Salem. *Coulee,* from the French, refers to the many steep-sided tributary valleys that may only have water flowing intermittently. At La Crosse the Great River Road intersects I-90, which crosses the Driftless Area, connecting Minnesota and La Crosse with I-94 at Tomah, 42 miles east. Cambrian sandstones of the Wonewoc formation crop out at the base of the river bluffs at La Crosse. Across the river a few miles is Dresbach, Minnesota, which long ago gave its name to the oldest division of late Cambrian time for North America. Such subdivisions were based upon different trilobite fossils in successive groups of sandstones. All but the oldest Cambrian formation, Mt. Simon, are exposed along I-90 within the first 8 miles into Minnesota; they are capped on the tops of the ridges by Ordovician dolomite. The same Cambrian succession is present on the Wisconsin side of the river around La Crosse but is not so well exposed. Grandad Bluff and two other bluffs loom above La Crosse. The higher Cambrian sandstones are exposed in the faces of the bluffs, which are capped by about 50 feet of early Ordovician Prairie du Chien dolomite. A road leads up to a park on Grandad Bluff, from which there are good views of the river valley 600 feet below.

Early Fossil Collecting

The earliest geological surveys of the upper Mississippi Valley in the 1830s and 1840s discovered many fossils diagnostic of different zones within the Cambrian and Ordovician strata of the region. So in 1884, U.S. Geological Survey collector Cooper Curtice already had leads to potential collecting localities, including some in the La Crosse area. There were no paved highways nor automobiles in his day, so he traveled mostly by railroad, wagon, and horseback. Along the Mississippi, he sometimes took advantage of steamboats, and at one landing in Minnesota he discovered a rich zone of fossils. Curtice sought particularly the Cambrian trilobites, which

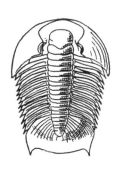

Conocephalites   Dikelocephalus

Two late Cambrian trilobite fossils. —Conocephalites from
Chamberlin, 1883; *Dikelocephalus* from Moore, Lalicker, and Fischer, 1952

are especially useful for identifying and tracing specific zones of strata all over the upper Midwest. One morning at Trempealeau, 15 miles northwest of La Crosse, he discovered a trilobite that interested him greatly. He provided this amusing account: "while pounding on limestone on the river bank I struck the beast [revealing] its tail and cheeks. It keeps company with *Dikelocephalus springer, D. minnesotensis.* . . . It resembles generically the pustular headed, binodose tailed species from Osceola Mills, Wis. called *Conocephalites binodosus*." Curtice found these same trilobites at a number of other localities, which allowed him to correlate the zone containing them.

La Crosse to Hudson

At La Crosse, Lock and Dam No. 7 forms a large lake, which is visible from the Great River Road just to the north at Onalaska. North of La Crosse, there are no steep cliffs for about 20 miles because of a broad valley of the Black River and wide floodplain. Around Holmen, Wisconsin 35 crosses Amsterdam Prairie, a broad, high outwash terrace. Erosion formed the rather hilly surface of this terrace. An outburst flood from a glacial lake in the upper part of the Mississippi drainage system may have created the erosional forms with up to 20 feet of relief. A thin veneer of finer, wind-blown sand covers the river sands and gravels within the erosional hills.

Three miles north of Holmen, the Great River Road bends westward and crosses the Black River, whose delta a few miles to the southwest partially dammed the Mississippi River. This was the outlet for drainage from Glacial Lake Wisconsin that covered the Central Plain during the last

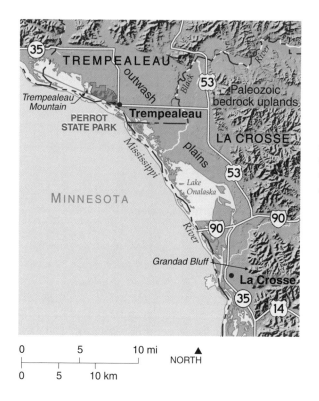

Landscape image of the area between La Crosse and Trempealeau Mountain.

0   5   10 mi   ▲
|—————|—————|—————| NORTH

0   5   10 km

glaciation. At Trempealeau, 4 miles west, is Lock and Dam No. 6 and a prominent bluff in Perrot State Park overlooking the river.

Perrot State Park

Perrot State Park lies just west of Wisconsin 35 at Trempealeau. It encompasses two isolated hills of Cambrian sandstone 500 feet high, overlooking the Mississippi River to the south and a broad wetland to the north. Woodland Culture art and burial mounds are highlights of the park, which was named for Nicolas Perrot, the first Frenchman in the upper Mississippi Valley. He established a trading post here in 1685. Trempealeau Mountain, the "mountain drenched by water" to the French or "bluff in the water" to the Indians, is now an island looming 500 feet above the river. The lowland north and east of the park was a former bend in the main channel of the Mississippi River, part of which is today the Trempealeau National Wildlife Refuge. A preglacial route of the river lay east of Trempealeau Mountain, but during glaciation, an outwash plain extended all the way across the valley. Subsequently, the modern Mississippi formed a new channel west of the mountain. The towns of Trempealeau and nearby Galesville have given their names to Cambrian strata. The Galesville sandstone, a subdivision of the Wonewoc formation, is exposed in the bluffs at Perrot State Park, where it contains marine fossils throughout. However, eastward toward central Wisconsin, for example at the Wisconsin Dells, it is comprised of nonmarine wind and river deposits formed during a partial retreat of the Cambrian sea. The Mississippi Valley region was lower then than the Wisconsin dome to the east, so marine conditions continued here even when small drops in sea level exposed the dome as lowland.

Cliffs and Meanders

Wisconsin 35 turns north at Trempealeau, but an alternate route from the Perrot State Park follows the edge of the wetland and rejoins the Great River Road 5 miles northwest. From that point, Wisconsin 35 follows the base of high bluffs, which expose all but the oldest Cambrian sandstones and are capped by the ever-present Ordovician dolomite. Here, as elsewhere, the dolomite is quarried in the uplands above the river to make crushed stone for roads and for other uses. The same geology extends eastward for 40 to 50 miles across the Driftless Area to I-94. A wayside 1.5 miles west of the Trempealeau River has outcrops of prominent crossbedding in the Cambrian Wonewoc sandstone. Across the river is Winona, Minnesota,

Trempealeau Mountain and the Mississippi River from Brady's Bluff in Perrot State Park. —Photo courtesy of the Wisconsin Department of Natural Resources

where Lock and Dam No. 5A is located. The river valley narrows somewhat above Winona, and the cliffs rise as much as 500 feet.

River channels tend to meander from side to side in their valleys. Where the main Mississippi channel nips at its valley side, erosion produces steep bluffs; the locks and dams are located at such points. Where the channel swings away from the opposite bank, deposition of sediment and wetlands produce more subdued topography. At Fountain City, the channel is on the Wisconsin side, but 2 miles farther north, beginning at Merrick State Park, the highway is on a river terrace alongside a long wetland. Here, the channel is on the Minnesota side, as is Lock and Dam No. 5. Twelve miles farther upstream the channel swings to the Wisconsin side again at Alma, which is dominated by Lock and Dam No. 4 and a power station.

At Fountain City, where cliffs also loom directly above town, a 55-ton rock suddenly dropped into a newly decorated bedroom of the Anderson home one April morning in 1995. This was the second such visitation known to this river town, for in 1904 a 5-ton boulder broke from the cliff and crushed a sleeping woman. The Andersons decided not to push their luck and sold their home—rock and all—to a local entrepreneur, who saw it as a profitable tourist attraction. The spring thaw facilitates the occasional falling of blocks from steep cliffs; ice in cracks in rock and in soil melts and helps lubricate the descent. Blocks scattered helter-skelter along the bases of steep cliffs provide mute testimony to the potency over geologic time of such occasional wasting of landscapes.

At Alma you can see Lock and Dam No. 4 from a tourist viewing point and also from Buena Vista County Park on top of the bluff only 2.3 miles northeast (via County E and a side road). Cambrian sandstones are exposed on the way up to the Prairie du Chien dolomite caprock. A walkway out to the park's overlook has flagstones cut from dolomite with conspicuous intertwined animal burrows. At the overlook, you can see lumpy stromatolites 1 to 2 feet in diameter in the caprock.

Lake Pepin

Two miles north of Alma, a highway causeway crosses the estuary-like mouth of the Buffalo River, which was drowned by the 1930s damming of the Mississippi at Alma. Between Nelson and Pepin, the Great River Road passes the mouth of the Chippewa River, the largest tributary of the Mississippi between here and the Wisconsin River to the south. The gradient of the Chippewa River is steeper than that of the Mississippi; therefore it can carry coarser sediment. When sediment-laden meltwater from the most recent glaciers ceased flowing, the Mississippi River began to erode downward through its outwash plain. This steepened the gradient of tributaries like the Chippewa River, causing massive erosion of sandy outwash. This

The Mississippi River viewed to the northwest from Buena Vista County Park above Lock and Dam No. 4 at Alma. The opposite river bluff is in Minnesota. —R. H. Dott, Jr., photo

Chippewa River delta blocks much of the Mississippi Valley, creating Lake Pepin.

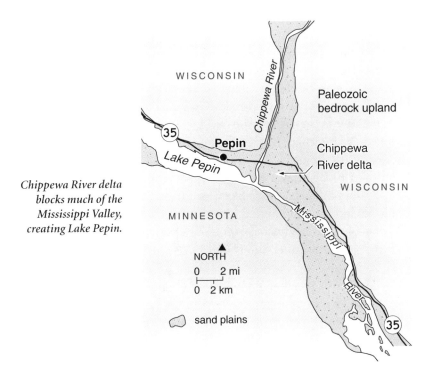

sediment choked the Mississippi and backed up water to create Lake Pepin, which now extends 20 miles upriver but once extended all the way to St. Paul. The lake began to form about 10,000 years ago.

Between Pepin and Bay City, the Great River Road provides many excellent views of Lake Pepin, whose beauty provoked a nineteenth-century opinion that every painter and poet should visit this lake. Seven miles north of Pepin on County CC is the 1867 birthplace of Laura Ingalls Wilder, author of *Little House in the Big Woods* and other popular children's books. Halfway uphill to the Little House, the Prairie du Chien dolomite is unusually disturbed. Dolomite and sandstone strata are steeply tilted and crumpled within a circular area about 1 mile in diameter. Geophysical measurements suggest that the disturbance extends downward at least 2,000 feet below the surface. How did otherwise nearly flat strata become so disturbed? Several hypotheses come to mind. First is a fault, of which several are known to cut Ordovician rocks between 15 and 40 miles to the northwest. The circular shape of the disturbance, however, does not favor this explanation. Two other possibilities involve groundwater. Perhaps the rocks collapsed into a hypothetical underlying cave system, or perhaps water under very high pressure shot upward and jostled the strata as it escaped to the surface, making a circular crater. Yet another, even more intriguing possibility is that a meteorite or comet plunged into the earth here. A similar circular disturbed area at Rock Elm only 16 miles north of here has more compelling evidence for such an impact. We discuss the Rock Elm disturbance at the end of this road guide.

Four miles northwest of Pepin, the road passes under Bogus Bluff capped by Prairie du Chien dolomite. Three miles farther is Maiden Rock Wayside, where legend has it that a Sioux Indian maiden jumped from the clifftop 300 feet above because her tribe had forbidden her marriage to the brave she loved. An alternate interpretation is that the first settlers to come to this area in the 1850s wished to promote the upper Mississippi Valley as "America's Rhineland," so adapted a myth from the Rhine Valley of Germany. Besides having an excellent view of Lake Pepin as she jumped, the mythical maiden would have flashed past the record of at least 20 million years of geologic time; that is, from early Ordovician at the top to mid-late Cambrian at the bottom. She landed on a Quaternary outwash plain. In the cliff opposite the wayside, the Tunnel City formation has fine sandstones containing small green pellets of the mineral glauconite. These alternate with layers of conglomerate with flat pebbles of sandstone, which must have been ripped from the seafloor by storm waves soon after the sandstone was deposited. At the wayside, the low walls contain large blocks of Prairie du Chien dolomite like that which caps the adjacent river bluffs.

These blocks show excellent examples of large pores that commonly form during the alteration of limestone to dolomite.

At the village of Maiden Rock and nearby Bay City at the head of Lake Pepin, sandstone of the youngest Cambrian formation, the Jordan sandstone, has been mined from a network of tunnels 25 feet wide and 25 feet high cut into the river bluffs. The poorly cemented sandstone is easily broken down to its individual quartz grains and then washed and strained. It is used in the petroleum industry for enhancing the flow of oil from wells. The sand grains are mixed in a slurry of clay and water and injected under very high pressure from a drill hole into an oil-bearing stratum. Small fractures in the rock are opened slightly and new fractures are created by the high-pressure fluid, and the quartz grains carried into those fractures by the fluid prevent their closing again. The grains from the Cambrian Wonewoc and Jordan sandstones are preferred in the industry for this "hydro-fracing" process. The sand is also used for sandblasting and could be used for foundry moldings. The mine at Maiden Rock is still active, but the former Bay City mine is now a protected bat cave refuge.

Just north of Maiden Rock village, the forested Rush River delta bulges into Lake Pepin at a major bend in the Mississippi Valley from a north-south to a nearly east-west orientation. Because of this change of valley trend, younger formations occur in succession at highway level from here westward. Although north of La Crosse the Wonewoc sandstone was at road level for many miles, along the upper end of Lake Pepin, the youngest Cambrian sandstone, the Jordan, descends to the highway, and 10 miles farther upriver, the overlying Prairie du Chien dolomite—from which our maiden jumped—is at river level.

You can see the Jordan sandstone with large-scale crossbedding in roadcut exposures at a historical marker explaining Lake Pepin 3 miles northwest of the town of Maiden Rock. West of Bay City, Wisconsin 35 passes over another river terrace surface that continues for about 10 miles. Four miles farther west is Hager City, opposite which is Red Wing, Minnesota, long a major shipping point for wheat grown on the southern Minnesota prairies; much grain is carried downriver from here by barges. Lock and dam No. 3 is 3.5 miles upriver from the U.S. 63 bridge, which connects Minnesota and Wisconsin. At Red Wing, a fault roughly parallel to the river has displaced the Cambrian and Ordovician strata 100 feet or so. It is one of several more that occur between here and Hudson, 30 miles to the north.

The Great River Road continues northwest along the river from Hager City to Prescott, with the uppermost Cambrian Jordan sandstone occurring at highway level most of the way. However, the overlying Prairie du Chien dolomite is at river level at Prescott, a late-nineteenth-century sawmill town and shipping point at the junction of the St. Croix and Mississippi Rivers.

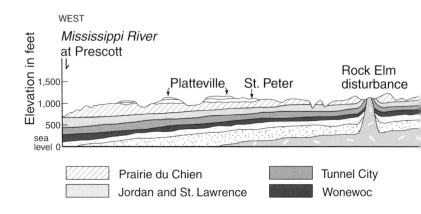

WEST

Mississippi River
at Prescott

Rock Elm
disturbance

Platteville   St. Peter

Elevation in feet

1,500
1,000
500
sea level 0

Prairie du Chien
Jordan and St. Lawrence
Tunnel City
Wonewoc

Older Glaciated Region

The area north of Hager City and Prescott to Hudson is within the west-central glaciated uplands, but the exact extent of glaciation along the route is unclear. There is evidence that glaciers advanced eastward across the Mississippi River into Wisconsin at least as far south as the mouth of the Chippewa River. And geologists have identified scattered patches of glacially transported material around the Buffalo River about 8 miles farther south. Near their southern limit, the glacial materials occur only as small erosional remnants like these. Thirty-five miles farther north around Hudson, however, these materials form a nearly continuous cover over bedrock, but erosion has destroyed glacial landforms. The glaciation that affected this part of Wisconsin occurred hundreds of thousands of years ago; some geologists have even suggested that it may have been as early as late Pliocene time, or about 2 to 3 million years ago. The eastward flow of ice in this area dammed a number of the westward-flowing streams in Wisconsin, forming lakes along the ice margin. Thick sequences of laminated, fine lake sediment are common in the lower parts of the river valleys.

Erosion by the steep tributary streams of the Mississippi River has stripped away most of the glacial deposits, exposing Paleozoic bedrock along many valleys. Because Wisconsin 35 rises about 300 feet from the Mississippi River to Hudson, it passes up through the succession of Ordovician strata. First is the Prairie du Chien dolomite, then the St. Peter sandstone, and finally the Platteville formation at the highest elevations. The tan or brown of the St. Peter distinguish it from the overlying and underlying gray limestone or dolomite in roadside exposures. You can see crossbedding in the St. Peter sandstone in deep roadcuts at the northeast edge of River Falls, where traces of fossil worm tubes are also present. In town, the city

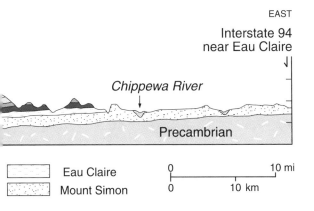

EAST

Interstate 94
near Eau Claire

Chippewa River

Precambrian

☐ Eau Claire

☐ Mount Simon

0 — 10 mi

0 — 10 km

Cross section of northwest Western Uplands between the Mississippi and Chippewa Rivers. Note the circular area of tilted rock known as the Rock Elm disturbance, a possible meteorite impact site.

park has a small waterfall over the underlying Prairie du Chien dolomite. River Falls is located at the confluence of two branches of the Kinnickinnic River, where waterfalls provided the natural site for an early mill to grind flour. Eight miles west is Kinnickinnic State Park, which encompasses the large, sandy delta of the Kinnickinnic River, where it empties into the much larger St. Croix River.

Rock Elm Disturbance

Twenty miles northeast of Hager City—13 miles east of Ellsworth (via U.S. 63 and Wisconsin 72) and 25 miles southwest of Menomonie—is a geologically enigmatic feature called the Rock Elm disturbance, a circular area 4 miles in diameter. The feature appears as a circle on air photos and subtle crescent-shaped ridges on topographic maps. Glacial deposits and vegetation greatly obscure the rocks.

Within the circular area, Cambrian and Ordovician formations have been tilted and jumbled together in a chaotic fashion. A domelike center has the oldest Cambrian formation (Mt. Simon) tilted as much as 22 to 44 degrees away from a heterogeneous breccia core. Angular fragments within the breccia include granite, other igneous rocks, metamorphic quartzite and amphibolite (a dark, banded rock composed only of amphibole minerals), and sedimentary chert and sandstones. Some of the fragments are enclosed by glassy material, which could have been formed either by sudden chilling of an igneous magma intruded from below or by melting of sandstones by impact from above by an extraterrestrial body such as a large meteorite. The igneous and metamorphic fragments are from Precambrian rocks 800 feet deep and the Cambrian sandstones are from 600 to 700 feet below the surface in this area. Surrounding the central dome are faulted and tilted

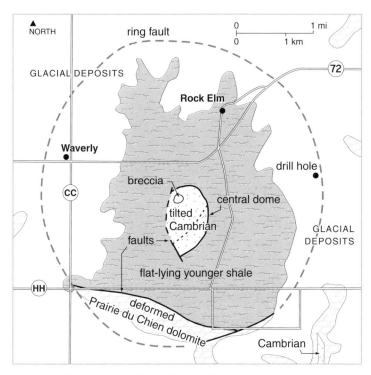

Geologic map of the Rock Elm disturbance southwest of
Menomonie in west-central Wisconsin. —After Cordua, 1987

Ordovician Prairie du Chien strata, which were overlapped by younger,
flat-lying shale and sandstone of later Ordovician age.

What caused the anomalous, local disturbance of rocks in a region famous for great stability since Precambrian time? Did an extraterrestrial
body fall into the Ordovician or later sea, or did a small but violent explo-
sion burst through the crust from below onto the seafloor to deform and
jumble the rocks? Microscopic studies reveal fine fracture patterns in quartz
grains like those known from shock metamorphism, giving greater weight
to the extraterrestrial impact theory. Similar anomalous areas of deformed
and faulted early Ordovician dolomite are present near Pepin 16 miles south
and at Glover Bluff in central Wisconsin near I-39.

The Rock Elm area has attracted the attention of mineral seekers for
more than a century. Small amounts of fine gold flakes were recovered in
the 1880s and a few diamonds were recovered as well. These minerals were
derived from the glacial drift surrounding the disturbed area rather than
from the Rock Elm structure itself. In the 1980s a few companies renewed
the search for minerals, but without success.

Wisconsin 60
Prairie du Chien—Gotham
50 miles (62 km)

Wisconsin 60 follows the north side of the lower Wisconsin River valley from Prairie du Chien all the way to its junction with U.S. 12 at Sauk City. Wisconsin 60 hugs the bluffs along the north margin of the river's alluvial plain much of the way, with excellent views of the river, the bluffs, and outwash plains. Many roadcuts expose Cambrian sandstones, some with conspicuous dark greensand bands rich in the mineral glauconite. You can see these especially well opposite Boscobel, 25 miles east of Prairie du Chien. These exposures reveal intervals of storm deposition. Ordovician Prairie du Chien dolomite caps the ridgetops. Kickapoo Indian Caverns is located 8 miles northeast of Bridgeport on a side road 2 miles northwest of Wisconsin 60.

Near Bridgeport, 5 miles above the mouth of the Wisconsin River, Wisconsin 60 is on a high bench with sandstone cliffs to the north and the river below it to the south. This bench, the Bridgeport terrace, is the dissected remnant of an outwash plain deposited by rivers flowing eastward from a

Landscape image showing remnants of the Bridgeport terrace in the lower Wisconsin River valley.

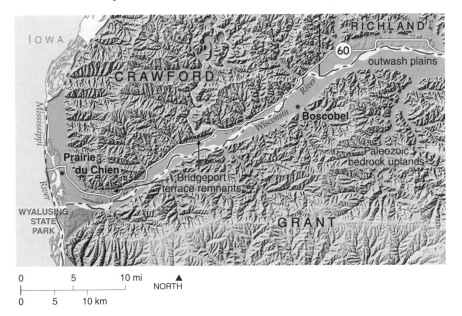

glacier that advanced from the west and blocked the mouth of the Wisconsin River. The exact time of the glacial advance is not well known but it was probably before 790,000 years ago because magnetic minerals in the sediment are oriented similarly to those deposited before that time, and also only the most resistant rock types in the outwash remain, the others having weathered away. This old outwash is preserved because it overlies a bedrock bench that is elevated above the river floodplain. The exact route of the meltwater drainage farther to the east is unknown.

As in other parts of the lower Wisconsin River valley and in the Mississippi Valley adjacent to Wisconsin, the steep bluffs owe much of their present

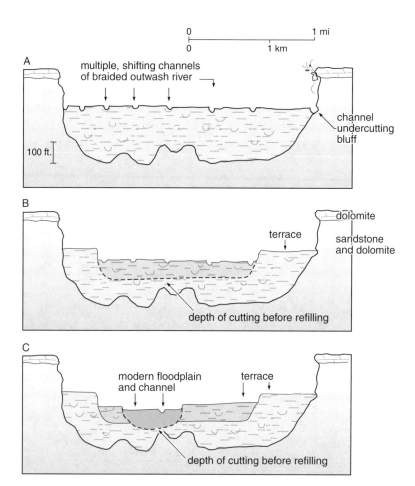

Sequence in the formation of a series of cut-and-fill terraces. A. Braided outwash river fills valley from wall to wall and at times undercuts bluffs. B. Outwash river erodes into outwash plain and partially refills the valley. C. Postglacial rivers erode into the outwash plains and refill to the modern level.

form to the braided outwash rivers and their floodplains, which stretched from valley wall to valley wall during the Quaternary Ice Age. These braided rivers tended to undercut the bluffs and remove rock that fell from them. Away from these major meltwater drainages, the rock formations do not tend to form such high, steep slopes. The modern Wisconsin River carries much less sediment than did those meltwater rivers and it flows in a much more stable channel. In most places, the modern channel and its floodplain are confined between flat, sandy plains, which are remnants of the dissected high floodplains of the outwash rivers. Only in a few places has the river flowed against the sandstone bluffs since the end of the Ice Age. Today, the only places where there are not accumulations of slope deposits at the base of the bluffs is where the river is now against the bluff. Such a place is along the highway opposite Boscobel.

Remnants of the outwash plains between Prairie du Chien and Gotham are much smaller than those upriver from Gotham. The lower Wisconsin River valley narrows toward its mouth, the opposite of what one would expect. The dominance of dolomite in the walls of the lower part of the valley explains the narrowing; less-resistant sandstone dominates the valley walls farther upriver. At many locations along Wisconsin 60 between Prairie du Chien and Gotham, you can see many sandbars, which are characteristic of the lower Wisconsin River. These bars were an impediment for early river travelers, but today they are a major attraction for canoe camping, swimming, and fishing along the river. Great care should be taken in swimming or wading around the sandbars because of strong currents, abrupt deepening at the margins of bars, and a potentially unstable bottom. These bars form during high-water stages that transport sand. During falling stages of the river, channels partially erode through them. At low stages, the sandbars emerge, forming islands. These processes respond to seasonal changes of flow, but there are also smaller, daily changes as upstream dams manipulate flow for hydroelectric power generation. Peak demand for electricity in the evening requires higher flow than reduced demand times. The corresponding daily rise and fall of river level is less pronounced in this dam-free, lower part of the valley, but nighttime flooding has rudely awakened people camped on sandbars.

Further discussion of the route from Gotham to Spring Green is presented in **U.S. 14: La Crosse—Madison.**

The upper Dells of the Wisconsin River at the mouth of Witches Gulch. Cambrian wind dunes formed the large-scale crossbedding to the left of the steamboat. Pioneer photographer Henry H. Bennett took the photo in the 1880s. —Bennett Collection No. 1086, Courtesy of H. H. Bennett Studio Foundation of Wisconsin Dells.

Baraboo, Dells, and Central Plain

The Baraboo, Dells, and Central Plain region straddles the boundary between the Driftless Area of the Western Uplands and the glaciated Eastern
Uplands. The Johnstown moraine marks this boundary, which separates
well-drained unglaciated landscapes characterized by deep valleys and
extensive Paleozoic bedrock outcrops to the west from the gently rolling
glaciated landscapes to the east. This region contains Wisconsin's oldest
and most famous tourist attractions, the Wisconsin Dells and Devils Lake
in the Baraboo Hills. The Dells of the Wisconsin River are a 7-mile-long
picturesque network of canyons as much as 100 feet deep carved into Cambrian sandstones by the rapid draining of Glacial Lake Wisconsin. The name
dells derives from the French *dalles,* meaning "deep ravine" or "vale"; the
English *dale* is related. Rocky Arbor and Mirror Lake State Parks are excellent places to see dells. Devils Lake State Park is the recreational focal point
for the Baraboo Hills. Besides providing scenic beauty for millions to ad-
mire every year, the Dells and Baraboo areas are also geologic meccas for
the annual field instruction of hundreds of students.

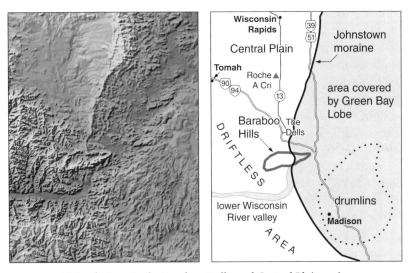

Major features in the Baraboo, Dells, and Central Plain region.

Native Americans have lived in the region for thousands of years, and French fur traders and missionaries used the Wisconsin River as a highway in the 1600s and 1700s. Logging during the 1800s denuded much of northern Wisconsin and some of the Baraboo-Dells region. Every spring, lumbermen floated huge rafts of logs down the river, but the constriction at the Dells caused great logjams, which were dangerous for the lumbermen. Floods have also been dangerous here, for the flow has been known to increase fifteenfold. In 1856, the river was first dammed at the site of the present city of Wisconsin Dells to generate power for the new settlement, but the lumbermen blew up the first dam because it obstructed their log rafts. The present hydroelectric dam built in 1909 raised the level of the upper Dells about 16 feet, which drowned some geological features.

Beginning in 1856, direct railroad service made the Dells easily accessible from the urban areas of Milwaukee, Chicago, Minneapolis–St. Paul, and St. Louis just as I-90/I-94 does today. During the late 1800s, special excursion trains and steamboat tours on the river brought droves of people "to experience the weird and gruesome formations, the grotesque and fantastic rock shapes, and occult caves of the Dells." Elaborate promotional pamphlets and hundreds of widely distributed pictures by pioneer photographer Henry H. Bennett created a romantic image of the Dells, inhabited first by the noble Indian and then by the heroic lumbermen rafters. After the turn of the twentieth century, however, the popularity of scenic tourism declined, and the Dells gradually evolved into a giant amusement park, which has made it a "pretty strange place" as one Chicagoan recently described it (Ostergren and Vale, 1997).

The Wisconsin River remains relatively intact thanks largely to the foresight of Henry H. Bennett's son-in-law, who became alarmed that the beauty of the river corridor might be lost to development—a very modern-sounding concern. Beginning soon after 1900, he bought river frontage and reforested it. Today, that property is a state natural area. Several companies offer boat trips, which allow you to enjoy the natural beauty of the river oblivious of the eclectic, Coney Island–like sideshows lining U.S. 12. The restored Bennett photo studio in downtown Wisconsin Dells, a state historical site, is well worth visiting to see early views of the Dells and to learn about early photographic techniques.

Devils Lake, nestled in the southern Baraboo Hills between 500-foot-high bluffs composed of Precambrian quartzite, also attracted the attention of early settlers and miners. The lake became accessible by a railroad in 1872. Today, I-90/I-94 skirts the northeast side of the Baraboo Hills and U.S. 12 bisects the area, passing within 2 miles of the lake. Early settlers had a field day naming topographic features here; besides the lake itself, there are Devils Lake Gap, Devils Nose, Devils Doorway, and Devils Alley. Why is the area so bedeviled? Winnebago Indian legends say the lake valley formed either by a meteor impact or lightning bolts hurled by thunderbirds. An early white settler thought that a volcanic eruption had blown out the center of the bluffs. Its early name was Spirit Lake, but touristic promotion substituted the modern name.

The Devils Lake area was set aside as one of Wisconsin's first state parks in 1910. Today, it attracts more than a million visitors per year. Parfreys Glen, a secluded canyon 4 miles east of the lake, is part of the park. Also of geologic as well as scenic interest is Natural Bridge State Park, 12 miles southwest of Devils Lake. Three other scenic gorges accessible by state highways are the Upper Narrows of the Baraboo River and Narrows Creek, both near Rock Springs in the northwestern part of the Baraboo Hills, 8 miles

Places of geologic interest in the Baraboo-Dells area.

west of the city of Baraboo, and the Lower Narrows of the Baraboo River, 5 miles east of the city. Piles of discarded red waste rock in brushy thickets are the only reminders of the important iron mining in the area between 1889 and 1925. Quarrying of quartzite, which began early in the 1900s, continues today at several localities.

The Baraboo Hills hold the largest forested area in southern Wisconsin and adjacent states. Because of the varied topography and geology, diverse biological communities inhabit the hills—from ridgetop prairies to both pine and hardwood forests. There are more than six hundred species of plants and many species of woodland birds in a typical square-mile area. Especially interesting are some plants growing in several deep canyons like Parfreys Glen, where a relatively cool microclimate has favored exotic species such as yellow birch, hemlock, and mosses, which are more typical today of cooler areas 100 miles or more farther north. They have managed to persist in these small, cool refuges as most of their kind shifted northward during postglacial warming.

Humans may have arrived in the area as early as 12,000 years ago; that is, soon after the end of the most recent glaciation of the region. These early hunting and fishing Paleo-Indians intermittently occupied several rock shelters in the western part of the hills. Best known is the Raddatz Shelter in Natural Bridge State Park near Leland, where artifacts were excavated in the 1950s. Those early hunters shared a landscape of tundra vegetation and spruce trees with deer, martin, possibly musk ox, and the now-extinct mastodon, mammoth, and giant beaver. Of much later origin are a few effigy mounds dating from A.D. 600 to 1200 found near Devils Lake. An exceptional example 4 miles northeast of Baraboo is Man Mound, a unique, large human shape originally about 50 feet long. By the time the Effigy Mounds people lived in the area, oak and pine forests dominated the vegetation, much as today.

The flat expanse of the Central Plain is saved from being monotonous by the Wisconsin River flowing through its eastern part and by many buttes, called *mounds*, with cliffs of Cambrian sandstone. The sand that blankets the Central Plain was deposited in and around Glacial Lake Wisconsin, which covered much of the plain during the most recent glaciation. The sand was derived from erosion of the local sandstones as well as carried from the north and east by rivers draining the glaciers.

Geologic studies of the Baraboo-Dells region began about 1850, but it was almost twenty years before geologists recognized that Precambrian rocks exist in the Baraboo Hills. It was another thirty years before geologists correctly deciphered the complex structure of those rocks beneath the hills. For more than a century, however, the area has been an outdoor laboratory for geology students from all over the upper Mississippi Valley region, who

Devils Doorway in Baraboo quartzite 600 feet above lake level in Devils Lake State Park. —Photo courtesy of the Wisconsin Department of Natural Resources

come by the hundreds every year to read from this exceptional textbook in the rocks the principles for unraveling the structural complexities of deformed strata. In a relatively small area, students can study many aspects of Precambrian, Paleozoic, and Quaternary geology. Thanks to pioneer Wisconsin geologists, who developed and wrote about those principles early in the twentieth century, the Baraboo Hills have become so famous that even earth scientists who have never visited know of them. A former president of the University of Wisconsin was surprised in the early 1960s to find geological diagrams of the Baraboo Hills displayed at a university in Pakistan.

Precambrian Record

The higher ridges of the Baraboo Hills are composed of the Precambrian Baraboo quartzite, a very homogeneous, red, metamorphosed quartz sandstone, which is about 4,000 feet thick. Overlying the quartzite, but concealed beneath the central lowland between the hills, are an additional 1,500 feet of less-resistant Precambrian strata. Along the outer flanks of both the North and South Ranges, the quartzite overlies igneous rocks, which are mostly a black to red volcanic rock called rhyolite. Coarser-grained, granitic intrusive rocks closely related to the rhyolites occur in places. Both crystallized about 1,750 million years ago. An example is the Baxter Hollow granite. Weathering for tens of millions of years produced clay-rich soils on the rhyolites and granites prior to deposition of the great volume of sand and fine gravel that today is the Baraboo quartzite.

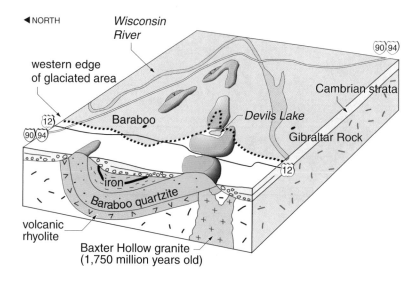

This block diagram of the eastern part of the Baraboo Hills shows the Precambrian Baraboo syncline and the western limit of glaciation.

Sometime between 1,650 and 1,465 million years ago, all of the rocks were crumpled into a series of wrinkles or folds. A single large down fold, or syncline, underlies the eastern Baraboo Hills, with the two eroded limbs of this fold forming the two Baraboo ranges; more complicated folds and faults underlie the western part of the area. During folding, the rocks were also metamorphosed—sandstones converted to quartzite and shales to slate. Exactly what caused the deformation is unclear, but our favorite idea is that a small continent collided with embryonic North America about 1,650 million years ago along a zone located somewhere beneath Illinois and Iowa. Another idea is that the deformation was somehow related to the intrusion about 1,450 million years ago of the very large Wolf River igneous complex centered 100 miles north of Baraboo.

NORTH   SOUTH

1,750 million years ago rhyolitic volcanism

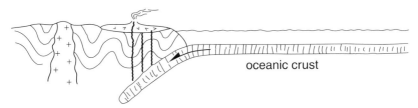

oceanic crust

1,700 million years ago Baraboo sandstone deposition

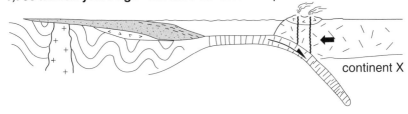

continent X

1,650? million years ago Baraboo Mountains

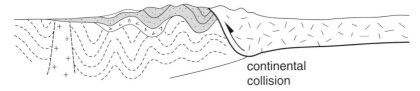

continental
collision

A tectonic plate collision may have folded the rocks in the Baraboo area.

What was the origin of the thick Baraboo strata? Tiny films of iron oxide on and between the quartz sand grains color the rock red. This oxidation indicates that the earth's atmosphere already contained considerable
oxygen. Rivers, whose channels were poorly defined and changed both rapidly and frequently, deposited the lower part of the quartzite. Such streams
are called *braided rivers* because of the complex patterns of repeatedly splitting and merging channels. Braided rivers carry coarse sediments. Native
Americans quarried a claystone near the base of the quartzite for the carving of ceremonial pipes. Red pipestone from Minnesota and Wisconsin
was so important that it was traded widely among the tribes of the upper
Mississippi Valley and Great Plains regions. The upper Baraboo quartzite

contains stratification characteristic of sediments deposited by marine processes. Wave ripples with sharp, straight crests are widespread, and features formed by reversing tidal currents are present in places. Together with overlying marine black mudrock (now slate), dolomite, and banded iron formation, these indicate that the sea gradually flooded the southern margin of embryonic North America during late Precambrian time.

The banded iron formation is particularly important because it was rich enough to be mined at three locations from 1889 until 1925. The cost of pumping water from the mine tunnels, which extended to depths of nearly 1,000 feet, finally made further mining uneconomical. None of the Precambrian strata that overlie the Baraboo quartzite, including the iron formation, crop out at the surface, so all that we know about them is from core drilling through the younger Paleozoic strata that blanket the central valley between the two Baraboo ranges.

Rhyolite and red quartzite like those of the Baraboo Hills appear in scattered outcrops for 40 miles east and northeast and have been penetrated in wells 75 miles east of Baraboo, indicating that these rocks originally covered a very large region. Red quartzite identical with the Baraboo is exposed 40 miles southeast at Waterloo, Wisconsin, and in southwestern Minnesota (as at Pipestone National Monument) and adjacent Iowa and South Dakota. These suggest an east-west expanse of more than 500 miles.

The quartzite has been quarried at several places within the Baraboo Hills for more than one hundred years. In the past, it was used for paving stone (cobblestones) and for making fire brick to line high-temperature steel-making furnaces. It is still quarried for piers and jetties on the Great Lakes and for railroad ballast, which is the gravel bed in which railroad track ties are laid.

Late Cambrian Strata

Cambrian strata surround the Precambrian quartzite cores of the Baraboo Hills and are exposed at the Dells, where Precambrian rocks lie 700 feet below the surface. The formations present are those that occur throughout the Western Uplands, but there is an important difference. Weathering and erosion wore down most of Wisconsin to a low, undulating land surface during the several hundred million years between the last Precambrian deformation and late Cambrian deposition, but high hills persisted wherever exceptionally resistant rocks occurred. The Baraboo quartzite formed an elliptical ring of hills as much as 1,000 feet high, which influenced dramatically the deposition of Cambrian sediments. From the distribution of outcrops of Cambrian formations, it is clear that the present topography closely reflects the terrain during Cambrian deposition. For example, patches of Cambrian strata occur between, and even at elevations below, many of the higher quartzite hills of today, as illustrated along the valley occupied by Devils Lake. Therefore, most of the present hills and valleys already existed in Cambrian time, and erosion is reexposing them. Luckily for geologists, the depth of erosion is just right to reveal very clearly the ancient geography of 500 million years ago.

The oldest Cambrian strata widely exposed in the Baraboo-Dells region are nonmarine sandstones deposited by wind and shallow streams with braided channels like those in which much of the lower part of the Baraboo quartzite was deposited. Large crossbedding—well exposed in the cliffs of the Dells—represent eroded, wind-formed dunes, whereas interlayered flat bedding represents areas between dunes, some of which were occasionally flooded by streams and ponds during wet spells. The orientation of the crossbedding indicates that Cambrian winds blew, on the average, from the present north and northeast. The Baraboo-Dells region was then at the edge of a lowland region, which included north-central Wisconsin and northern Michigan. It was dotted with hills of resistant Precambrian rocks surrounded by vast, sandy plains washed by small rivers and whipped by winds.

During Cambrian time, North America was rotated 90 degrees clockwise from its present position and lay along the equator; Wisconsin was in the southern tropics. Therefore, Cambrian winds actually blew from the southeast as do modern trade winds in the southern hemisphere. The

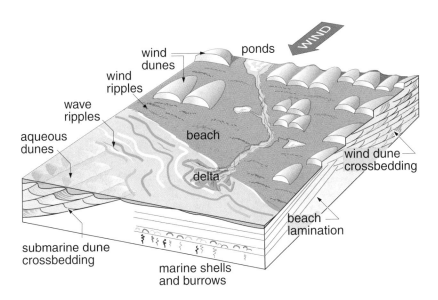

The Cambrian strata of the Wisconsin Dells area were deposited in these shoreline environments.

presence of some coarse sand grains indicates that those winds must have been very strong at times, for most present-day windblown sand grains are considerably finer. The lack of sizable land vegetation in Cambrian times made it easier for wind to pick up and transport sand.

The region must have been a pretty strange place 500 million years ago just as the Dells is today in a different sense. It was a sandy, windblown desert almost barren of life, but not dry like deserts today. Subtle aspects of stratification indicate that there were temporary ponds, streams, and wet sand flats among the dunes. There were no trees, shrubs, or grasses. Only lowly microbes had learned how to live above sea level, although very rare tracks suggest that a few small crablike animals were beginning to experiment with occasional walks on the moist beaches and dune flanks.

Meanwhile, a shallow, sandy-bottomed Cambrian ocean had been gradually encroaching upon the central part of the continent for millions of years. When it began to flood Wisconsin about 500 million years ago, hills were converted to islands and most of the former lowlands became sandy intertidal flats inhabited by a variety of burrowing and crawling animals. As the sea deepened, a completely submerged sandy seafloor 10 to 50 or more feet deep replaced the tidal flats. Marine sandstones deposited in such environments overlie the wind deposits.

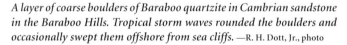

A layer of coarse boulders of Baraboo quartzite in Cambrian sandstone in the Baraboo Hills. Tropical storm waves rounded the boulders and occasionally swept them offshore from sea cliffs. —R. H. Dott, Jr., photo

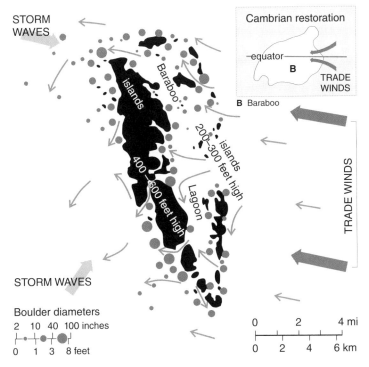

Boulders and cobbles of quartzite were eroded from cliffs on the Baraboo Islands and were dispersed by tropical storms in Cambrian time. In Cambrian time, the Baraboo Islands were oriented north-south, and prevailing trade winds blew from the east.

Marine Cambrian deposits are prominent in the Baraboo area, where an elliptical ring of quartzite islands was gradually buried by quartz sand. Surrounding the old islands is a rim of Cambrian conglomerates containing red quartzite fragments. Powerful waves of tropical storms attacked the sea cliffs, tearing blocks of red quartzite from them. The waves rounded many of the blocks by repeated tumbling against each other and polished them by sandblasting. Strong undertow from the waves and brief bursts of strong currents generated by the storms occasionally swept some of the boulders short distances away from the cliffs, but when mild, fair weather conditions returned, the ongoing deposition of sand simply buried the boulders. Although the conglomerate fragments range up to 25 feet long, well-rounded ones are no more than 5 feet in diameter. By comparing rugged modern shorelines like those of the Pacific Coast, we find that storm waves capable of moving and rounding quartzite boulders up to 5 feet in diameter must have been at least 25 feet high when they crashed onto the Baraboo Islands 500 million years ago. Even the greatest storm waves, however, were not able to move and round the largest, angular blocks, which must have simply fallen from the sea cliffs to be buried in place.

Today, we can see the results of those ancient tempests at many places around the Baraboo Hills, but especially in Parfreys Glen and along the East Bluff Trail at Devils Lake. Conspicuous layers of conglomerate, formerly called "puddingstone," contain rounded red quartzite cobbles and boulders interstratified with white or tan sandstones. The size of the fragments diminishes abruptly away from the islands so that at distances greater than 1 mile, only rare, fine pink quartzite pebbles are found, and the Cambrian formations look the same as they do in the Western Uplands. Similar coarse conglomerates occur elsewhere in Wisconsin where Cambrian strata abut against buried islands of resistant Precambrian rocks, for example at Interstate Park in northwestern Wisconsin.

Ordovician Strata

As the sea flooded more and more of the continent, Cambrian strata partially buried the Baraboo Islands. The higher islands persisted through Ordovician time, when the sea flooded almost all of North America, but they were so diminished in size that they no longer shed much gravel. Consequently, the change from sand to dolomite deposition so characteristic of early Ordovician time throughout the Mississippi Valley region happened here as well. Indeed, at several places around the hills, Prairie du Chien dolomite occurs next to Precambrian quartzite and contains only a few small, pink pebbles. Many stromatolites and oolites attest to the shallowness of the sea, so shallow that waves were much more feeble than in Cambrian time. The distinguished geologist L. L. Sloss once bragged that "The early Ordovician sea was so shallow I could have walked through it."

Sea level dropped slightly after deposition of the early Ordovician dolomite, and erosion partially reexposed some of the buried quartzite. As a consequence, the St. Peter sandstone, which was deposited over the eroded dolomite here as elsewhere in the Midwest, contains some quartzite gravel like that found in the Cambrian sandstones. Gibraltar Rock, a county park 5 miles south of the eastern Baraboo Hills, has a 100-foot-high cliff of St. Peter sandstone on its west face. The top of this cliff is 1,250 feet above sea level. The highest Baraboo Hills are 200 to 300 feet higher, so would have still been islands during the later Ordovician rise of sea level when the St. Peter and younger fossiliferous limestones and dolomites were deposited everywhere. Although erosion has removed the record of the younger limestones and dolomites from the Baraboo-Dells region, patches of them occur 10 to 20 miles south and southeast of the hills. As best we can judge by projecting those strata back toward Baraboo, the ancient quartzite was almost entirely buried by the end of Ordovician time about 440 million years ago.

Gibraltar Rock is a bold cliff of Ordovician St. Peter sandstone. View looking northwest toward the Baraboo Hills, which show on the right skyline. —R. H. Dott, Jr., photo

Silurian Strata

No Silurian rocks occur in the Baraboo Hills—the nearest preserved marine Silurian strata are 25 miles south on Blue Mound and 55 miles east in the Eastern Uplands near Lake Winnebago. We feel sure, however, that the sea covered all of Wisconsin then as well as during subsequent Devonian time because the strata of those ages still preserved in Wisconsin show no hint whatsoever that any land existed to be eroded within central Wisconsin. It was probably not until about 200 million years ago that Wisconsin became permanently dry land. Since that time, erosion has stripped all Devonian, Silurian, and much of the Ordovician strata from the area, exposing the ancient Baraboo Hills. By the time of the Quaternary Ice Age, the overall shape of the landscape was much as it is today.

Quaternary Glaciation

Although the Baraboo-Dells area may have been glaciated several times during the Quaternary Ice Age, evidence remains only for the most recent advance of the Wisconsin Glaciation. The Baraboo-Dells area was glaciated about 18,000 years ago when ice of the Green Bay Lobe flowed westward into the area. The north-south-trending edge of the Green Bay Lobe, marked today by the nearly continuous Johnstown moraine, wrapped around the eastern end of the Baraboo Hills, advancing as far as the Devils Lake area. At its maximum extent, the Green Bay Lobe blocked both ends of the Devils Lake gorge, forming a high-level ancestor of the modern lake. Ice also dammed the Wisconsin River to form Glacial Lake Wisconsin over the present Central Plain. Although the exact timing of the advance and retreat of the margin of the Green Bay Lobe is not closely dated by radiocarbon analyses, it is generally thought that by about 15,000 years ago the ice had begun to retreat eastward.

Although generally over half a mile wide and up to 60 feet high, the Johnstown moraine is smaller where it wraps up and over the uplands of the Baraboo Hills. It looks higher when viewed from the east because the western flank of the moraine is partly buried by thick deposits of sand and gravel carried from the ice sheet by meltwater rivers. These outwash deposits are commonly over 100 feet thick and form the broad sandy plains

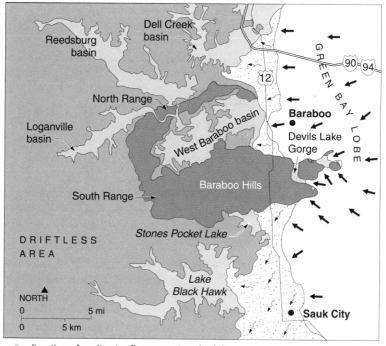

The western edge of the Green Bay Lobe wrapped around the Baraboo Hills, blocking both ends of Devils Lake gorge. The lakes in the Dell Creek, Reedsburg, Loganville, and West Baraboo basins connected to Glacial Lake Wisconsin to the north.

along the western edge of the Johnstown moraine. The till in the moraine is very sandy and contains many fragments of dolomite because much sand and dolomite were incorporated into the bed of the glacier as it flowed westward across a broad region of Paleozoic sandstone and dolomite bedrock. The till also contains a variety of igneous and metamorphic rocks derived from distant northern Precambrian rock sources, but it also has much locally derived Baraboo quartzite where it lies on the Baraboo Hills. As is typical of moraines, the surface of the Johnstown moraine is very hummocky and contains many depressions that hold lakes or wetlands. This hummocky surface formed when ice masses that were buried by sediment melted. A complex network of small ridges and meltwater channels cross the surface.

A conspicuous feature of the Johnstown moraine in the central part of Wisconsin is a series of tunnel channels now filled with sand and gravel. Typically about a quarter of a mile wide, up to a few miles long, and tens of feet deep, these channels were cut by meltwater flowing beneath the glacier and discharging at the ice margin. The water in at least some of these was moving upslope to the margin of the glacier much as water under pressure moves upward in a pipe. With permafrost beyond the ice margin, it is likely that a zone along the margin of the glacier was frozen to the underlying

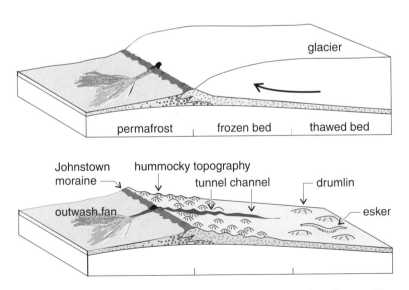

Block diagrams show the typical distribution of landforms along the west side of the Green Bay Lobe. Beneath thick areas of ice, geothermal heat and friction from sliding warm the glacial bed and permit meltwater to flow. Near the margin, cold penetrates the thin part of the glacier, freezing the ice to the ground and inhibiting water flow. —Modified from Attig, Mickelson, and Clayton, 1989

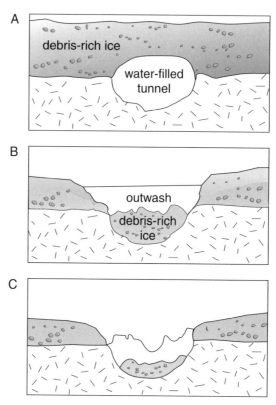

Sequence in the formation of a tunnel channel. A. Water flowing in a tunnel erodes into the material underlying the glacier. B. The roof of the tunnel made up of debris-rich ice collapses and is covered by sand and gravel deposited by outwash rivers flowing through the low area. C. Buried ice melts and the outwash collapses.

material, inhibiting water movement from beneath the glacier to the margin. The tunnel channels may have served as meltwater conduits from areas farther beneath the Green Bay Lobe, where the base of the glacier was warmer than near the margin, where cold penetrated the thinning ice. When flow through a tunnel channel ceased, the ice roof over the channel collapsed and was buried by outwash. Many of these tunnel channels show up in the modern landscape as a string of lakes and wetlands that occupy the depressions formed when the buried ice melted. Large fans of sediment deposited where the tunnel channels discharged from beneath the Green Bay Lobe extend up to a mile beyond the Johnstown moraine. These fans coalesce, forming the broad outwash plains west of the Johnstown moraine. The areas near the mouths of these tunnel channels are commonly the sites of pits where sand and abundant gravel are mined and used for a variety of aggregate products.

Glacial Lake Wisconsin

When the Green Bay Lobe flowed onto the east end of the Baraboo Hills, it dammed the Wisconsin River and formed Glacial Lake Wisconsin. The level of the lake rose until it began to drain out through a low gap along its northwest margin through the Black River to the Mississippi. At its greatest extent, Glacial Lake Wisconsin occupied much of central Wisconsin, and was about the size of modern Great Salt Lake.

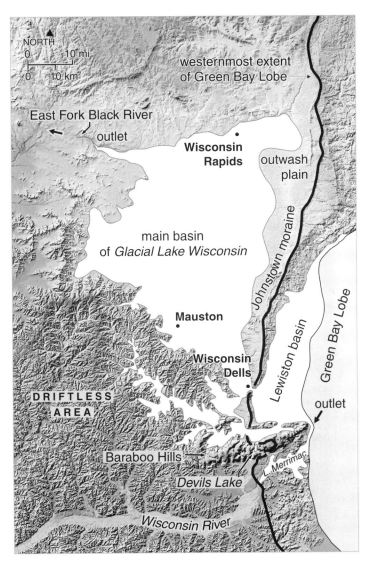

Glacial Lake Wisconsin formed when the Green Bay Lobe blocked the Wisconsin River. Map shows the extent of the Green Bay Lobe as an outlet opened around the east end of the Baraboo Hills. —Modified from Clayton and Attig, 1989

By about 14,000 years ago, the western edge of the Green Bay Lobe had melted back from the Johnstown moraine to the east end of the Baraboo Hills. As it melted, lakes formed between the ice margin and that moraine north of the Baraboo Hills in the Lewiston basin and south of the Baraboo Hills in the Merrimac basin. As the ice dam at the east end of the hills became narrower, it failed, allowing water from the Lewiston basin to rush into Lake Merrimac and down the lower Wisconsin River. The outflow from Lake Merrimac first cut a gap in the Johnstown moraine and spilled across the outwash plain near the former Badger Ammunition Plant. Soon, however, it cut a deeper channel farther east, which is now flooded by modern Lake Wisconsin.

Once the water level in the Lewiston basin dropped, the only thing impounding the main basin of Glacial Lake Wisconsin to the north was the sandy sediment of the Johnstown moraine and the weakly cemented Cambrian sandstones beneath the moraine at Wisconsin Dells. When this moraine dam failed, water from that huge lake rushed through the area, stripping away most lake or glacial sediment from the surface of the sandstones and cutting a network of deep gorges—the Wisconsin Dells.

We know that modern ice-dammed lakes tend to drain very rapidly. The draining, first of the series of ice-dammed and moraine-dammed lakes and then of the main basin of Glacial Lake Wisconsin, likely happened in just a

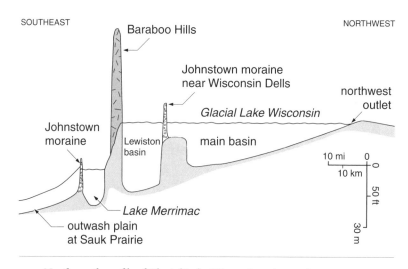

North-south profile of Glacial Lake Wisconsin at its maximum extent. The vertical scale is exaggerated. —Modified from Clayton and Attig, 1989

few days or weeks. It would have dwarfed even the greatest historic floods of the Wisconsin River.

The broad, flat sand plain of central Wisconsin is the most visible testimony to the former existence of Glacial Lake Wisconsin. Up to 300 feet of sandy and silty sediment was deposited in the lake, forming the flat lakebed. Meltwater rivers flowing westward from the Green Bay Lobe and the Wisconsin River draining meltwater from ice lobes in northern Wisconsin carried sand into the lake. Conspicuous bedrock bluffs like Roche-A-Cri, which stick up through this plain, were islands in the lake. Waves eroded these steep-sided bluffs, much like they erode the bedrock stacks along modern steep, rocky coastlines. The Paleozoic sandstones of these bluffs and surrounding areas provided much of the sand deposited in the lake. In a number of places, permafrost polygons formed in the lake deposits, indicating that after the lake drained, the climate was still cold enough to form permafrost.

Geological Fieldwork in the 1880s

U.S. government fossil collector Cooper Curtice spent about a week in the summer of 1884 around the Baraboo Hills collecting Cambrian fossils. His weekly letters back to Washington D.C. provide interesting insights into the hazards of fieldwork over a century ago (unpublished, U. S. Geological Survey archives). At Madison he rowed a boat 2 or 3 miles across Lake Mendota to collect from a cliff there. He reported that "I got fairly well sun burnt and blisters on my hands rowing. My boat was a small one, and the wind blew a gale. I have dried off since and of course did not drown as I half expected." A couple of weeks later, Curtice wrote that "Since last Sunday I have been in Baraboo the land of the Devils Lake and of thunder storms and in Reedsburg the country of cyclones [tornadoes]. The cyclone had its own way in that country over an area many miles in length and one mile in width a week ago Saturday. The ruins in its path attest to the fact." He reported a difficulty even more vexing than weather, however, while staying at a farm south of the Baraboo Hills. "Old Man Parker's boarding house [in Georgia last year] is a paradise beside this place which I am just leaving. They do not charge for board. Kind people but I guess they think that I have fatted their [bed] bugs up enough to pay for my board. Their intentions are good." About a week later he wrote that "I stayed at the Wisconsin House last night [a hotel at Devils Lake] and struck another nest of bugs." In spite of such trials and tribulations, Curtice was successful in his mission, for he shipped many crates and barrels of fossils back to Washington. Some of those fossils are on display in the Smithsonian National Museum of Natural History.

Interstate 39/U.S. 51
Coloma—Stevens Point
35 miles (57 km)

Coloma is at the junction of I-39/U.S. 51 with Wisconsin 21. Three miles west, Wisconsin 21 crosses the Johnstown moraine, the terminal moraine of the Green Bay Lobe, onto the Central Plain. To the east, Wisconsin 21 traverses wetlands and lakes of glaciated terrain in the Eastern Uplands. Within the 5 miles north of Coloma, I-39 crosses diagonally over the terminal moraine onto the edge of the Central Plain. Just south of County C, the overgrown gravel pits east of I-39/U.S. 51 are in a tunnel channel where it cuts through the Johnstown moraine. From here to Stevens Point, the

Landscape image along I-39/U.S. 51 between Coloma and Stevens Point.

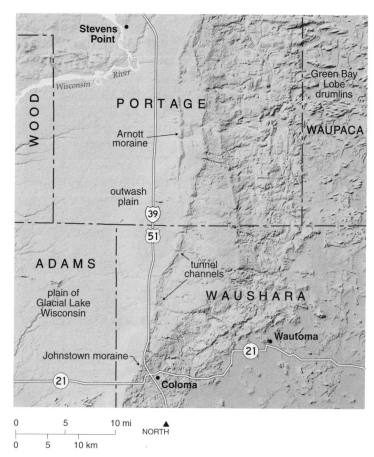

highway is flat and straight as it crosses the outwash plain deposited beyond the western edge of the moraine. The Johnstown moraine is visible east of the route as a forested ridge, becoming more distant farther north. In this area, the Green Bay Lobe reached its maximum extent about 18,000 years ago 3 to 4 miles east of the highway. Between Bancroft and the Plover area, another moraine, the Arnott, was deposited during an earlier glaciation; it is visible about 2 miles east of the highway. These moraines are very similar in size and shape except that the older Arnott has a much smoother surface than the younger moraine, presumably because it has suffered longer erosion. These moraines are the wooded ridges that you can see across the flat, cultivated outwash plain east of the highway. To the west of the highway, the outwash plain drops gradually in elevation and merges with the former floor of Glacial Lake Wisconsin. This section of highway provides excellent views of the lake plain to the west. Locally, wind has reworked the sand of the outwash plain and lake plain into small dunes that are now vegetated.

Only in one area near the highway does older bedrock peek through the Quaternary materials. Mosquito Bluff and the Ledge, about 17 miles north of Coloma and just east of the highway, are two isolated buttes formed of Cambrian sandstone, but dense forest conceals the bedrock.

Stevens Point marks the boundary between the Central Plain, dominated by sandy glacial outwash and lake deposits with local Cambrian sandstone buttes, and the Northern Highlands, dominated by Precambrian igneous and metamorphic rocks. The I-39/U.S. 51 discussion continues in the Northern Highlands chapter.

Interstate 90/Interstate 94
Wisconsin River—Camp Douglas via the Wisconsin Dells
55 miles (88 km)

Near Portage, I-90/94 crosses the Wisconsin River over the upper end of Lake Wisconsin, a section of the river dammed at Prairie du Sac, 16 miles downriver to the west. When the dam was built in 1911–1915, it was the largest hydroelectric project west of Niagara, New York. Moreover, it was the first large dam built upon a sand bed, a major engineering triumph.

As you approach the river crossing, the South Range of the Baraboo Hills looms on the northwest skyline. The highway swings around the easternmost end of the hills and turns toward the west to run parallel to the

North Range along the southern edge of the Central Plain, which was made famous by Aldo Leopold's classic book about ecology and conservation, *A Sand County Almanac*. The Leopold shack is just across the river to the north.

The Baraboo quartzite and other Precambrian rocks have been warped into a large syncline that resembles a canoe. The quartzite in the eastern point of the hills is like the prow of the canoe, which broadens westward and whose sides incline downward beneath the land surface. Here at this eastern end of the Baraboo Hills, the Green Bay Lobe formed an ice dam against the hills, thus blocking the Wisconsin River to form both Glacial Lake Wisconsin and the glacial lake in the Lewiston basin. When that ice dam failed, the huge amount of water in these lakes rushed through this area in a torrent, moving boulders up to 6 feet across that you can find in gravel pits east of the highway in this area.

Wisconsin 33 provides an opportunity to see more of the Baraboo Hills. Exit to Wisconsin 33 and proceed west into the Lower Narrows valley between the two ranges toward Baraboo and Devils Lake. A roadside interpretive sign at the north end of the narrows describes the geology. You can see vertical stratification in the quartzite there on the north limb of the Baraboo syncline within which the rocks are vertical or even slightly overturned toward the south. The underlying volcanic rhyolite is poorly exposed both west and east of the narrows. The Ice Age National Scenic Trail crosses the North Range just west of the Lower Narrows.

Continuing past the Wisconsin 33 exit, the interstate parallels the Wisconsin River, first crossing an area of sand plain deposited on the floor of Glacial Lake Lewiston and then crossing over the Johnstown terminal moraine to enter the unglaciated Driftless Area half a mile before the intersection with U.S. 12. Between the moraine and this intersection, I-90/94 passes over an outwash plain deposited just in front of the moraine.

Two miles west of U.S. 12, the interstate crosses over Mirror Lake, which occupies a gorge cut into Cambrian sandstones during the draining of Glacial Lake Wisconsin. A human-made dam on Dell Creek formed picturesque Mirror Lake. You can reach it either from U.S. 12 just south of I-90/94 or from the town of Lake Delton.

Wisconsin Dells

Our route bypasses Lake Delton and the Dells, a very popular resort area with special geological significance. Roadcuts along the interstate expose flat-lying, white to tan Cambrian sandstones, but these are much better exposed along the Wisconsin River just to the east in the network of scenic canyons known as the Dells of the Wisconsin River. The best way to see the Dells is by boat. Commercial tours depart from the city of

Wisconsin Dells. Exit the interstate on Wisconsin 13 if you wish to avoid the touristy strip of U.S. 12.

The Wisconsin Dells consist of a branching network of steep-sided gorges cut into Cambrian sandstones, which display large-scale crossbedding formed in wind dunes that covered the region 500 million years ago. The gorge of the Wisconsin River is the largest and best known of these. It is about 7 miles long and is typically several hundred feet wide but only about 50 feet wide at its narrowest point. Tributary gorges, such as Witches Gulch and Coldwater Canyon, offer the surprise of a cool, shaded environment very different from that of the main gorge. Although tens of feet deep, they are only a few feet wide in many places. Some of the gorges cut across local drainage divides and most appear too large to have been cut by the small streams that now occupy them; several contain no stream at all.

The gorges that make up the Wisconsin Dells were mostly cut when Glacial Lake Wisconsin drained about 14,000 years ago. The sandstone bedrock is not well cemented so was susceptible to rapid incision by floodwaters.

Witches Gulch, one of several deep, narrow tributary ravines of the Wisconsin Dells, exposes Cambrian sandstone.
—Photo courtesy of the Wisconsin Department of Natural Resources

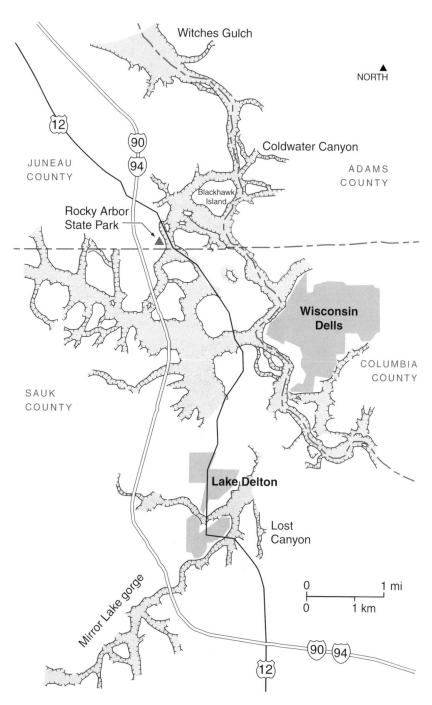

The deluge of water from the sudden draining of Glacial Lake Wisconsin cut the intricate pattern of gorges that make up the Wisconsin Dells. —Modified from Clayton and Attig, 1989

The lake in the Lewiston basin drained first when the ice dam at the east end of the Baraboo Hills failed. Then the Johnstown moraine, which had dammed the main basin of Glacial Lake Wisconsin, was breached in the Dells area. We believe that most of the cutting of the gorges occurred when the torrent of water from Glacial Lake Wisconsin tore through the area, stripping out the Johnstown moraine, cutting the Dells, and flooding down the Wisconsin River valley.

Rocky Arbor State Park to Camp Douglas

Rocky Arbor State Park, 1.5 miles north on U.S. 12 from the Wisconsin 13–U.S. 12 intersection in the city of Wisconsin Dells, contains an excellent example of one of the gorges that make up the Wisconsin Dells network. You can see the north wall of this gorge from a loop hiking trail.

Half a mile north of Rocky Arbor, the interstate diverges from the Wisconsin River and passes along the margin between the very flat Central Plain and the Western Uplands. In the next 25 miles, several isolated wooded hills known in Wisconsin as *mounds* are erosional remnants of once more-extensive Cambrian sandstones, which must have extended clear across the state until erosion removed all but these remaining hills from central Wisconsin; they, too, will eventually be victims of erosion. In the uplands to the west of the interstate, Cambrian and Ordovician strata are continuous to and beyond the Mississippi River. Eight miles west from either the Mauston or New Lisbon exits is the Elroy-Sparta State Trail, the nation's first rail-to-trail conversion for bicycling and hiking. It has exposures of, and tunnels through, Cambrian sandstones.

Fossil Tracks from New Lisbon

Cooper Curtice roamed through this region during the summer of 1884 collecting Cambrian fossils for the U.S. Geological Survey. He went from Camp Douglas to New Lisbon to see and collect flagstones with the spectacular tracks of an extinct Cambrian animal. These tracks, which resemble tire tracks, are as much as 5 or 6 inches wide and yards long. This very distinctive track, which in 1860 was named *Climactichnites,* meaning "ladderlike," has been found only in sandstones of Cambrian age in Wisconsin, New York, Quebec, Ontario, and Missouri. No fossil has ever been clearly identified as the trail maker, but there are several possible candidates. The most recent hypothesis is that an animal lacking a preservable skeleton but having a muscular foot made the track as it moved across sandy tidal flats, sucking up sand to obtain microorganisms living therein; the foot probably secreted a mucous trail like that of modern snails, which would have helped preserve the trackways. When Curtice arrived in New Lisbon, he found the best specimens on sidewalk flagstones, so resourceful fellow that he was, he arranged with the owners that three of these should be replaced by new stones from the nearby quarry. He also collected a 5-by-3.5-foot slab weighing about 700 pounds and arranged to have all shipped back to Washington.

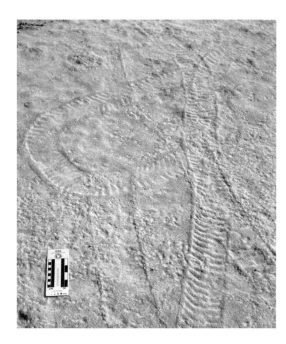

Tire-track-like trails of an extinct Cambrian animal (Climactichnites), *which had no skeleton and thus left no fossil.* —R. H. Dott, Jr., photo

Climactichnites *was probably a sluglike animal.* —From Yochelson and Fedonkin, 1993

Madison—Lake Delton
via the Baraboo Hills

50 miles (80 km)

For 15 miles northwest from Madison, U.S. 12 parallels closely the farthest western extent of the Green Bay Lobe, which lies west of the route. The hills are Paleozoic sandstone and dolomite with a patchy, thin cover of material transported by the glacier. A few bedrock roadcuts and some hilltop dolomite quarries are visible from the highway. The valleys have thicker accumulations of glacial outwash and lake sediment. Here at the edge of the glacier, the ice could not smooth out the bedrock hills as much as it did farther east where the glacier was thicker. Where U.S. 12 descends to cross the Wisconsin River, it crosses the Johnstown moraine, which is quite indistinct here. Large gravel pits north of the highway just east of the river exploit sand and gravel deposited by meltwater rivers right where they emerged from the glacier.

From Sauk City there is an excellent view westward across the Wisconsin River valley to the hills of the Driftless Area beyond and the Baraboo Hills to the north. Between the Wisconsin River and the southern edge of the Baraboo Hills, U.S. 12 crosses several broad, nearly flat outwash plains deposited by the rivers that drained the western edge of the Green Bay Lobe. Those rivers had complex, constantly shifting braided systems of channels that rapidly filled the lower Wisconsin valley from wall to wall with sand and gravel carried from the glacier. In places in this area the outwash is over 300 feet thick. Tundra polygons, evidence of permafrost, can be seen on air photos of the outwash plains near Sauk City. Between Sauk City and the Baraboo Hills, U.S. 12 rises onto higher and higher outwash plains. The low ridge that you can see to the east of U.S. 12 is the Johnstown moraine. A historical and geological marker on the east side of the highway about 7 miles north of Sauk City describes the terminal moraine. Here, the moraine stretches across a restored prairie that is on the highest of the outwash plains, the site of the former Badger Army Ammunition Plant (1942–1998). This high-level outwash plain once filled the valley from wall to wall and was deposited when the Green Bay Lobe stood at the Johnstown moraine. The lower outwash plains were deposited after the glacier margin had receded eastward and the outwash rivers had eroded much of the highest outwash plain.

The steep cliffs visible across the plain to the west of U.S. 12 are in the Driftless Area and they expose Paleozoic strata, but their shape is a product of the great outwash rivers. The channels undercut the bedrock hills and removed rock that fell, creating the steep cliff faces that we see. The thick accumulations of outwash sand and gravel in the main valley blocked smaller stream valleys west of here, creating lakes. The Wisconsin River cut through the outwash deposits, and erosion whittled away at the outlets, eventually draining the lakes.

As U.S. 12 leaves the outwash plains to climb over the South Range of the Baraboo Hills, the lower part of the Precambrian red Baraboo quartzite appears in roadcuts on the long uphill grade. A small exposure of Cambrian sandstone and conglomerate, visible alongside the west ditch of the highway just south of the summit, was deposited against eroded quartzite in a narrow inlet between two large quartzite islands that loomed more than 200 feet above Cambrian sea level. Many similar patches of these strata occur around the Baraboo Hills, and they provide clues to the geography of the area during late Cambrian time. In the South Range, the quartzite is inclined 25 degrees downward toward the north. You can see this inclination and the red color of the rock in a roadcut 2.5 miles north of the summit. This is near the top of the mile-thick quartzite. Ripple marks and other stratification features here suggest that tidal currents influenced the deposition of the upper part of the quartzite.

Half a mile farther north, Wisconsin 159 leads eastward to Devils Lake State Park. It passes right over the Johnstown moraine a mile east of U.S. 12, but you can also see the moraine clearly from U.S. 12 just north of the Wisconsin 159 intersection. The best and safest viewpoint is at a historical marker turnout on the east side of U.S. 12, which commemorates the founding of the Ringling Brothers Circus at the nearby city of Baraboo. The moraine is the wooded ridge extending diagonally from southeast to northwest and crossing the highway a little north of the sign. The field between the sign and the ridge is on the outwash plain. Hills west of the highway are in the Driftless Area.

Continuing north, U.S. 12 next crosses the Johnstown moraine, re-enters the glaciated area, and then crosses the Baraboo River in West Baraboo. Next the route climbs over the North Range of the Baraboo Hills, which is more subdued than the South Range. Throughout the North Range, the quartzite has been tilted to a vertical position, but to see it in this range, you must make a 7-mile side trip either east on Wisconsin 33 to the Lower Narrows of the Baraboo River or to the west on Wisconsin 136 to the Upper Narrows of that river at Rock Springs.

As U.S. 12 crosses the North Range, it also crosses the Johnstown terminal moraine again, and for the next 6 miles traverses a smooth, sandy outwash plain with the wooded moraine visible half a mile away on the eastern skyline and parallel to the highway. Three low gaps visible in the moraine are places where tunnel channels cut through it. At the intersection with I-90/94, you can see the Johnstown moraine just to the east.

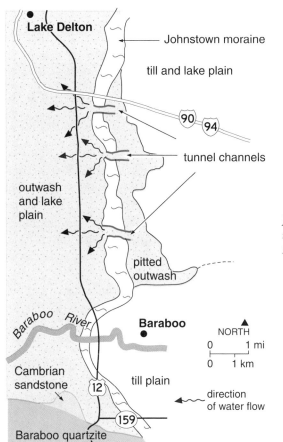

Johnstown moraine and tunnel channels between Baraboo and Lake Delton.

Devils Lake State Park

To visit Devils Lake State Park, which is a unit of the Ice Age National Scientific Reserve, head east on Wisconsin 159 from U.S. 12 or south on Wisconsin 123 from Baraboo. The park headquarters and nature center are at the north end of Devils Lake. You can reach the south end from Wisconsin 113 on South Shore Drive. Several hiking trails are of considerable geological interest; obtain maps and trail guides at the headquarters.

Devils Lake is 1.3 miles long, half a mile wide, and a maximum of about 50 feet deep. It lies within an abandoned river valley and is largely spring fed. The lake level fluctuates considerably with variations of annual precipitation. The West, East, and South Bluffs rise 500 feet above lake level; add to that at least 300 feet of sediment fill beneath the valley, and we find that this ancient gorge was once at least 800 feet deep. The bluffs expose

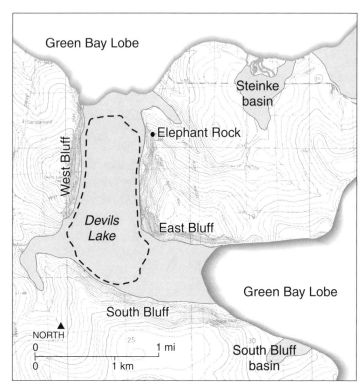

Devils Lake was larger and deeper when ice blocked both ends of the gorge.

much of the Baraboo quartzite plus a few patches of Cambrian conglomerate and sandstone on the sides of the valley. These patches prove that a gorge already separated two islands of quartzite during Cambrian time, and that the modern gorge is an excavated ancient one.

From viewpoints along the East Bluff Trail, you can clearly see the northward tilt of the quartzite across the lake. Remember that the South Range of the Baraboo Hills has been carved from the south limb of the Baraboo syncline. About one-fourth of the way up the trail from the north and next to Elephant Rock, an oddly shaped boulder of quartzite, is a large patch of Cambrian strata lying upon eroded quartzite and containing red boulders of that rock as much as 8 feet long. This patch of Cambrian sediments is more than 200 feet below the highest nearby quartzite hills, so it must have been deposited on the slope of a quartzite island in the Cambrian sea. Many of the boulders are rounded; they were probably deposited here by very powerful storm waves pounding against an ancient sea cliff of quartzite.

The Johnstown moraine, which marks the maximum extent of the Green Bay Lobe, divides the glaciated eastern part of Devils Lake State Park from the western unglaciated part of the park. The ice lobe covered the east end of the Baraboo Hills, wrapped around the high hills to the north and east of Devils Lake, and filled both ends of the ancient gorge.

Devils Lake formed when the ice blocked both ends of the gorge; its water level was about 90 feet higher than the present lake. Water from this

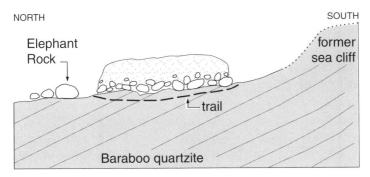

A patch of Cambrian conglomerate and sandstone rests on Precambrian Baraboo quartzite at Elephant Rock on the East Bluff Trail in Devils Lake State Park.

View looking southeast from West Bluff across Devils Lake at Baraboo quartzite inclined downward to the left in East Bluff. The Johnstown terminal moraine blocks the southern end of the lake in the distance behind the tree limbs. —Photo courtesy of the Wisconsin Department of Natural Resources

high phase drained out the northwest corner of the lake near the present north entrance road to the park. When the ice melted, the Johnstown moraine remained to dam the ends of the gorge and retain the lake at its present lower level. The ice margin also dammed lakes in a number of other smaller basins such as Steinke and South Bluff. When the ice margin retreated, these small lakes drained. Flat surfaces of silty sediment mark the lakebeds.

Nearly continuously through the area, the Johnstown moraine is about a quarter of a mile wide and 50 to 60 feet high where it crosses the north end of the gorge. The park's nature center is located on the crest of the moraine. The moraine is about three-quarters of a mile wide at the east end of the gorge and when viewed from the east is almost 150 feet high. You can see the moraine at both the north and east ends of the gorge from the boat landing at the southwest corner of Devils Lake as well as from the top of West Bluff. Throughout the rest of the area, the moraine is typically much smaller.

A short hike north of County DL from the parking lot at the Steinke Basin Trailhead takes you to the crest of the Johnstown moraine and a junction with the Johnson Loop Trail (named for the Johnson family who farmed this area for several generations). This trailhead also provides access to the Ice Age National Scenic Trail. The Johnstown moraine trends east-west in this area and the southern edge of the ice was near the old windmill you can see a short distance north of County DL. You can also see several conspicuous boulders of pink rhyolite that the glacier transported from the Lake Superior basin. In this area the uneven hummocky topography is typical of moraines. The north-south-trending lowland containing ponds and wetlands just east of the windmill is the location of a tunnel channel, through which water flowed out from beneath the glacier. The Steinke Basin parking lot is on the outer edge of the sediment fan deposited at the mouth of that tunnel channel.

A notable feature of Devils Lake gorge is the accumulation of a large mass of angular quartzite blocks along its walls. This accumulation, called *talus*, ends abruptly at the Johnstown moraine at the east end of the gorge, suggesting that most of the talus accumulated before the Green Bay Lobe began to recede from its maximum extent in the area. The talus probably accumulated throughout Quaternary time, but especially during the periods of colder climate and glaciation. Repeated freezing and thawing of water in cracks loosened blocks of quartzite in the cliffs walling the gorge. Some of the talus blocks are over 10 feet across. On a hot summer day, cool air draining from the base of the talus can provide a welcome relief to a hot vacationer or geologist! This cool air sustains vegetative communities one would expect to find only in cooler climates. The presence of many large trees growing on the talus suggests that these slopes have not changed for a

Looking west from the junction of Wisconsin 113 and County DL into the east end of Devils Lake gorge. The ridge crossing the valley between the quartzite uplands to the right and left is the Johnstown moraine. —J. W. Attig photo

Toe of the talus on the north side of Devils Lake gorge. The largest blocks of quartzite are more than 6 feet across. —J. W. Attig photo

very long time. The Grottos Trail provides access to the talus at the base of East Bluff.

From the Potholes Trail that extends from the top of East Bluff to the beach area at the southeast end of Devils Lake, you can see a number of well-formed potholes. Stones moving within the bottom of a long-lived river eddy drilled these cylindrical holes into the quartzite along the walls of the gorge. A nearly spherical millstone found in the bottom of one of these potholes is on display at the park nature center. Geologists do not know if a glacial or preglacial river carved the potholes. We know that rivers flowing from glaciers do carry large amounts of coarse sediment and commonly form potholes where they spill over bedrock. Nonglacial rivers can form potholes as well, however, and because we know of no evidence that a glacier ever advanced to a position where it could have spilled meltwater over East Bluff in the vicinity of the potholes, we think they were more likely formed by the preglacial river that carved the gorge.

Pollen and seeds that accumulated in sediments at the bottom of Devils Lake provide a record of how vegetation in the area has changed since glaciation. The sediment also contains other organic material that geologists can date using radiocarbon. The pollen record in Devils Lake shows that,

Pothole in quartzite along the Potholes Trail in Devils Lake State Park. Note leaves for scale.
—J. W. Attig photo

Kenneth Lange, longtime naturalist for Devils Lake State Park, holds a quartzite millstone found in a park pothole. —J. W. Attig photo

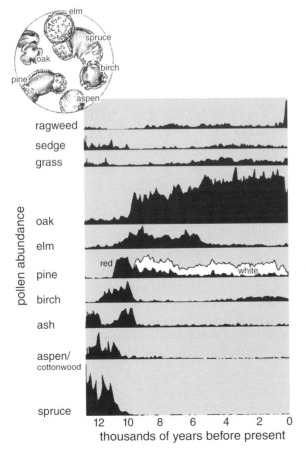

The abundance of different plant pollens in a sediment core from the bottom of Devils Lake shows the change in vegetation during the last 12,000 years.
—Modified from Attig, Clayton, Lange, and Maher, 1990

from about 12,000 to 10,000 years ago, spruce, aspen, birch, and ash were common in the area. Around 11,000 years ago red pine reached the area, but white pine took another thousand years or so to become prominent. Elm trees were very abundant from about 10,000 to 6,000 years ago. Maple, basswood, and ironwood were also more abundant then than now. Between 6,000 and 3,000 years ago, oak savannas became common, indicating a warmer and dryer climate. Around 3,000 years ago, oak forest became more common, suggesting that the climate cooled and became moister. An increase in the amount of ragweed pollen marks the impact of clearing of land by European settlers in the mid-1800s.

Parfreys Glen

Parfreys Glen, 4 miles east of Devils Lake via County DL, should be a "must" stop for any park visitor. This 100-foot-deep gorge was Wisconsin's first designated state natural area and provides superb scenery as well as geologic and botanical rewards. It is one of several deep glens in the Baraboo Hills that have a cool microclimate favorable for species of plants normally found only in cooler, northern Wisconsin. The glen was named for an English immigrant who lived here from 1865 to 1876. A mill pond was created in 1846 by building an earth-and-log dam at the mouth of the narrow, rock-walled inner glen. Both sawmills and gristmills operated here for many years.

The walls of Parfreys Glen expose Cambrian sandstones with many layers of conglomerate similar to those at Devils Lake. Fragments of red Baraboo quartzite vary from many small pebbles to some great rounded boulders 5 feet in diameter within the most prominent conglomerate layer. The finer, more angular fragments in the lower layers did not get tumbled and abraded by waves as long as did those in the upper layers. The sea cliff from which the Parfreys Glen boulders were eroded lies mostly concealed by soil and vegetation only a few hundred feet west of the narrowest part of the glen. As you stand here, try to imagine a tropical storm throwing up a wall of water 25 feet high to crash against that cliff; then listen for the rattle of the boulders tumbled by the backwash of water at the base of the cliff.

Sandstones in the upper 30 or 40 feet of the Glen wall have the fossil worm burrows called *Skolithos*. Animals were finally able to inhabit this locality only during the deposition of these upper strata.

What about the origin of the gorge? Surely it was not cut by the modest trickle now flowing here, for it is unable to reduce the blocks that have fallen from the gorge walls during the past century or so. We believe that it was cut largely by meltwater from the glacier as it receded eastward from Devils Lake. Souvenirs of the downcutting are visible high on the east wall at the upper, narrowest point where there are two large concave, cylindrical

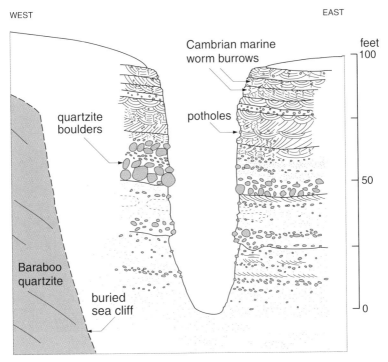

Cambrian conglomerate and sandstone exposed in Parfreys Glen. Red boulders in the walls of the glen were derived from a sea cliff largely buried west of the trail.

scourings into the sandstone. These are partially preserved potholes bored into the rock as the gorge was deepened. After the ice front retreated eastward past Parfreys Glen, downcutting practically ceased, and since that time, the creek has been fed by a small spring located above the Glen.

Natural Bridge State Park

Twelve miles southwest of Devils Lake via U.S. 12 and County C, between the villages of Leland and Denzer, is a spectacular natural bridge carved from Cambrian sandstones. In the 1890s, the Leland Natural Bridge was a favorite summer gathering place for locals. A dance floor was built below the bridge with an adjacent bar sheltered by an overhanging sandstone cliff.

The Leland Natural Bridge lies within the Driftless Area 2 miles south of the South Range of the Baraboo Hills. Rare, pink pebbles of Baraboo quartzite in the Cambrian sandstone were derived from a wave-eroded quartzite pinnacle or sea stack one-half mile north, and were swept here by storm-driven ocean currents. The natural arch is 35 feet long and 25 feet high at

The Leland Natural Bridge eroded from Cambrian sandstone of the Tunnel City formation. The overhang below was a shelter for prehistoric people, and in the 1890s, it sheltered a bar during weekend social events. —Photo courtesy of the Wisconsin Department of Natural Resources

its center. It stands on a low ridge 170 feet above and 1,500 feet away from the nearest small stream, which is by the road entrance to the park. It does not seem likely that running water could have formed the bridge in this location, so what else could? Weathering by seepage and repeated freezing and thawing of water in the pores and cracks of the permeable sandstone probably weakened a less-resistant layer for thousands of years. This slow destruction was no doubt aided by the harsh climate prior to about 15,000 years ago when the glacier stood only 12 miles away above Devils Lake. Undermining from both sides of a thin rib of sandstone finally opened a hole, creating the bridge as we now see it. This process is well known in the canyon country of Utah today, where there are a number of such natural bridges.

The large, cavelike amphitheater beneath the bridge illustrates the slow erosion of a less-resistant layer. Long before it housed a bar, it provided a rock shelter for the first Paleo-Indian people who lived in the region. Archaeological study of this Raddatz Shelter, so named for the former property owner, shows that prehistoric people may have been here as early as 8,000 to 10,000 years ago.

Ableman Gorge on the Baraboo River at Rock Springs

To reach Ableman Gorge, or the Upper Narrows of the Baraboo River, head 7 miles west from West Baraboo on Wisconsin 136 to Rock Springs. The gorge provides an accessible and scenic, half-mile-long geologic cross section through the North Range—a vest-pocket model for the Precambrian and Cambrian geology of the entire Baraboo Hills. Here, you can see an ancient island of Precambrian quartzite buried by Cambrian strata.

Rock Springs has been a center for stone quarrying since 1868. Quartzite is still exploited here for railroad ballast, the crushed stone in which railroad ties are set. There is a large, active, quartzite quarry (off limits to the public) on top of the east side of the valley. You may have seen this red quartzite along railroad tracks throughout the upper Midwest.

An abandoned quartzite quarry on the west side of the gorge next to Wisconsin 136 is accessible public land and provides a sample view of the vertical north limb of the Baraboo syncline. The ancient, red Baraboo quartzite was turned up on end throughout the North Range. In the old quarry wall, we can see crossbedding in nearly every stratum, and at the

The north end of Ableman Gorge as it appeared in the 1930s. Flat-lying Cambrian conglomerate overlies the eroded edges of vertical quartzite. —Photo courtesy of the Milwaukee Public Museum

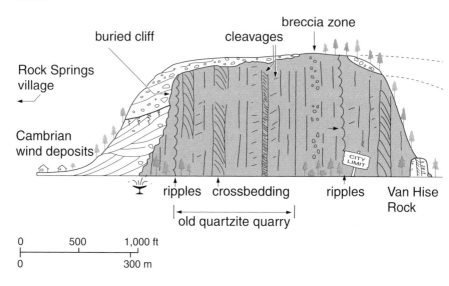

SOUTH

Rock Springs village

buried cliff

cleavages

breccia zone

Cambrian wind deposits

ripples   crossbedding   ripples   Van Hise Rock

old quartzite quarry

```
0        500      1,000 ft
├────────┼────────┤
0                 300 m
```

south end, there is a high wall studded with ripple marks, the largest of several such exposures in the Baraboo Hills. Although we see only the bottom impression of the ripples here, their straight crests suggest that they were formed by waves. Both crossbedding and wave ripples also can help us tell which way was up in vertical or overturned strata; here the "up" or top direction is toward the south.

In the northern part of the old quarry, there is a zone of angular red quartzite fragments encased by white quartz veins, making a rock called *breccia*. Faulting or some explosive process fractured the rock, and then hot solutions precipitated quartz and clay. The breccia formed either during or soon after the deformation of the Precambrian rocks because pebbles eroded from this zone occur in Cambrian conglomerates. In places, cavities within the zone contain small quartz crystals 1 to 2 inches long, some of which are partially coated by a fine, cream-colored, clay mineral.

Near the north end of the gorge along the east side of the highway at a small parking lot is **Van Hise Rock National Historical Landmark**, a prominent pinnacle of quartzite about 15 feet high. Plaques commemorate the rock's importance and fame in the research and teaching by Wisconsin's early great geologist and university president, Charles R. Van Hise. Around 1900, he refined principles for interpreting the origin of slate and its relationship to larger folded structures in layered rocks, such as the Baraboo syncline. The central dark band in Van Hise Rock contains closely spaced, diagonally inclined slate layers defined by what geologists call *slaty cleavage*.

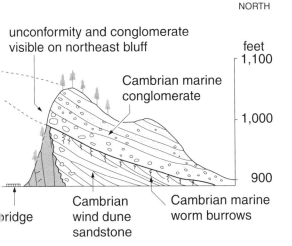

NORTH

unconformity and conglomerate visible on northeast bluff

Cambrian marine conglomerate

feet
1,100

1,000

900

Cambrian wind dune sandstone

Cambrian marine worm burrows

ridge

Ableman Gorge, the Upper Narrows of the Baraboo River, just north of Rock Springs. Exposures here provide a clear picture of the burial of the Baraboo quartzite islands by Cambrian deposition. The inclined cleavage in the quartzite tells us this is part of the north limb of the Baraboo syncline. —After Dalziel and Dott, 1970

This contrasts with vertical, pink layers of quartzite on either side. Slaty cleavage forms in fine-grained strata sandwiched between coarser ones when the rocks are squeezed into folds. As the strata are bent, individual layers slide past one another as occurs when we bend a ream of paper. The stress produces cleavage in weaker, shaly layers. Van Hise demonstrated here that the geometric relationship between the diagonal slaty cleavage and the vertical stratification has a predictable relationship to the entire, larger structure, which is invisible beneath the central Baraboo Valley to the south. The cleavage tells us that Van Hise Rock lies on the north limb of a syncline. The geometric relationship of crossbedding in the two adjacent pink quartzite layers as well as the ripple marks at the south end of the gorge verify this conclusion. Geologists all around the world apply the principles of structural geology developed here by Van Hise and his students.

Besides its importance to understanding the overall structure of the quartzite, the small area of Ableman Gorge also provides a miniature model for understanding the Cambrian history of the entire Baraboo Hills. In the woods on private land south of the abandoned quarry, Cambrian sandstones and conglomerates abut against a buried, sloping cliff of quartzite. At the very top of the old quarry wall, boulders of quartzite within sandstone form a veneer across the eroded edges of vertical quartzite layers (binoculars help). At the north end of the gorge, beyond Van Hise Rock in cliffs across the river (northeast) and above the railroad tracks, flat-lying Cambrian sandstones and conglomerates are visible from the highway.

Wave-formed ripple marks on a vertical face of Baraboo quartzite in an abandoned quarry on the west side of Ableman Gorge. This is the bottom of a rock layer, so you are looking at the molds or impressions of the ripples.
—Nancy R. Dott photo

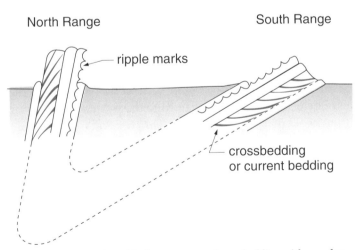

North Range

South Range

ripple marks

crossbedding
or current bedding

Wave-formed ripples with sharp crests and crossbedding with angular truncated or cutoff tops indicate the original top direction in vertical strata (left limb). The diagram shows the relationships of these features across the Baraboo Hills from the North Range to the South Range.

Van Hise Rock in Ableman Gorge. Stanley A. Tyler, former University of Wisconsin professor, demonstrates the origin of the dark, slaty portion of the rock. —Photographer unknown

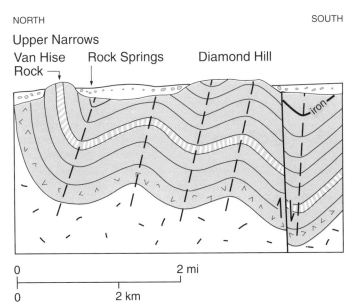

Folds in the Baraboo quartzite south of Ableman Gorge.
Van Hise Rock is on the north limb of a syncline.

These exposures provide a mirror image of those in the woods at the south end of the gorge. The first deposits of sandstone have large-scale crossbedding visible beside the railroad track. Wind blew sand against a quartzite cliff, forming dunes there—just as wind was simultaneously forming dunes in the Wisconsin Dells 12 miles north. Conglomerate appears abruptly about halfway up the cliff face and continues to the highest exposures. Subtle marine worm burrow structures called *Skolithos* are found within sandstone immediately beneath the lowest conglomerate, recording the arrival of the advancing Cambrian sea in this area as well as at the Dells. Here, as at Devils Lake and Parfreys Glen, we see evidence of the dramatic work of Cambrian storm waves in the form of rounded boulders of quartzite derived from ancient sea cliffs and tumbled for short distances. Finally, when deposition completely buried the local "Rock Springs" island, no more quartzite gravel was available, so only sand was deposited above the now-buried quartzite. Although this and other Cambrian islands along the present North Range had disappeared by the end of Cambrian time, a few higher quartzite islands persisted along the present South Range through Ordovician time.

In many places, the surface of the quartzite is exceptionally smooth to the touch. A good example is just across Wisconsin 136 diagonally southwest from Van Hise Rock. We believe that such exceptional polish was accomplished through sand and silt blasting by wind during Quaternary glaciation. Sparse vegetative cover on the land beyond the ice sheets would have greatly enhanced both wind erosion and transport. In places, windblown particles abraded flattish faces and small grooves on quartzite surfaces. The orientation of such features indicate the local wind direction at the time they were abraded.

Wisconsin 21
Tomah—Coloma
60 miles (95 km)

Tomah lies at the western edge of the Central Plain and Wisconsin 21 heads east across the heart of that lowland region, which was the floor of Glacial Lake Wisconsin. Silt and fine sand were deposited on the floor of that lake. Wisconsin 21 passes through patches of the typical oak, pine, and birch forest of central Wisconsin, which can tolerate long dry spells. The sandy soil is so permeable here that natural rainwater sinks too quickly to sustain crops, making agriculture dependent upon constant irrigation by huge sprinklers, which resemble some giant insect like a praying mantis.

At Necedah, Wisconsin 80 to the north provides access to the Necedah National Wildlife Refuge. A driving tour through the refuge is an excellent way to get a feel for the landscape and vegetation of the area. Wetlands and lakes abound, and in surrounding areas, because of a high water table, there are many commercial cranberry bogs.

Several bedrock mounds or buttes composed of resistant Cambrian and some Precambrian rocks add interest to the otherwise very flat landscape along Wisconsin 21. An example is Necedah Mound in Necedah, 150 feet high and composed of red Precambrian quartzite flanked by Cambrian sandstone and cobbles and boulders of the quartzite. The rock, which is quarried here, is identical in appearance to the Precambrian Baraboo quartzite 60 miles to the south. Petenwell Rock, a 100-foot-high butte of Cambrian sandstone, looms up 4 miles east of Necedah, where Wisconsin 21 crosses the Wisconsin River between Castle Rock Lake to the south and Petenwell Lake to the north. Both of these lakes are impoundments of the river called *flowages*. A Native American legend of Petenwell Rock tells of lovers being pursued by elders opposed to their association. In hopeless despair, they jumped from the top into the river and disappeared forever.

About 10 miles east of the river, Wisconsin 21 intersects Wisconsin 13, and a short 1.5-mile diversion to the south takes you to Roche-A-Cri State Park. Although said to refer to "rock with crevices," the name given to this prominent butte of Cambrian sandstone by early French trappers translates literally as "crying or shrieking rock." We guess that it referred to shrieking hawks, which like to nest on rocky prominences. On the south face of the butte is a fine cluster of varied prehistoric Indian petroglyphs and pictographs, whose presence was first recorded by a government surveyor in 1851.

Like Petenwell Rock, Roche-A-Cri is typical of the many bedrock mounds that rise above the very flat sand plain. Your visit would not be complete without climbing the 303 wooden steps to the top of the butte, from which magnificent views extend across the Central Plain to the Western Uplands and eastward to the terminal moraine. In all directions, you can see other bedrock mounds, all of which were islands in Glacial Lake Wisconsin; Roche-A-Cri is very near the center of that former lake. Wave erosion certainly contributed to the steep slopes that characterize the mounds.

All of the mounds or buttes expose Cambrian sandstones, which formerly covered the entire Central Plain and the Northern Highlands as well. What we see today are simply the last remnants of a once-continuous sheet of sandstone, which has been eroding away for millions of years. The lower portions of the sandstones in this area were deposited over 500 million years ago by rivers that wandered aimlessly across a sandy Cambrian plain in ill-defined braided channels, which changed with every increase of flow.

Roche-A-Cri, one of several buttelike pinnacles of Cambrian sandstone looming above the Central Plain. —Photo courtesy of the Wisconsin Department of Natural Resources

During drier periods, seepage into the permeable sandy riverbed greatly reduced the flow. Then, wind picked up and transported much sand, forming dune fields such as those displayed in the sandstone walls of the Dells of the Wisconsin River 25 miles to the south. Cambrian river deposits prevailed in the central Wisconsin region while more dunes formed downwind to the south. Fossiliferous marine strata occur in the upper parts of the highest buttes, which you can see, for example, in the topmost 20 feet or so at Roche-A-Cri beneath the viewing platform. Here, there are zones of worm burrows, some of which resemble a cluster of short soda straws crowded together side-by-side; these fossil burrows are called *Skolithos.*

Seven miles east of Roche-A-Cri is picturesque Ship Rock Wayside, another butte of Cambrian sandstone, which rises about 75 feet above the plain. The strata exposed here are unfossiliferous river deposits formed during the early part of late Cambrian time about 500 million years ago.

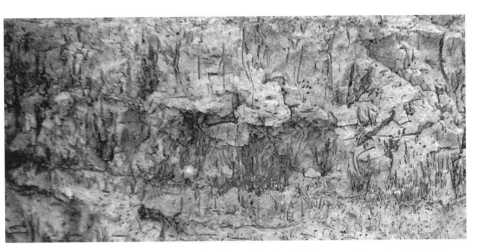

Densely packed Skolithos *fossils, the dwelling tubes in which a wormlike animal lived in shallow, agitated waters of the late Cambrian seas that lapped against the Baraboo Islands.*
—R. H. Dott, Jr., photo

Five miles east of Ship Rock, Wisconsin 21 leaves the plain of Glacial Lake Wisconsin and begins to rise onto the outwash plain deposited beyond the Green Bay Lobe. From the intersection of Wisconsin 21 with County G, there is an excellent view of a moraine—possibly the Johnstown moraine, though several moraines intersect near here—deposited along the west edge of the Green Bay Lobe. The moraine rises about 50 feet above the outwash plain. From the crest of the moraine to the intersection with I-39/U.S. 51 at Coloma, Wisconsin 21 crosses a hummocky glacial landscape of sandy till and outwash. In this area, the Johnstown moraine forms the drainage divide between the Mississippi River and Lake Michigan watersheds. One mile west of the intersection is the turnoff to the south onto Fourth Avenue, which gives access to the Glover Bluff disturbance described in **I-39/U.S. 51: Portage—Coloma** in the Eastern Uplands chapter.

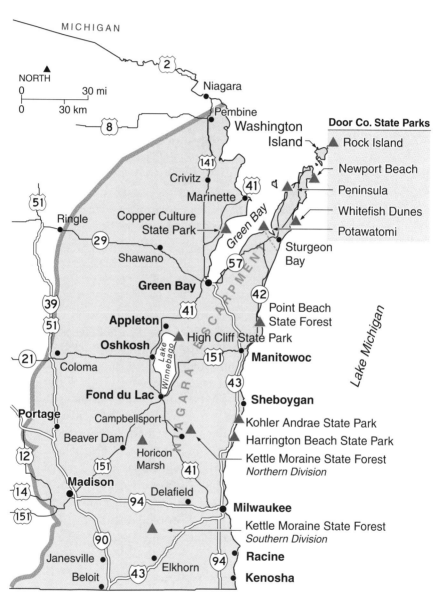

Roads and points of geologic interest in the Eastern Uplands and the Door Peninsula.

Eastern Uplands and Door Peninsula

The Eastern Uplands contain more than half of the total population of Wisconsin and at least three-fourths of the state's industry. These are both concentrated in the Milwaukee-Racine-Kenosha corridor in the southeast and along the Fox River from Oshkosh to Green Bay in the central part of the region. What is left of a once-large commercial fishing industry is concentrated along the Lake Michigan shore. Great Lakes shipping from the St. Lawrence Seaway continues to use ports such as Milwaukee, and there is still a small shipbuilding industry, which is concentrated at Sturgeon Bay on the Door Peninsula.

Lake Michigan bounds the region on the east, and it was from the lake that the first European explorers, French fur traders and missionaries led by Jean Nicolet, entered Wisconsin via Green Bay in 1634. The French established the first permanent European settlement in Wisconsin at Green Bay in 1683. From Green Bay, the Eastern Uplands extend northward through the Door Peninsula to upper Michigan and southward to Illinois. Prominent glacial moraine ridges, which mark the westernmost advance of the most recent Wisconsin ice sheet, topographically define the complex western margin. This topographic boundary, however, overlaps different bedrock provinces. In the north, for example, it crosses Precambrian bedrock typical of the Northern Highlands, whereas in the south it crosses over the same Paleozoic strata that are exposed widely throughout the Western Uplands. The boundary also marks a major divide between rivers that drain eastward through the Great Lakes to the Atlantic Ocean and those that drain through the Mississippi River to the Gulf of Mexico. Glacial deposits and landforms dominate the Eastern Uplands; it is the meeting place of two lobes of the last glacier, one named for Green Bay and the other for Lake Michigan.

From the broad upwarped Wisconsin dome centered in the Northern Highlands, the poorly exposed Paleozoic strata of the Eastern Uplands plunge eastward beneath Lake Michigan into a circular, depressed portion of the earth's crust called the Michigan basin. Both the Wisconsin dome and the Michigan basin are such large features, each covering most of an entire state, that the eastward inclination of the strata beneath the Eastern Uplands is imperceptible to the eye. The half-degree tilt means that a given rock layer decreases in elevation by a few tens of feet for every mile traversed from west to east. Although not much like a steep, breath-

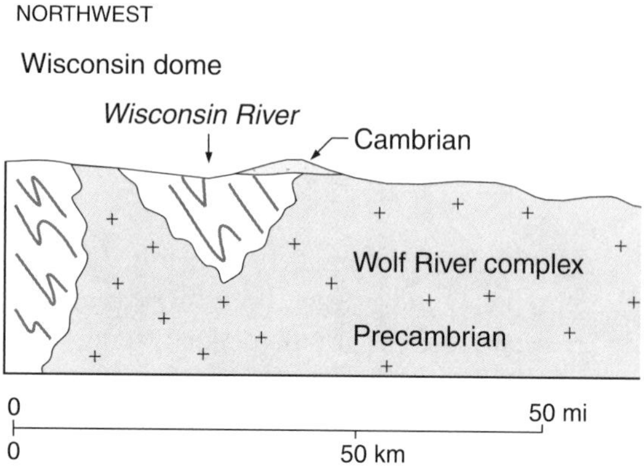

NORTHWEST

Wisconsin dome

Wisconsin River

Cambrian

*Section across the
Eastern Uplands
from the Wisconsin
dome to the
Michigan basin.*

Wolf River complex

Precambrian

0   50 mi

0   50 km

taking roller coaster, this slope does carry the base of the Paleozoic strata to a depth of more than 13,000 feet beneath central Michigan.

Precambrian and Paleozoic Rocks

Precambrian rocks—mostly volcanic rhyolite, granite, and quartzite—are exposed at scattered localities within the Eastern Uplands. The Cambrian and Ordovician exposures are discontinuous and mostly covered with glacial material. Although you can see the Cambrian strata in very few places along highways in eastern Wisconsin, drilling indicates that they are much the same here as farther west. As the late Cambrian sea gradually lapped onto the eastern flank of the Wisconsin dome, Precambrian rocks formed islands just as they did around Baraboo and several other places in western Wisconsin. The more widely exposed early Ordovician Prairie du Chien dolomite caps many hills and looks the same as in the Western Uplands. The overlying St. Peter sandstone is also present but is known primarily from quarries and wells. The younger Ordovician Platteville and Galena formations are even better known thanks to their being quarried extensively for limestone and dolomite. The youngest Maquoketa shale, being soft, is rarely seen at the surface but extends from Green Bay south along the base of the Niagara Escarpment past Lake Winnebago and beyond into Illinois. It underlies the lowlands of Green Bay, the Fox River valley, Lake Winnebago, and the Horicon Marsh.

Niagara Escarpment

A long ridge called the Niagara Escarpment, composed of resistant Silurian strata, extends from the Milwaukee area to the Door Peninsula and

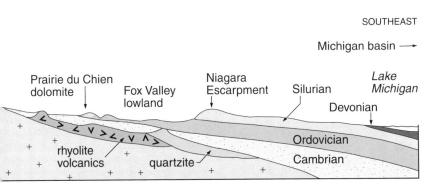

SOUTHEAST

Michigan basin →

Prairie du Chien dolomite | Fox Valley lowland | Niagara Escarpment | Silurian | *Lake Michigan* | Devonian | Ordovician | Cambrian | rhyolite volcanics | quartzite

northeast across Michigan and then southward through Ontario to the Niagara Falls region of New York, which explains its name. According to an overly dramatic 1973 account from Ontario, the escarpment was the result of some ancient cataclysm. "There must have been an unearthly screeching. How the ground must have shivered! And what a relief it must have been when quiet was once more restored." In reality, the escarpment had a very tranquil origin due simply to slow erosion over millions of years of the gently tilted strata that surround the Michigan basin; the Niagara dolomite is simply more resistant to erosion than the strata beneath and above it.

Neda Ironstone

Along the base of the Niagara Escarpment within the uppermost part of the late Ordovician Maquoketa shale, a thin, discontinuous but very distinctive layer is known as the Neda ironstone. It was named for a small town 20 miles south of Fond du Lac at the base of the escarpment. The ironstone was the basis for a thriving iron smelting industry for sixty-five years, which was important during the early days of settlement in eastern Wisconsin. The ore consisted of lens-shaped bodies of a granular rock as much as 55 feet thick composed of millimeter-scale pellets called *oolites*, which formed by calcium carbonate precipitation around a rolling nucleus on shallow shoals. Oolites occur widely at the top of the Ordovician strata across the upper Midwest, and in places, as around Neda, iron oxide replaced the calcium carbonate sometime after deposition. The source and timing of introduction of the iron has long been a mystery, but the most plausible explanation is that a tropical soil rich in iron developed on the oolite shoals when they were exposed as lowland. A worldwide fall in sea

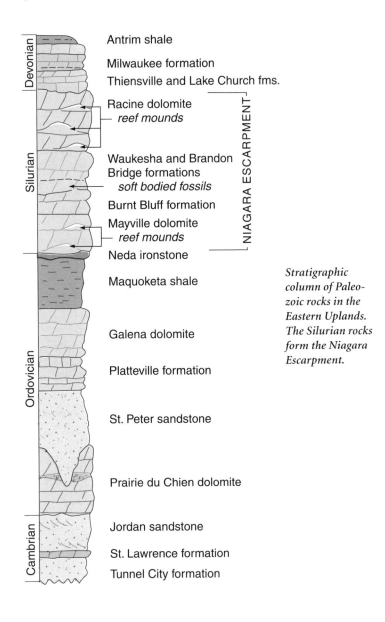

Devonian	Antrim shale
	Milwaukee formation
	Thiensville and Lake Church fms.
Silurian	Racine dolomite — *reef mounds*
	Waukesha and Brandon Bridge formations *soft bodied fossils*
	Burnt Bluff formation
	Mayville dolomite — *reef mounds*
	Neda ironstone
Ordovician	Maquoketa shale
	Galena dolomite
	Platteville formation
	St. Peter sandstone
	Prairie du Chien dolomite
Cambrian	Jordan sandstone
	St. Lawrence formation
	Tunnel City formation

NIAGARA ESCARPMENT

Stratigraphic column of Paleozoic rocks in the Eastern Uplands. The Silurian rocks form the Niagara Escarpment.

level during a late Ordovician glaciation centered in what is now northwestern Africa formed and exposed the shoals. A very different arrangement of continents at that time placed western Africa at the south pole while a tropical North America lay on the equator. The more recent Quaternary Ice Age provides an analogy, for we know that when huge continental glaciers tied up a lot of earth's water around 18,000 years ago, sea level dropped as much as 400 feet.

Microscopic view of the Neda iron formation. Pressure of burial elongated the concentric oolite grains, which average about one-half millimeter long.
—Photo courtesy of J. A. Emerick and R. A. Paull

Silurian and Devonian Deposition

Silurian strata were deposited in eastern Wisconsin between about 440 and 415 million years ago at tropical latitudes (about 20 to 30 degrees south) on a shallow seafloor that sloped gently southeastward toward the Michigan basin. This was but a part of a tropical ocean that covered all of North America. Broad tidal flats dominated from Lake Winnebago northeast through the Door Peninsula into northern Michigan. Finely laminated dolomite, algal mats, and some small, domal algal stromatolites were deposited practically at sea level under dominantly calm conditions; rare storms scattered some shelly layers. The dolomite has cracks from occasional drying during exposure of the flats. The tidal and very shallow marine deposits have relatively few fossils, which are not very diverse. Various shy creatures who preferred to live on or just below the sea bottom left microscopic skeletons and formed burrows. From Lake Winnebago southward into Illinois and Indiana, the environment deepened gradually and was more hospitable for organisms, so the strata deposited there contain more diverse and abundant fossils. Silurian reefs and their associated fossils have long been known in this region, especially from Milwaukee and Racine. Around 1980 a rare and exciting find, the impressions of a variety of soft-bodied animals, was made in a quarry in Milwaukee.

In the Silurian and Devonian strata, erosional episodes produced many subtle breaks, or unconformities. Small, worldwide falls of sea level exposed the land surface; each fall caused the intertidal environment to move southeastward away from the Wisconsin dome, only to retreat back northwestward when sea level rose again. Geologists have recognized at least half a dozen major cycles of such sea level changes. Some of the rises of sea level probably drowned all of the Wisconsin dome, but during part of Silurian and Devonian time, the dome may have been a low island.

Farther southeast in Michigan, Silurian rocks are deep beneath the surface, and samples obtained by drilling suggest that the depth of water there was somewhat greater than in Wisconsin. Near the end of Silurian time,

Depositional environments 433 to 417 million years ago in Silurian time when reefs grew in the shallow sea. Several sea level fluctuations shifted these environments back and forth. Inset map shows the tropical latitude of Wisconsin. R, reefs.

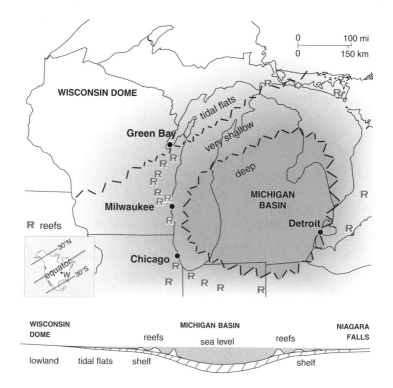

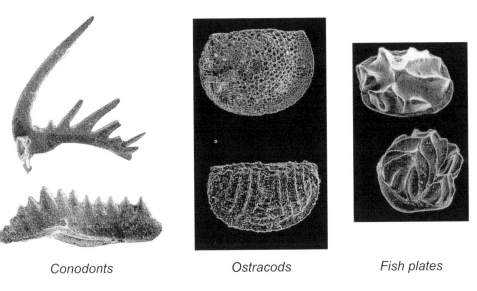

Conodonts   Ostracods   Fish plates

Microscopic marine fossils from Silurian rocks in the Eastern Uplands. —Photos courtesy of J. Kuglitsch

gypsum and salt were deposited in Michigan when the seawater evaporated. These deposits are more than 2,000 feet thick, but the precipitation of such deposits could have occurred in the surprisingly short span of a few thousand years if evaporation was intense. A major, continent-wide erosion surface separates the Silurian Niagara dolomite from younger Devonian strata. If late Silurian sediments were ever deposited in Wisconsin, erosion removed them before deposition of the Devonian strata.

Devonian strata around 400 million years old are the youngest preserved bedrock in Wisconsin, but they are present only in the greater Milwaukee area. Limestone and dolomite dominate the strata, but there is also shale. Some layers are richly fossiliferous with brachiopods, bryozoans, and crinoids being most abundant. Like the Silurian dolomites, these rocks formed in intertidal to shallow ocean environments. The youngest Devonian strata are black shales that occur beneath the Lake Michigan floor; they were discovered during the drilling of a Milwaukee water-intake tunnel. These shales formed in a deeper marine environment lacking oxygen.

Most of the Silurian and Devonian (and some Ordovician) strata were originally deposited as limestone and were later converted to dolomite. We are not sure exactly how or when this alteration occurred, but we suspect that soon after deposition, very briny waters migrated upward from the Michigan basin. Such fluids can carry more dissolved magnesium than

Impressions of soft-bodied Silurian fossils from Waukesha. —Photos courtesy D. E. G. Briggs

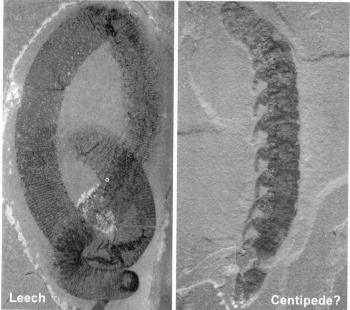

normal seawater, so when they percolate through limestones ($CaCO_3$), magnesium atoms replace some of the original calcium to form dolomite ($CaMg(CO_3)_2$).

Reefs That Made Milwaukee Famous

The Silurian rocks of the Milwaukee area contain the first ancient reefs recognized in North America, perhaps even in the entire world. That was in 1862, and later studies showed that countless reefs grew in the shallow Silurian ocean that covered most of North America approximately 420 million years ago. They were particularly abundant in the Milwaukee-Chicago-Indiana region. Silurian reefs formed a roughly circular ring around the Michigan basin with deeper-water deposits inside the ring in central Michigan and very shallow, largely intertidal dolomite outside.

Reefs are the urban areas of the seafloor. The Silurian reef rocks are especially fossiliferous, with more than two hundred species known. Corals caught the attention of early workers, but many other kinds of animals also lived in these densely populated areas of the seafloor. Extinct spongelike creatures called *stromatoporoids* were important reef constructors along with corals and bryozoans. Others who dwelled around the reefs included brachiopods, crinoids, cephalopods, trilobites, snails, and clams. One of the trilobites, named *Calymene*, is the Wisconsin state fossil. The flat rock layers between reef masses have fossils similar to those in the reefs, but there are fewer of them, much like our rural areas between modern cities. A robust brachiopod called *Pentamerus* was prominent in both environments. Some of the reefs were built up as rigid frameworks of interlocking skeletons on the shallow seafloor, but others began as patches of corals or other colonial animals whose skeletons disrupted currents, causing fine, limy mud to accumulate between animal colonies. Over time, muddy mounds grew with only scattered skeletons.

In Wisconsin, the reef masses are a few feet high and up to 80 feet in diameter. The reefs become larger southward from Milwaukee toward Racine and especially in Illinois and Indiana. Their shapes vary from broad, low mounds to steep-sided, and even mushroom-shaped masses. Typically, an unstratified, massive core rich in diverse fossil skeletons is surrounded by dolomite with layering inclined away from the core at angles of about 30 degrees. The flanking deposits consist of fragments of skeletons and core rock broken from the reef by waves. Both core and flank rocks formed in water probably less than 20 feet deep that waves occasionally stirred. A

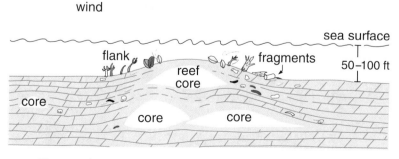

The central massive core of a Silurian reef grades into dipping flank strata with fragments of core rock and fossils broken by waves.

Brachiopod *(Pentamerus)*

Coral *(Halysites)*

Trilobite *(Calymene)*

Stromatoporoid

Silurian fossils associated with reefs. —Coral and stromatoporoid photos courtesy of the Milwaukee Public Museum; brachiopod photo by R. H. Dott, Jr.; trilobite photo courtesy of the University of Wisconsin Geology Museum

Reconstruction of a Silurian reef on display at the Milwaukee Public Museum. Large tentacled animals are cephalopods; flowerlike creatures on stalks are crinoid animals; bottom surface has mostly coral and stromatoporoid colonies. —Photo courtesy of the Milwaukee Public Museum

third, rock type is flat, well-stratified, fine dolomite deposited between the reefs in quieter water perhaps as much as 100 feet deep.

Quaternary Glaciation

A series of Quaternary glaciations have shaped the landscape of the Eastern Uplands and the Door Peninsula. Moraines, drumlins, eskers, and poorly drained wetlands and lakes abound. Geologists do not know exactly how many times the area has been glaciated because late Wisconsin ice sheets reached all but the far southwest part of the region, obliterating much of the evidence of earlier glaciations. Prior to the Quaternary glaciations, rivers had eroded a valley into the northeast-trending belt of easily eroded shale and sandstone that underlies the center of the Green Bay–Fox River lowland. The first glacier flowed southward in the valley and enlarged it. Subsequent glaciations continued to deepen and broaden the lowland and accentuate the steep western face of the Niagara Escarpment. In similar fashion, rivers probably began to form the lowland now occupied by Lake Michigan, and glaciers broadened and deepened it. Today, the bedrock floor of Lake Michigan is in places hundreds feet below the adjacent land. In most places thick glacial and lake deposits cover the lake floor. As the ice retreated, meltwater flooded this broad, low region. The lake level fluctuated by tens of feet with the waxings and wanings of the ice. Although the glacier is long gone, lake level continues to vary several feet as drought years alternate with wet periods. When the lake is high, wave erosion attacks steep bluffs composed mostly of glacial till and lake sediment, causing the bluffs to collapse in small landslides. Both flooding and landslides offer ever-present threats to lakeshore properties. Hard bedrock cliffs, as on the Door Peninsula, resist erosion more effectively, but nonetheless are gradually being worn back, too.

The early advances of the Green Bay and Lake Michigan Lobes covered nearly all of the Eastern Uplands at times during the Quaternary Period. Evidence for these early glaciations consists of a patchy cover of glacial sediment over the bedrock in the far southwestern part of the region and the local presence of glacial sediment from these early advances beneath younger late Wisconsin glacial deposits in the southeastern part. The most extensive of these earlier advances were southwestward advances out of the Lake Michigan basin. Well-preserved glacial landforms are lacking there and the landscape mainly reflects the shape of the underlying bedrock. However, geologists have recognized subdued drumlins (as east of Beloit) and a subdued moraine. The exact timing of the early glaciations is not well known. The earliest probably occurred hundreds of thousands of years ago, but the most recent likely occurred not long before the late Wisconsin advance of the Green Bay and Lake Michigan Lobes into the area, which reached its maximum extent about 18,000 years ago.

The Green Bay Lobe reached as far south as the Janesville area, where it deposited the Johnstown moraine, but the Lake Michigan Lobe expanded southward into Illinois and Indiana, and only the western edge of the Lake

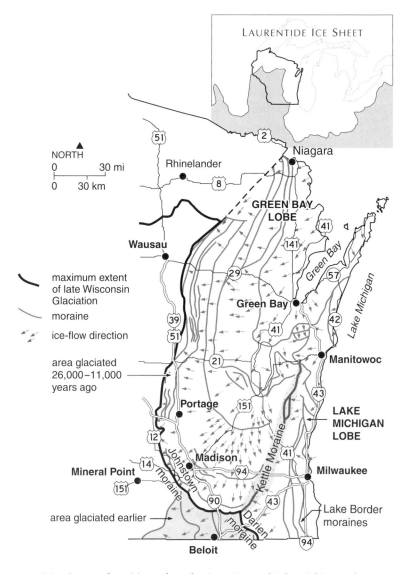

Moraines mark positions where the Green Bay and Lake Michigan Lobes remained stationary in eastern Wisconsin. The Kettle Moraine marks the position where the lobes met. Inset shows the maximum southern extent of the Laurentide Ice Sheet during the Wisconsin Glaciation.

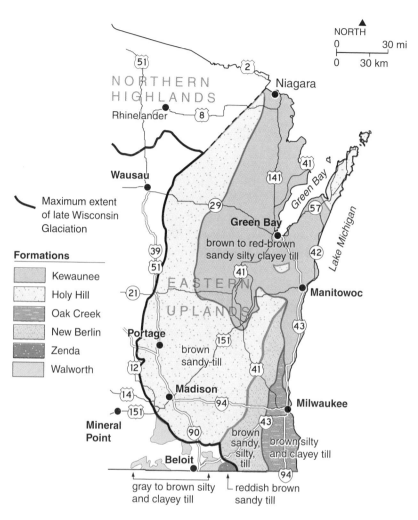

Characteristics, extent, and formation names of glacial tills in eastern Wisconsin.

Michigan Lobe flowed into easternmost Wisconsin. The Darien moraine marks the maximum extent of the Lake Michigan Lobe in southeastern Wisconsin. The till deposited by both advances is typically brown and very sandy.

Glacial and Postglacial Lakes

About 15,000 years ago, the Green Bay and Lake Michigan Lobes began to recede from their maximum coverage of the area. By 11,000 years ago these two ice lobes were gone from eastern Wisconsin and the Lake Michigan basin, but their retreat was not without event. On many occasions they readvanced southward after periods of shrinkage, each readvance a complex interaction of glaciers and meltwater lakes.

Several readvances of the Lake Michigan Lobe about 14,000 years ago reached a bit beyond the present southern shore of Lake Michigan and deposited a series of north-south-trending moraines, the Lake Border moraines, in the southeastern part of Wisconsin. The till deposited during these advances is brown and rich in silt and clay, whereas earlier advances had deposited sandy till. The ice was advancing through lakes along its margin so it incorporated silty and clayey lake sediment. Whenever the margin of the Lake Michigan Lobe was far enough south to block the northeastern outlet of the lake basin at the Straits of Mackinac in Michigan, a lake formed south of the ice margin and filled until it reached the lowest available outlet near Chicago, which funneled the water across Illinois to the Mississippi River.

Shortly before 13,000 years ago, the ice receded north far enough to open the northeastern outlet once again. The lake that drained northeastward at that time was much smaller than modern Lake Michigan. The northern end of the basin and the outlet were low because the ice, which had been thicker and had remained longer there, had depressed the earth's crust more there than it had farther south. After the ice was gone, the earth's crust began to rebound and it is still rebounding today, although at an ever slower rate. Today, the earth's crust at the northern end of the basin is rising about 1 foot per century faster than at Chicago. Because of this differential rebound of the crust, the shorelines of late glacial lakes, which were horizontal when formed, are tilted so they rise northward.

Soon after 13,000 years ago, the Lake Michigan Lobe readvanced as far as east-central Wisconsin, again blocking the northeastern outlet. The lake that formed at the edge of the ice in the southern part of the basin now drained again through the outlet near Chicago. The till deposited in the Green Bay–Fox River lowland and in the Lake Michigan basin by this and later advances is much redder than that of earlier advances. Water containing red clay from the Lake Superior basin spilled across the Upper Peninsula of Michigan into the northern Lake Michigan basin prior to this advance, and this red clay was then incorporated by the glacier as it advanced southward. Only a minute amount of iron-bearing red clay can turn a lot of till reddish brown.

By about 12,000 years ago, the Lake Michigan basin was again free of ice as was the northeastern outlet. Spruce thickets called the Two Creeks Forest grew in the east-central part of the region from about 12,000 to 11,750 years ago. Many radiocarbon dates on wood established the age of the forest. About 11,750 years ago, the ice margin again advanced and blocked the

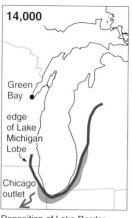

14,000

Green Bay •

edge of Lake Michigan Lobe

Chicago outlet

Deposition of Lake Border moraines

13,500

Recession from Lake Border moraines

13,000

red clay enters Lake Michigan basin through Au Train-Whitefish channel

North outlet open: Low lake level

12,800

Chicago outlet

Readvance deposition of red till

12,000–11,750

North outlet open: Two Creeks Forest grows

11,750

Chicago outlet

Ice advance blocks north outlet, buries Two Creeks Forest

11,000

Lake Algonquin confluent in Lake Michigan and Lake Huron basins

10,000

Low phase: Advance in Superior basin

5,000

Straits of Mackinac

Lake Nipissing

Sequence of lakes and ice advances in the Lake Michigan basin. Light brown shade shows the extent of open water. Dark gray line shows the southern extent of the Lake Michigan Lobe. —Modified from Hansel, Mickelson, Schneider, and Larsen, 1985

northeastern outlet. The lake rose until it spilled out the Chicago outlet, and the Two Creeks Forest was buried first by lake sediment and later by till as the glacier plowed over it.

By about 11,000 years ago, the ice margin receded north of the Straits of Mackinac and water in the Lake Michigan basin joined that in the Lake Huron basin at a level about 20 feet above the modern level. This combined lake is known as Lake Algonquin. As the ice margin continued to retreat, lower northern outlets emerged and so the water level in Lake Algonquin again fell to below modern levels in the two lakes. About 5,000 years ago, crustal rebound of outlets again raised water level to about 20 feet above the modern lake level to create Lake Nipissing. Waters of this new lake connected the Michigan, Huron, and Superior basins. Subsequently, water level dropped through several lake phases to its modern position as crustal rebound, the erosion of outlets, and climatic conditions interacted.

Today, shoreline features of Lake Algonquin and Lake Nipissing are visible in a number of places along the Wisconsin shore of Lake Michigan, especially in the Door Peninsula. Because the shore features of Lake Algonquin are about 6,000 years older than those of Lake Nipissing, they have experienced much more rebound. Shoreline features of the two lakes are at similar levels in the south part of the Lake Michigan basin, but farther north on the Door Peninsula, Lake Algonquin shorelines are tens of feet above those of Lake Nipissing.

And what of the Green Bay Lobe? Whenever it advanced south past Sturgeon Bay in the central Door Peninsula, a lake called Glacial Lake Oshkosh formed at its margin in the Green Bay–Fox River lowland. This lake drained eastward across the base of the Door Peninsula through one of several outlets when they were not blocked by ice of the Lake Michigan or Green Bay Lobes. When they were blocked, however, the lake rose until it drained out a southwestern outlet near Portage to the Wisconsin River. As the Green Bay Lobe receded from the lowland, a combination of rebound and the opening of the outlets across the base of the Door Peninsula controlled the water level and extent of the lake. Glacial Lake Oshkosh formed and drained several times as the Green Bay Lobe waxed and waned in much the same sequence as lakes in the Lake Michigan basin.

Diamonds, Copper Nuggets, and Driveway Rock

Erratics, or foreign minerals and rocks, provide important clues to the flow directions of ancient glaciers. The ice that flowed over the Eastern Uplands carried materials from far to the north in Michigan and Canada. The most distinctive are diamonds, copper, and a handsome red volcanic rock.

About 15,000 to 13,000 years ago: Green Bay Lobe recedes, opening a sequence of lower and lower outlets for Glacial Lake Oshkosh.

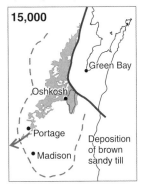

Outlet at Portage
to Wisconsin River

Outlet through Manitowoc
River valley

Outlet through Neshota/West
Twin River valley

Outlet through Kewaunee
River valley

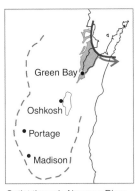

Outlet through Ahnapee River
valley

Green Bay Lobe north
of the lowland

About 13,000 to 11,500 years ago: Green Bay Lobe readvances to the central part of the lowland at least twice, resulting in reuse of outlets and burial of Two Creeks Forest

⟶ outlet

⌣ Green Bay Lobe margin

˙⌣ ＿ maximum extent of Green Bay Lobe

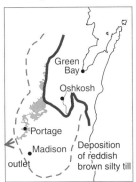

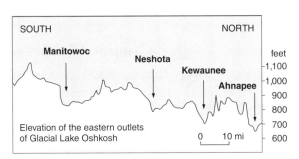

Sequence of outlets of Glacial Lake Oshkosh. Light brown shade shows the extent of open water. Dark gray line shows the southern extent of the Green Bay Lobe. —From unpublished material courtesy of Thomas S. Hooyer

Diamonds have been found in glacial deposits in several places in south-eastern Wisconsin since the late 1800s. The first and most famous of these was a 16.25 carat diamond found near Eagle in 1876 by a man digging a well in glacial sand and gravel. This diamond was on display at the American Museum of Natural History in New York City until it was stolen in 1964. As you might expect, once diamonds were found, there were a number of hoaxes of apparent finds in following years. It is clear, however, that some diamonds are present in the glacial deposits of southeastern Wisconsin. The source for these is a rare, diamond-bearing igneous rock called *kimberlite* that occurs in the Upper Peninsula of Michigan. When glaciers flowed across the area they incorporated and transported diamonds into Wisconsin. In recent years a kimberlite found by drilling near Kenosha raises the possibility of a local source for some of the diamonds in the glacial sediment of that area.

Nuggets and slabs of nearly pure copper weighing as much as hundreds of pounds have also been found in glacial deposits in many parts of northern and eastern Wisconsin. Copper in late Precambrian rocks of the Lake Superior region was the source for the nuggets transported by glaciers into the Eastern Uplands of Wisconsin. Glacial transport striated and polished many of the larger pieces.

You are not likely to see either diamonds or copper along the roadside, but you will have plenty of opportunities to see another far-traveled glacial erratic. An attractive, light red rock is so commonly placed as a landscaping accent at the edge of driveways that we call it "driveway rock." This mostly fine-grained volcanic rhyolite is speckled with large crystals of orange feldspar and smaller bluish quartz grains. Like the copper, this rock was also derived from late Precambrian rocks in the eastern part of the Lake Superior basin. Also look for this distinctive glacial erratic in yards and stone walls. In recent years, operators of sand and gravel pits have gotten premium prices for large specimens.

Trenton Meteorite

In 1868, Wisconsin's most famous meteorite was discovered on a farm 30 miles northwest of Milwaukee and was named for the nearest town. It is not known when the meteorite fell. A cluster of five pieces was found within a small area. The largest was 14 inches long and weighed 62 pounds. Of the smaller pieces, two weighed 16 pounds each and the others 10 and 8 pounds. They are composed of iron and nickel, so belong to the metallic meteorite clan rather than the rare stony clan. The largest mass is at the Milwaukee Public Museum.

Interstate 39/U.S. 51
Portage—Coloma
35 miles (57 km)

Portage is historically significant because, as its name implies, the city lies at a point where the southwestward-draining Wisconsin River is only 1.5 miles from the headwaters of the northeastward-draining Fox River. Long before Wisconsin was settled by European immigrants, Native Americans and French explorer-trappers, such as Jacques Marquette and Louis Joliet in 1673, canoed up the Fox River from Green Bay on Lake Michigan to cross the intervening wetland and proceed down the Wisconsin River to the Mississippi. With settlement, Fort Winnebago was established and a canal was dug to facilitate the movement of boats between the two rivers. Remains of the fort are almost invisible today, but you can see the old canal and a lock at Portage. The Portage canal, which took forty years to complete, was never very successful, and as with other canals in the eastern states, its death knell was sounded by the arrival of railroads.

Portage lies on a broad outwash plain deposited by the Wisconsin River. Between Portage and Coloma, I-39/U.S. 51 crosses a landscape shaped by westward-flowing ice of the Green Bay Lobe. The maximum extent of the lobe lies about 15 miles west of Portage, where it deposited the Johnstown moraine. I-39 gradually converges northward with the moraine and crosses it a few miles north of Coloma. Bedrock has also influenced the terrain, and at several points near the route, rock protrudes through the glacial till. The lower part of the Ordovician Prairie du Chien dolomite forms a discontinuous ridge that defines the western hilly area within the Eastern Uplands.

North of Portage, I-39/U.S. 51 passes through an upland for about 4 miles. The hills in this area are east-west-trending drumlins, each about a half mile long and 50 to 100 feet high, formed by the westward-flowing Green Bay Lobe. The road then descends onto a broad, swampy flat near the Columbia-Marquette County line blanketed with sediment deposited beneath the southwestern part of Glacial Lake Oshkosh. The Lewiston basin of Glacial Lake Wisconsin drained when the margin of the Green Bay Lobe receded to an area about 4 miles west of the highway here. As the lobe continued to melt, Glacial Lake Oshkosh flooded this area and expanded northward as the ice margin receded. Between the county line and the intersection with Wisconsin 82 and Wisconsin 23, the road traverses flat low areas of sand deposited on the floor of Glacial Lake Oshkosh and uplands of till-covered bedrock.

Five miles north of Portage, a roadcut provides a window through the glacial till, revealing Cambrian sandstones. Another window appears at

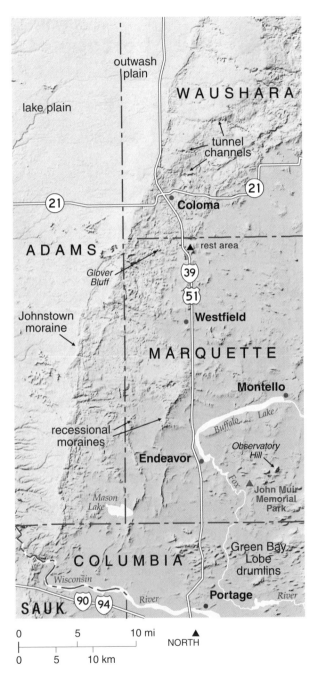

Landscape image of the area between Portage and Coloma.

Endeavor, 6.5 miles farther north, where a Precambrian volcanic rock (rhyolite) is exposed in a low ridge 0.5 mile east of the town on the south bank of the Fox River. This rock type is widespread across east-central Wisconsin and is the same as that underlying the Baraboo quartzite 15 miles southwest.

Four miles southeast of Endeavor is a point of special historic interest, John Muir Memorial County Park at Ennis Lake, which is accessible via County T, O, and F. This area was the boyhood home of the man who was destined to become the father of the American conservation movement. At the age of eleven in 1849, John emigrated with his father from Scotland to homestead here in a wilderness that spawned his interest in nature. After attending the University of Wisconsin for four years, he "wandered away on a glorious [lifetime] botanical and geological excursion . . . I was only leaving one university for another, the Wisconsin University for the University of the Wilderness" (Muir 1965). He arrived in California in 1867 where his fame soon blossomed. Muir contributed significantly to geology, especially by recognizing the glaciation of Yosemite Valley and southeast Alaska, where he discovered a glacier that now bears his name. With hindsight, John Muir could have advised his father against trying to farm in this part of Wisconsin, for the old homestead lay on a bouldery moraine with poor soil.

On Observatory Hill only 2.5 miles northeast of Ennis Lake, Muir very likely saw glacially scratched Precambrian rhyolite. Young Muir may also have seen granite at the small town of Montello only 7 miles northeast of the old homestead. A now-abandoned quarry in the center of Montello provided stone for Grant's Tomb in New York City and for polished slabs that decorate some of the pillars in the state capitol in Madison. This granite was also used for making paving stones early in the 1900s. It was formed 1,750 million years ago in close association with the eruption of the rhyolites exposed at Endeavor and Observatory Hill.

Between the Wisconsin 82 and Wisconsin 23 exit and Westfield, the highway crosses a hummocky till upland. Between Westfield and the Marquette-Waushara County line the highway parallels a recessional moraine of the Green Bay Lobe. At Westfield the ridge just east of the road is a recessional moraine deposited when the margin of the Green Bay Lobe stabilized for a period of time during its wastage from the area. The moraine crosses the highway about 1 mile north of Westfield; it is the wooded ridge just west of the highway.

At milepost 118, a rest area for northbound traffic displays a large boulder of Cambrian sandstone that has fine examples of a tire-track-like impression called *Climactichnites*. It is a track made by an extinct animal lacking any skeleton. It crawled over moist sandy tidal flats sucking up microbes from the wet sand. A southbound rest area 2 miles farther north has a large slab of ripple-marked Cambrian sandstone of the sort in which *Climactichnites* occurs.

From the rest area to Coloma, the highway crosses a hummocky till upland. Three miles west of Coloma, Wisconsin 21 descends the outermost moraine of the Green Bay Lobe onto the westward sloping outwash plain and the basin of Glacial Lake Wisconsin in the Central Plain. About 2.5 miles north of Coloma, I-39/U.S. 51 also descends this same moraine onto the outwash plain beyond the maximum position of the Green Bay Lobe. This moraine marks the western boundary of the Eastern Uplands along this route.

Glover Bluff Disturbance

The ridge-forming Prairie du Chien dolomite surfaces at a wooded hill 2 miles west of the highway rest areas and about 4 miles south of Coloma. Generations of geology students brought here to map the confusing structure named this unique site Mystery Hill. (The site is on private land and visitors should ask for permission.) Quarries on top of the hill provide a window through the glacial moraine and reveal disturbed uppermost Cambrian sandstone and lowermost Ordovician dolomite in a circular area about 1 mile in diameter. Faulting has steeply tilted and complexly jumbled the rock layers in a manner very unusual for Wisconsin. The formations exposed here are also about 100 feet lower in elevation than would be expected for this area. Very rare specimens of dolomite display a structure called *shatter cones*, which are found at many known meteorite sites and are attributed to very high velocity impact. The rarity of shatter cones and the apparent absence of other features typical of impacts, however, makes this disturbed

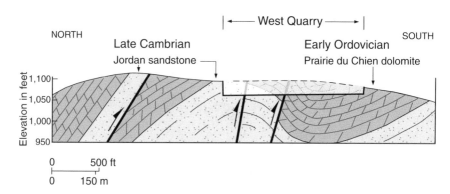

Anomalous structure in the west end of Glover Bluff, 4 miles south of Coloma. Some geologists have attributed the deformation to the impact of a large meteorite.

Shatter cones in Ordovician dolomite from the Glover Bluff disturbance. High velocity impacts upon rocks generally cause such structures. —R. H. Dott, Jr., photo

locality even more mysterious than the Rock Elm disturbance in northwestern Wisconsin or a similar, buried Des Plaines anomaly in northeastern Illinois near Chicago's O'Hare airport.

Interstate 43

Beloit—Milwaukee

73 miles (118 km)

From the intersection with I-90 at Beloit eastward to Darien, I-43 crosses a till upland with northeast-southwest-trending drumlins formed during an early advance of the Lake Michigan Lobe. At Darien I-43 crosses the Darien moraine, which marks the outermost extent of the late Wisconsin advance of the Lake Michigan Lobe. For about 2 miles west of Darien, the highway crosses the westward sloping outwash plain deposited beyond the Darien moraine. East of Darien, the highway crosses a broad area of pitted outwash and hummocky till before crossing a gently rolling till plain near Delavan. From Elkhorn, Wisconsin 67 north will take you to Eagle and the Southern Unit of the Kettle Moraine State Forest, which is discussed in **I-94: Milwaukee—Madison.** Lake Geneva south of Elkhorn lies just east of the Darien moraine and occupies what was a tunnel channel. The till deposited by several glaciations in this area is more than 300 feet thick at one site. The lake, a popular resort area, is also the home of the Yerkes Astronomical Observatory established by the University of Chicago in 1892.

The wayside about 4 miles east of Elkhorn is on the south bank of a glacial meltwater channel in which Sugar Creek flows today. I-43 continues across the till upland to near East Troy, where the hills south of the road are northeast-southwest-trending drumlins formed beneath the ice of the late Wisconsin Lake Michigan Lobe. The highway continues across this till upland with drumlins to the New Berlin area and then enters suburban Milwaukee. Here, the highway crosses several of the north-south-trending Lake Border moraines formed at the margin of the Lake Michigan Lobe, but they are difficult to recognize amidst all of the urbanization.

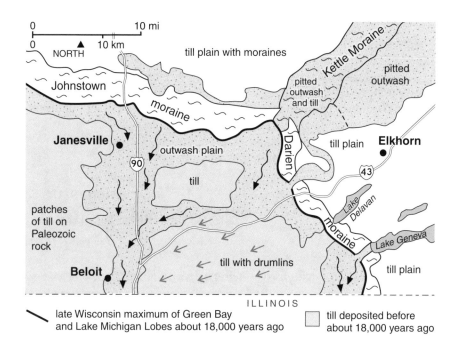

Glacial geology of the area north and east of Beloit. The Green Bay Lobe deposited the Johnstown moraine at its maximum late Wisconsin extent. The Lake Michigan Lobe deposited the Darien moraine at its maximum late Wisconsin extent. Both moraines were deposited between about 18,000 and 15,000 years ago.

Interstate 43
Milwaukee—Green Bay via Manitowoc
117 miles (186 km)

This section of I-43 begins at a major interchange in the center of Milwaukee on the north side of the Menomonee River just west of its confluence with the Milwaukee River and runs north through urban areas for 12 miles. The Milwaukee Public Museum is downtown only three blocks east of I-43 on Wells Street. Farther north, exits 74 and 75 provide access east about twenty-five blocks to the University of Wisconsin–Milwaukee, where the Greene Museum with the Greene Fossil Collection is located. Exit 77 gives access to Estabrook Park where fossiliferous Devonian strata are exposed along the Milwaukee River. Entrance to the park is five blocks east on Hampton Road. From the main park shelter and concession stand, a stairway leads down to riverbank exposures of the Milwaukee formation that were quarried here one hundred years ago for making cement. See "Milwaukee Geology" in **I-94: Illinois Border—Milwaukee.**

Lime Kiln Park

North of Milwaukee at Thiensville, Cedarburg, and Grafton, there are quarries in Silurian dolomite. Two miles west of the interstate from exit 92, you can see an abandoned quarry and old kilns at Lime Kiln Park along the Milwaukee River at Grafton. Quarrying began here in the 1870s and continued to about 1930. The stone was used to make lime by cooking it in three large kilns, which have been restored. Prior to being converted to a park, part of the adjacent old quarry was used as a landfill site, which has contributed some pollution of the local groundwater. Nearby, another quarry produced stone blocks used in the construction of many handsome historic buildings in the Cedarburg-Grafton area.

Wells in the area indicate that the total Silurian sequence is about 600 feet thick, but quarrying has exposed only the upper 40 to 50 feet, all within the Racine dolomite. Although there are some richly fossiliferous coral reef masses, most of the stone represents limestone deposited between the scattered reefs. Much of the stone is made of skeletal fragments, which vigorous ocean currents abraded, winnowed, and transported, converting them to lime sand. Deposition occurred on very shallow shoal areas. You can find this material on the old quarry face in the south part of Lime Kiln Park and in some of the older stone buildings in the area.

From Milwaukee to Manitowoc, I-43 crosses a very gently rolling till plain deposited by the westward-flowing Lake Michigan Lobe. The north-south-trending hummocky uplands in this area are moraines formed along the western edge of the Lake Michigan Lobe. The lowlands between moraines are outwash plains. I-43 crosses one of these nearly flat plains for about 2 miles on either side of the intersection with Wisconsin 33 near Port Washington. Here, sediment-laden meltwater from the Lake Michigan Lobe flowed southward between the edge of the glacier and the moraine to the west. Today, the Milwaukee River flows in this lowland only one-half mile west and parallel to the highway. For 30 miles it flows parallel to the Lake Michigan shoreline before it is finally enters the lake at Milwaukee harbor.

At Port Washington, the Dodge House provides an example of architectural construction with rounded cobblestones transported to the area by glacial ice. The builder introduced this fieldstone construction style around 1840 from his native upstate New York, which was also glaciated. The building now houses the Port Washington Chamber of Commerce.

Harrington Beach State Park

Six miles north of Port Washington, exit 107 at Belgium provides access to Harrington Beach State Park, 1.5 miles east by Lake Church Road and County D. Although a sandy bathing beach on Lake Michigan is the chief attraction, there is also a small lake in an abandoned quarry in Devonian dolomite (Lake Church formation). Because the water table is very shallow in this area, the 45-foot-deep pit filled quickly with water when quarrying (and pumping) ceased. Together with exposures at Milwaukee in Estabrook Park and a few outcrops along the Lake Michigan lakeshore, this is one of the few places in Wisconsin where Devonian rocks still exist, although there can be no doubt that they once covered the entire state.

In the late 1800s, this quarry provided stone for making lime. Beginning in 1901 and continuing until 1925, a much larger operation supplied stone for shipment on the Great Lakes to steel mills near Chicago and cement plants at Milwaukee. A company town called Stonehaven was built here for workers, mostly recent immigrants from Italy, Austria, and Luxembourg. Some foundations for buildings are still visible, but there is little evidence today of the large crushers and a long, elevated pier built into the lake for loading ships. A historic trail with explanatory signs gives a vivid impression of the Stonehaven operation, however.

The low sandy ridges parallel to and just above the present lake level are beach ridges deposited during the Nipissing phase of Lake Michigan about 5,000 years ago. We discuss beach ridges further in **Wisconsin 42: Manitowoc—Sturgeon Bay**.

Kohler-Andrae State Park

Exit 120 provides access to Kohler-Andrae State Park (3 miles via County V and KK), which has a sandy bathing beach on Lake Michigan with wind

Lake in an abandoned quarry in Devonian dolomite of the Lake Church formation at Harrington Beach State Park. —Photo courtesy of the Wisconsin Department of Natural Resources

dunes behind the beach. Be sure to visit the Sanderling Nature Center where there are displays, other interpretive material, and trails.

The Kohler Dunes blocked the Black River, forming a wetland to the west and forcing the river to flow northward for 5 miles before emptying into Lake Michigan near Sheboygan. Though somewhat vegetated, the dunes are good examples of wind dunes composed of beach sand blown a short distance inland. Prevailing winds over this part of North America are from the west; therefore sand is only blown westward from the beaches during storms with temporary easterly winds. On the eastern side of Lake Michigan, however, the prevailing wind blows onshore, so dunes on the Michigan shore are nourished continually and are much larger, less vegetated, and more active than their Wisconsin cousins.

A core from a deep hole drilled in 1961 at Sheboygan penetrated an entire Paleozoic sequence of Silurian, Ordovician, and Cambrian strata before reaching a Precambrian granitic rock at 1,875 feet. Such deep drill holes are rare in eastern Wisconsin, making our knowledge of the deeply buried lower Paleozoic and Precambrian rocks very limited here.

Between Sheboygan and Manitowoc, I-43 is 1 to 2 miles inland from the lakeshore and traverses rather flat, agricultural land with little visible geology. Between Manitowoc and Green Bay, I-43 crosses a broad gently rolling till upland. The till here is typical of the later advances of the late Wisconsin Green Bay and Lake Michigan Lobes; it is reddish brown and rich in silt and clay. Four miles north of Manitowoc and east of the interstate at Rockwood are dolomite quarries, which have been active for one hundred years. The Silurian stone is crushed and roasted to make lime. Old kilns made of stone and timber similar to those at Grafton still survive alongside modern kilns.

A short trip to the east on Wisconsin 147 provides a good view of the Neshota–West Twin outlet channel of Glacial Lake Oshkosh, now occupied by the Neshota and West Twin Rivers. A little over a half mile east of I-43, the road descends the steep western side of the channel. You can see the eastern side to the east about a half mile farther. When the Green Bay Lobe receded past the west end of the outlet, water from Glacial Lake Oshkosh spilled eastward across the drainage divide, located a few miles to the north, into the valley of the West Twin River and thus into Lake Michigan.

Maribel Caves County Park

At Maribel Caves County Park, a five-minute drive from I-43 via exit 164 to Wisconsin 147, the steep face of a cliff 20 to 30 feet high of Silurian dolomite is the western wall of the channel cut by water draining from Glacial Lake Oshkosh through the Neshota–West Twin outlet. The road to the parking lot descends part of the channel wall, and a boardwalk and

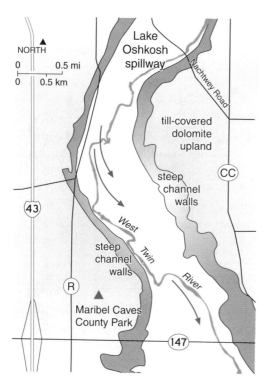

The water draining from Glacial Lake Oshkosh cut the steep channel now occupied by the Neshota and West Twin Rivers near Maribel Caves County Park. Arrows show direction of drainage from Glacial Lake Oshkosh.

stairs take one down the rest of the way. The erosion of the channel inter-sected caves formed by groundwater dissolving dolomite along fractures; some of these extend well over 100 feet into the cliff face. The former Maribel Caves Hotel was a health spa in the early 1900s with spring water that was reportedly of "great therapeutic value." The cedar, hemlock, and birch for-est of the valley contrasts sharply with the dense hardwood forest of the upland.

Near the Manitowoc-Brown County line and the village of Denmark, I-43 crosses hummocky moraine topography and then continues across a dolomite upland thickly covered by till before descending the west-facing Niagara Escarpment to Green Bay. Where it descends the escarpment, the highway follows the western end of the Neshota–West Twin outlet of Gla-cial Lake Oshkosh. Thanks to the erosion of this channel, the escarpment is low and not very impressive at this point. A large quarry 2 miles west of I-43 along County MM exposes the lowest Silurian strata and provides a fine view from the escarpment across the Green Bay lowland.

Interstate 90
Beloit—Wisconsin River
78 miles (125 km)

The bedrock of the Beloit area is Ordovician dolomite and sandstone, but it is exposed only in quarries and a few roadcuts. Dolomite appears along I-90 about 8 miles south of the border in Illinois, but there is no bedrock at the surface again until Madison, where Cambrian as well as Ordovician strata are exposed. Otherwise, the landscape that the traveler sees along this route is entirely the result of Quaternary glaciation.

Between the Illinois border and Janesville, I-90 crosses a broad outwash plain deposited in the Rock River valley by meltwater rivers flowing south-ward from the Green Bay Lobe. By about 18,000 years ago, this lobe reached its maximum late Wisconsin extent about 3 miles north of Janesville and deposited the Johnstown moraine, which is named after a small commu-nity about 10 miles east of Janesville.

East of Beloit, both south and north of the intersection with I-43, the highway rises off the outwash plain onto the west end of a till-mantled bedrock upland. The nearly continuous till cover on these uplands was deposited by an early glaciation that advanced southwestward over the area. The till surface here has many northeast-southwest-trending drumlins. Still earlier glaciations deposited till on the bedrock uplands west of Beloit. In these uplands the till cover is patchy, having been eroded from most areas, so bedrock controls the shape of the landscape.

The outwash plain between Beloit and Janesville is a broad, nearly flat, southward-sloping surface of thick sand and gravel deposited by meltwater streams draining the Green Bay Lobe. There are many commercial sand and gravel pits in this area. About 3 miles north of Janesville, I-90 leaves the flat outwash plain and rises onto the Johnstown moraine, a more hilly landscape. This part of the moraine consists mostly of outwash that was deposited on top of ice. When the buried ice melted, the overlying outwash collapsed to form the hills. I-90 continues across a similar landscape to the vicinity of the Rock-Dane County line. Although several recessional moraines of the Green Bay Lobe cross this area, they are indistinct where they cross I-90. The hummocky landscape just south of Edgerton is part of one of these moraines. About 3 miles north of the county line, I-90 rises onto a till-covered dolomite upland. Here, the till is brown and sandy, typical of that deposited by the late Wisconsin Green Bay Lobe. The surface of this upland has many well-formed, northeast-southwest-trending drumlins, which are generally longer and better formed east of the highway.

Interstate 94 joins I-90 at Madison and continues to cross the till-mantled bedrock upland to the Wisconsin River near Portage. North of Madison, the best drumlins are several miles east of the highway. For a discussion of the Madison area, see **I-94: Milwaukee—Madison.**

Interstate 94
Illinois Border—Milwaukee
35 miles (56 km)

Interstate 94 enters Wisconsin from the Chicago urban complex. The geology as well as the urbanization and traffic are indistinguishable as one crosses the border. The bedrock of the route between Chicago and Milwaukee is primarily Silurian dolomite, which is mostly concealed beneath glacial deposits. The glacial veneer becomes thinner northward, so the bedrock becomes more obvious. The Silurian strata of the Chicago-Milwaukee corridor include ancient reefs. One of the largest examples is exposed in a big quarry at Thornton, Illinois. I-294 crosses it just west of the Indiana border on the south edge of Chicago; conspicuous reef flank strata inclined 30 to 40 degrees are visible along the highway. Unfortunately, no such large or accessible example is available in Wisconsin.

Just south of the border in Illinois Beach State Park at Zion, spectacular beach ridges mark successive shorelines formed as the lake level fell to its present elevation following the last advance of the Lake Michigan Lobe.

Similar ridges occur farther north along the Wisconsin shore at Point Beach State Forest and at the Ridges Sanctuary on the Door Peninsula.

I-94 between the Illinois border and Milwaukee lies about 7 miles inland from Lake Michigan. Urbanization has obscured the geology, especially within Milwaukee. The highway crosses the Lake Border moraines, north-south-trending, nearly parallel, somewhat hummocky features deposited by the westward-flowing ice of the Lake Michigan Lobe. The till in this area is typically brown or gray and rich in silt and clay. Farther west, the Lake Michigan Lobe till is more sandy. The abundant silt and clay in this area indicates that the Lake Michigan Lobe receded far enough back

Landscape image of the north-south-trending Lake Border moraines south of Milwaukee. Dashed lines show the moraine crests.

into the Lake Michigan basin for lakes to form along its western margin before readvancing to form these moraines. When the ice readvanced it incorporated silt and clay that had accumulated on the floor of the lakes.

One mile north of the border at the south edge of Kenosha (between Wisconsin 32 and the lakeshore) is Chiwaukee Prairie, which is remarkable for a great diversity of plants due in part to the moderating climatic influence of Lake Michigan. The prairie lies on a glacial lake plain formed during a higher phase of Lake Michigan.

Between the Illinois border and the Des Plaines River (about 4.5 miles), I-94 crosses hummocky topography on a north-south-trending moraine. Here, the river cuts eastward through several north-south-trending moraines. Farther west the river, like other rivers in the area, flows in a lowland between two of the north-south moraines. Where crossed by I-94, the Des Plaines River valley contains a pitted outwash plain about a mile wide. North of this valley, the highway crosses several more miles of hummocky moraine upland before descending onto a flatter till plain near the intersection with Wisconsin 142 northwest of Kenosha.

Just west of Kenosha (half a mile east of I-94 and north of Wisconsin 50), drilling in 1994 encountered a small body of the unusual igneous rock called *kimberlite.* Its mineral composition indicates an origin in a region of very high pressure, namely the earth's mantle at a depth of at least 70 miles. The material was blasted suddenly up through the entire overlying crust in thin, pipelike intrusions—like spikes driven through a plank of wood. The intrusions blasted into Silurian dolomite at some unknown time between the Silurian period and the Quaternary Ice Age. Kimberlites may contain diamonds, but none have been found at Kenosha. Diamonds have been found in glacial deposits elsewhere in eastern Wisconsin for many years. Presumably, glacial ice carried these diamonds to Wisconsin from kimberlites in northern Michigan.

Wisconsin 158 east provides access to the beautifully developed waterfront on Lake Michigan (Fifty-Sixth Street and Second Avenue) and the Kenosha Public Museum, which houses a number of fine displays related to geology. Perhaps the most spectacular of the exhibits is a reconstructed woolly mammoth skeleton, one of two skeletons recently found in Kenosha County. Radiocarbon dates on the bones indicate that the animals died about 12,300 years ago. Archeologists believe that markings on the bones may have been made when the animals were butchered. If this interpretation is correct, the markings coupled with abundant arrowheads provide the earliest definite evidence for humans in Wisconsin. At that time, the southern edge of the Laurentide Ice Sheet was probably near the northern end of the Lake Michigan basin.

North of the Wisconsin 142 intersection, I-94 continues to cross a till plain between moraines for about 5 miles. The north-south-trending moraines, the slightly higher land to the east and west of the highway, are about 1 mile wide and rise 50 to 100 feet above intervening lowlands. About a half mile north of the intersection with Wisconsin 11 the highway rises onto a hummocky moraine and follows it as far as the Racine-Milwaukee County line. One mile north of County K, I-94 passes between two flat lake plains that are high in the landscape. These lake plains are composed of sediment that accumulated on the floors of ice-walled lakes. Northward to Milwaukee, I-94 continues to cross hummocky, north-south-trending moraines and intervening till plains.

Between Kenosha and Racine and 4 miles east of I-94 adjacent to the University of Wisconsin Parkside Campus is Petrifying Springs County Park. In the 1850s, a settler remarked that these springs turned vegetation to stone. Although the name suggests fossils, precipitation from the mineral-rich springwater simply coats modern sticks, leaves, and acorns with lime. Weakly acidic rainwater dissolves calcium carbonate from the limy soil and glacial till. Where the underground water emerges in springs, it precipitates lime around plant debris. True petrifaction occurs when chemicals replace organic matter. For example, to make petrified wood, silica carried in fluids percolating through sediments completely replaces the cellulose tissue of a buried log.

In the Racine area, a few outcrops and quarries expose Silurian dolomites containing fossil reefs. Since the 1830s, these have yielded the largest known assemblages of Silurian fossils from both reef and inter-reef strata of the Racine formation. There is a natural outcrop at Wind Point on Lake Michigan at the north edge of the city. Two and one-half miles southwest of Wind Point at the north edge of Racine, a large active quarry exposes both reef and nonreef rocks. This quarry has two parts on either side of Wisconsin 32 near Three Mile Road with a tunnel connecting them.

Another accessible locality is Quarry Lake Park in the northern suburb of Horlicksville; the entrance is from Northwestern Avenue just south of its intersection with Green Bay Road and County MM. This unique city park has an artificial sandy bathing beach at the south end of a lake that partly fills an abandoned quarry; the other three sides are vertical rock walls. Within those walls, especially the eastern one, you can see strata inclined 30 degrees, which were deposited on the flanks of a reef; they dip away from the massive reef core at the center of the wall. These exposures are only accessible by small boat or across winter ice, but you can see their general structure from the edge of the old quarry. Ten miles northwest at Franklin, an active quarry exposes 280 feet of Silurian strata and a few feet of underlying Maquoketa shale of Ordovician age; fossil reefs are present there, too, in the Racine dolomites.

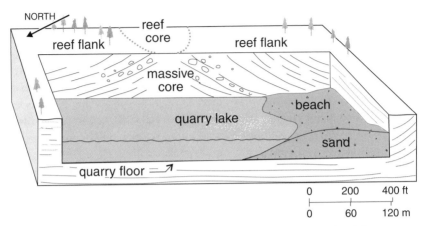

Silurian reef exposed in the eastern wall of the quarry in Racine dolomite at Quincy Lake Park. Inclined strata in the southwest corner of the old quarry indicate another reef beyond that corner.

MILWAUKEE GEOLOGY

Milwaukee was established where three rivers—the Milwaukee, Menomonee, and Kinnickinnic—join and form a suitable harbor with a broad valley bottom extending 3 miles inland. *Milwaukee* means "good earth" in Indian languages. The *waukee* part of the name means "earth" and is encountered repeatedly in Wisconsin; Pewaukee just west of Waukesha means "swampy earth." Chiwaukee at the Illinois border east of I-94 is a curious exception; it's a made-up name, reflecting a location halfway between *Chi*cago and Mil*waukee*.

The Milwaukee harbor provided an important point of entry into southern Wisconsin for thousands of European immigrants arriving by ship. Some of these struck out for the lead mining district while others took up farmland nearby. With the flood of immigrants in the late 1800s, the city grew rapidly and soon became Wisconsin's largest community. Lumber from the northern part of the state provided building material, but stone was also needed, especially for bridges, harbor piers, large municipal buildings, and for making lime and cement. Although glacial material mostly conceals the bedrock, Silurian and Devonian dolomites visible in places were quickly exploited.

Early in the 1900s there were brickyards throughout Wisconsin, but Milwaukee was the most important center of brick making with six major companies in 1906. Made from clay-rich lake sediment and till that had a very low iron content, the bricks obtained a distinctive cream color when fired in kilns. Although more typical, iron-bearing red brick was also produced in the area, Milwaukee Cream Brick became the fashion favorite for the construction of many buildings throughout the upper Midwest. Lake Michigan water quenches the city's great thirst, but industries such as Milwaukee's famous breweries use groundwater from deep wells drilled into the bedrock.

By the 1840s, a few curious amateurs were beginning to explore the natural history of their new urban home. Especially important was Increase Lapham, who arrived in 1836 and soon recognized rocks and fossils that were identical with the Silurian ones that he knew from his native western New York. He sent some fossils to a famous New York paleontologist, James Hall, who confirmed that, indeed, the dolomite of the Niagara area extends to Milwaukee. Lapham also recognized two different types of dolomite, massive, very fossiliferous, moundlike bodies, which were quarried for making lime, and well-stratified rock quarried for building stone. In 1862 Hall visited Milwaukee and recognized that the massive mounds were the cores of ancient reefs—the first ever recognized in North America if not the world.

The only reef accessible in the city today is next to the parking lot for the Milwaukee County Stadium, home of the Milwaukee Brewers baseball team. To reach this locality, leave I-94 at Exit 308A and turn south on Mitchell Boulevard for a short distance, then east onto Miller Parkway. This road passes the reef-flank at the west edge of the parking lot before reaching the stadium. Steeply dipping reef flank strata are visible at the east end of the exposure. Because of its scientific significance to the early recognition of ancient reefs, this locality has been designated a national historic landmark.

Impressions of soft-bodied animals were discovered as recently as the 1980s in dolomite in a quarry in Waukesha. Fossils of animals lacking skeletons are extremely rare, and these are the only ones known from Silurian rocks in the world. They give us a window into a portion of life of the past that we almost never can know about. Considering how many modern creatures lack any preservable hard parts (insects, spiders, worms, jellyfish), you can understand why such a find is so important.

Devonian dolomite and shale with fossils are exposed along the Milwaukee River in Estabrook Park, which you can reach from I-43, exit 77. A resistant dolomite layer crops out at the bottom of a stone stairway leading down from the refreshment building near Picnic Area 5 and forms a low waterfall in the river. One layer in the rock here proved ideal for making water lime, a cement that would harden even underwater. Unlike the Silurian dolomites, just enough shale is associated with the layer of Devonian limestone to make high-quality cement. For thirty years, beginning in the 1870s, an important cement industry occupied this site, but the Milwaukee Cement Company quarries, crushers, and huge kilns were long ago replaced by a large green park. The youngest bedrock known in Wisconsin is the Antrim formation, late Devonian black shale containing fish and plant fossils. It was discovered during tunneling under the Milwaukee waterfront and in drill holes near the lakeshore.

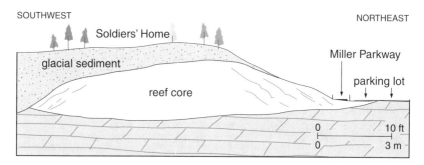

Reef exposed next to the parking lot for the Milwaukee County Stadium, home of the Milwaukee Brewers. —Adapted from a Milwaukee Public Museum handout

Photo circa 1913 of the historic Schoonmaker Quarry in Wauwatosa shows a Silurian reef in Racine dolomite. It was here that James Hall first recognized the Silurian reefs of the Milwaukee area in 1862. The quarry has since been completely filled in. Lens-shaped reef core is in the center; flank strata are to the right behind the crane. Line shows the top of the reef. —Photo courtesy of the Milwaukee Public Museum

Waterfall over Devonian strata at the base of the Milwaukee formation on the Milwaukee River in Estabrook Park in Milwaukee. —Photo courtesy of the Milwaukee Public Museum

A major fault, which is a rarity in Wisconsin Paleozoic strata, is exposed in a quarry on the north side of Waukesha, 1 mile south of I-94 at the intersection of Blue Mounds Road (County JJ) and Wisconsin 164. It trends northeast and has 33 feet of visible displacement. Using rare surface exposures and well records, geologists have traced this Waukesha fault for 80 miles from the Illinois border to Lake Michigan at a point about 10 miles north of Milwaukee. Drilling indicates that the fault has dropped Precambrian rocks to depths of more than 2,000 feet below the surface. Once again we see how important subsurface information is for supplementing surface exposures. In both Milwaukee and Chicago, tunnels 35 feet in diameter and 250 to 300 feet below the surface have been excavated in Silurian dolomites for metropolitan sewer networks during the 1980s and 1990s. Seventeen miles of tunnels beneath Milwaukee and 100 miles beneath Chicago have provided additional valuable information about the Silurian bedrock.

Milwaukee Museums

The Milwaukee Public Museum in the city center at 800 West Wells Street between Seventh and Ninth streets has fine collections of minerals and fossils of all ages, including local Silurian ones. An excellent diorama portrays Milwaukee as a tropical reef paradise some 400 million years ago. Imagine snorkeling over this ancient sea bottom. Outstanding reconstructions also display dinosaurs and other important fossil types.

The University of Wisconsin at Milwaukee, 3 miles northeast of the city center, houses the Greene Collection—the best Silurian fossils from the area. Thomas A. Greene moved to Milwaukee from Rhode Island in 1847 and founded a successful wholesale drug company. He became an avid collector and built his own museum building and display cases for his huge collection, which is now owned by the university. The original brick building on Downer Avenue between Kenwood Boulevard and Edgewood Avenue has deteriorated badly, so the collections are now in modern facilities in the university's Geology Department in Lapham Hall, where the public can view them at certain times. The campus can be reached from I-43 by either exit 74 or 75; Lapham Hall is at the south edge of the campus adjacent to Kenwood Boulevard.

Saratoga of the West

From the 1860s to the early 1900s, Wisconsin was a leading producer of mineral water. Before emerging from springs, groundwater seeped through glacial deposits and bedrock, slowly obtaining its dissolved mineral content. In 1911, Wisconsin bottlers sold almost 6 million gallons of mineral water. By 1913 there were thirty springwater bottling companies, and people flocked to resorts at some of those springs to gain the presumed health benefits of "taking the water."

Several of the bottling companies and spas were in the Waukesha area, dubbed the "Saratoga of the West," a reference to the famous old spa at Saratoga, New York. In downtown Waukesha you can visit a number of sites with names that harken back to the springwater era, including Waukesha Spring Park, Horeb Spring Park, and Bethesda Spring Park. At Frame Park, there is a flowing spring and a historical marker about the spas. These Waukesha springs are probably related to the Waukesha fault in the dolomite and sandstone bedrock. Other of the early 1900s bottling companies, such as Minnehaha Springs Bottling Company at Eagle in the Kettle Moraine, likely took water from springs issuing from a shallower source in the glacial deposits. It goes without saying that in Wisconsin beer was also a common product of many of the bottling companies.

Interstate 94
Milwaukee—Madison
80 miles (130 km)

From central Milwaukee, I-94 gradually climbs westward over the Niagara Escarpment. Glacial deposits from the western edge of the Lake Michigan Lobe obscure the underlying Silurian bedrock of the escarpment. Between the Lake Michigan shore and Brookfield (10 miles), the landscape consists of a series of north-south-trending moraines, called the Lake Border moraines, but they are difficult to recognize from the highway in this urbanized area. West of Brookfield, the hills south of the highway are north-east-southwest-trending drumlins formed beneath the southwestward-flowing Lake Michigan Lobe. At Waukesha, Silurian dolomite has been quarried for many years.

Landscape image showing drumlins formed by the southward-flowing Green Bay Lobe and the southwestward-flowing Lake Michigan Lobe, and the Kettle Moraine, where the two glacier lobes met.

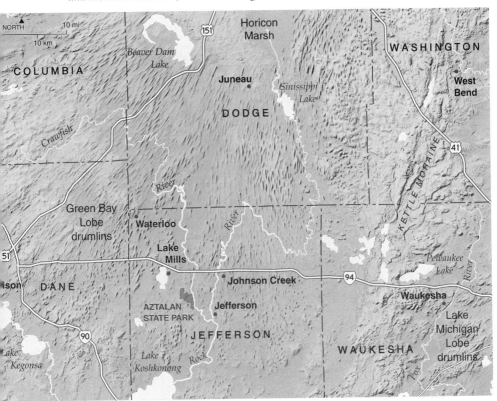

About 20 miles west of Brookfield at the summit of the escarpment in the vicinity of Delafield and Oconomowoc, I-94 crosses the Kettle Moraine, which formed between the Lake Michigan Lobe and the Green Bay Lobe. Both lobes spread southward through lowlands on either side of the escarpment, the ice margins butting together along its top. Rock debris from both lobes collected to form the Kettle Moraine, which extends from about 50 miles north of Milwaukee southwest to I-43 near Elkhorn. This complex collection of landforms and sediment got its name from its abundant round-bottomed depressions, which formed where blocks of ice were buried by outwash or other types of sediment. When the buried ice melted, the overlying sediment collapsed to form a pit resembling the widely used cast-iron kettles of the 1800s.

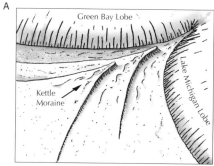

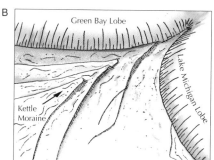

Stages in the formation of the southern part of the Kettle Moraine. A and B. A series of outwash fans are deposited in the area between the receding margin of the Green Bay and Lake Michigan Lobes. C. Buried ice melts and parts of the outwash fan collapse into round-bottomed pits, or kettles.
—From Clayton, 2001

Two portions have been reserved as the Kettle Moraine State Forest, one 25 miles north and the other 5 miles south of I-94. Both units have interpretive centers and well-marked hiking and ski trails. A portion of the Ice Age National Scenic Trail provides access to some of the better glacial features. The Northern Unit of the Kettle Moraine State Forest and the Ice Age National Scientific Reserve at Campbellsport are described in **U.S. 41: Milwaukee—Marinette**.

Kettle Moraine State Forest: Southern Unit

For a brief taste of the Kettle Moraine, take exit 285 at Delafield and follow Kettle Moraine Scenic Drive, or County C, south of the interstate 1.5 miles to Lapham Peak State Park with an observation tower providing fine views of the landscape. This hill, 1,233 feet above sea level, was named for Wisconsin's earliest naturalist, Increase Lapham, who is described by a marker at the tower as "Eminent scientist and useful citizen." Lapham made many important early contributions to geology and other natural sciences but is remembered especially as the father of the United States Weather Service. He settled in nearby Oconomowoc in the 1830s and made weather observations from this hill.

For a fuller taste, continue south about 15 miles on Kettle Moraine Scenic Drive for views of the landscape and several hiking trail access points. The headquarters for the Southern Unit of the Kettle Moraine State Forest is about 3 miles west of Eagle on the south side of Wisconsin 59. Here, there are maps of hiking trails, interpretive materials and programs, and a nature center, which has excellent displays about the geology of the Kettle Moraine area. Among many items displayed, there is a large nugget of copper carried from the Lake Superior basin by the Quaternary glaciers. Also near Eagle is Old World Wisconsin, a living museum of early farming by various ethnic groups who settled in the state.

The southern part of the Kettle Moraine consists of a series of moraines and outwash plains. As the margins of the Green Bay and Michigan Lobes receded, meltwater deposited a series of outwash plains between the lobes, undoubtedly burying moraines and other accumulations of till. Much of the outwash sand and gravel was deposited on top of ice and over and around moraines. With the eventual melting of the buried ice, the nearly flat outwash plains became pitted and in some places collapsed to form hilly areas of sand and gravel.

Drumlin Showplace

A conspicuous hill about 1 mile north of the I-94–Wisconsin 67 intersection is man-made. It was constructed in the early 1970s as a ski hill. The material for construction was excavated from the outwash plain that surrounds it. West of Oconomowoc, I-94 crosses spectacular drumlins of the southern Green Bay Lobe all the way to Madison. This region is one of the most famous drumlin fields in the world. Nearly every hill crossed is a drumlin, but from the highway, their distinctive elongate shape may not be obvious. Around Johnson Creek the drumlins trend northwest-southeast, but farther west near Lake Mills they trend north-south, and near Madison they trend northeast-southwest. The spreading flow of ice toward the southern margin of the Green Bay Lobe created a regional fan-shaped pattern of drumlins. Many of the lowlands between drumlins are wetlands, which were much more common prior to the construction of drainage systems to provide more land for agriculture.

Several I-94 exits provide access to the Glacial Drumlin State Trail, a hiking and biking trail along a former railroad bed that crosses many drumlins and provides excellent views. At the eastbound rest area near Johnson Creek, an interpretive sign discusses drumlins. I-94 also crosses several small recessional moraines of the Green Bay Lobe between Madison and the Kettle Moraine but they are not easy to recognize.

Twenty miles east of Madison and only 2 miles south of I-94 near Lake Mills is Aztalan State Park, Wisconsin's most important archaeological site. This fortified Native American village, a northern outpost of the Mississippi Valley Culture, was occupied from approximately A.D. 900 to 1200. The name *Aztalan* was coined in the nineteenth century by enthusiasts who thought the site had some connection to the Aztec people of Mexico. Instead, it was related to a major center, Kahokia, at East St. Louis, Illinois.

Fifteen miles east of Madison and 5 miles north of the interstate at Waterloo is the only area of exposed bedrock near this route. A window through the Pleistocene deposits reveals Precambrian red quartzite and Paleozoic conglomerate composed of boulders of that quartzite. The rocks and their relationships to each other are the same as at the Baraboo Hills to the northwest though not as well exposed. The quartzite was deformed, metamorphosed, and eroded prior to the flooding of Wisconsin by seas in Cambrian and Ordovician time. Storm waves in the ancient sea pounded islands of quartzite, tumbling and rounding the boulders that would become conglomerate. At Waterloo, the conglomerate appears to be of younger, Ordovician age than at Baraboo but is otherwise similar. The Baraboo geology appears to extend at least 40 miles southeastward to Waterloo, and drilling indicates that similar red quartzite extends even farther toward Milwaukee.

MADISON GEOLOGY

Madison, the City of Four Lakes, grew up on the narrow land between the two largest of the lakes in the area, which together occupy the valleys of a preglacial river system much modified by the ice. The earliest Native

American inhabitants of the area built more than 1,500 effigy mounds around the lakeshores. In 1837, the shrewdest land speculator in Wisconsin Territory persuaded the legislature to establish the capitol on the hill between Lakes Mendota and Monona at the junction of several Indian trails. He named the town after former President James Madison, who had died recently.

Indians of the Woodland Culture built effigy mounds along rivers and lakeshores in Wisconsin approximately A.D. 650 to 1200. Some mounds have recognizable shapes like birds and animals, but many are simple linear ridges.

Glacial deposits obscure bedrock in Madison, but some natural outcrops and quarries reveal that Cambrian and Ordovician strata underlie the area. During early settlement in the middle 1800s, Cambrian sandstones exposed on several hillsides in the western part of the city were exploited by quarrying for building stone. Most of the oldest buildings on the University of Wisconsin campus, several elegant old houses, and many walls were built of this stone. The increasing popularity of brick in the early 1900s, however, caused a decline in sandstone quarrying, which finally ended by World War II. Ordovician dolomite was quarried and crushed for road surfacing, especially when automobiles became more and more popular in the early 1900s. Crushed dolomite is still produced in large quantities all over the state for road surfaces and for mixing with cement to make concrete.

The overall shape of the landscape in the Madison area reflects the shape of the underlying bedrock surface. Uplands are typically till-covered sandstone and dolomite. Low areas are filled with locally thick sequences of till, outwash, and lake sediment. Northeast-southwest-trending drumlins and small northwest-southeast-trending moraines are common on uplands. There are several drumlins on the isthmus between Lakes Mendota and Monona, the site of the state capitol. Perhaps the most notable features of the area are the Madison lakes, which were much larger when the Green Bay Lobe receded northeastward across the area. Before being artificially filled, much of the lowland around the Madison lakes was wetland, which was a remnant of the floor of the larger lake system. The Dane County Regional Airport and part of the University of Wisconsin Arboretum rest on lake sediment deposited in the larger ancestors of the present Madison lakes. The higher part of the arboretum is on a recessional moraine.

Bascom Hill on the University of Wisconsin campus, which was established in 1849, is also a drumlin. On its western end, a historical marker mounted on a large erratic boulder of gneiss, a metamorphic rock, commemorates Thomas Chrowder Chamberlin, a distinguished geologist, educator, and leader in the late 1800s. He served as president of the University of Wisconsin, as state geologist, and developed many of the early concepts of glaciation. The site next to the old university observatory provides a fine view across Lake Mendota.

The Geology Museum at the university displays minerals, rocks, and fossils not only from Wisconsin but from other parts of the world. It is located in Weeks Hall at the corner of Dayton and Charter Streets. One of the highlights of this museum is a large mastodon skeleton found 65 miles west of Madison in 1897.

The elegant, classical-style state capitol, located on a drumlin hill in the center of the city, contains a wonderful variety of rock types from several parts of North America and Europe—it is a geologic museum in its own right. Its exterior is white granite; it is said that Wisconsin bought an entire quarry near Bethel, Vermont, to assure an adequate supply of this stone. The interior has five different types of Wisconsin granite in polished decorative panels; tan-colored limestone or dolomite wall panels from Minnesota; limestone stair steps, base boards, and railings from Tennessee, Illinois, and Missouri; various marbles and serpentine from Italy, France, and Greece; and surrounding the rotunda, pillars of polished black Norwegian larvikite (a variety of the igneous rock syenite) with iridescent feldspar crystals. A booklet describing the building includes lists of the decorative stones. Why not test your rock identification skills here and look for fossils in the limestones?

U.S. 41
Milwaukee—Marinette via Oshkosh and Green Bay
186 miles (300 km)

U.S. 41 extends northwestward from the center of Milwaukee to Fond du Lac, then bends around the western side of Lake Winnebago through Oshkosh to Appleton, where it heads northeast to Green Bay and then continues north along the western shore of the bay to the Michigan border at Marinette.

For most of the way to Fond du Lac, the highway crosses diagonally over the dolomite bedrock of the Niagara Escarpment, which is obscured by the

Kettle Moraine. Five miles northwest of Milwaukee and a few miles south-west of Menomonee Falls, a major building stone industry quarries Silurian dolomite. Called "Lannon Stone," it is one of the state's most popular building stones because it breaks easily into layers that are very even in thickness. Lannon Stone is from an interreef deposit, but some reef cores are also present here.

In the Milwaukee area, U.S. 41 cuts across several north-south-trending moraines that mark former positions of the western margin of the Lake Michigan Lobe during a series of readvances. North of the intersection with Wisconsin 167 in Germantown, the highway crosses a pitted outwash plain. The till upland to the east has a number of nearly east-west-trending drumlins formed beneath the westward-flowing Lake Michigan Lobe. Near the intersection with Wisconsin 60 at Slinger, the highway enters the north-ern part of the Kettle Moraine (see **I-94: Milwaukee—Madison** for more discussion of the Kettle Moraine). In this northern part of the moraine, the outwash plains that dominate much of the southern part give way to more eskers, gravelly moraine ridges, and narrow pitted outwash plains depos-ited between walls of glacial ice to the east and west. The original nearly flat surface of some of these outwash plains, which were deposited on top of ice, are now sandy hills.

Between Slinger and Allenton, U.S. 41 leaves the western side of the Kettle Moraine and crosses a pitted outwash plain along the East Branch of the Rock River. The uplands here are till-mantled dolomite and have many poorly formed, northwest-southeast-trending drumlins formed beneath the southeastward-flowing Green Bay Lobe. North of Allenton, the high-way continues across a till upland with drumlins. Nearly all of the hills in this area are drumlins whose orientation gradually swings around to nearly north-south at Lomira.

Neda Iron Mining District

At Allenton, Wisconsin 33 leads 10 miles west to the old Neda iron min-ing district at the western margin of the Niagara Escarpment. Thin, dis-continuous lenses of ironstone occur within the Maquoketa shale where iron oxide replaced calcium carbonate, probably when shoals were exposed during a fall in sea level. Mining began in 1845 by tunneling underground into the base of the escarpment at the east edge of Neda, 1.5 miles south of Wisconsin 33 on Wisconsin 67. Later, an open pit mine was also developed a mile north. Blast furnaces smelted the ore at Mayville, 5 miles farther north, using lime from a quarry halfway between the two towns at the in-tersection of the two highways. The Neda mines closed in 1914 because the ore contained too much phosphorous and sulfur for making steel, but the Mayville furnaces continued for another twenty-four years processing ore from northern Michigan. The old lime quarry is the only surviving part of

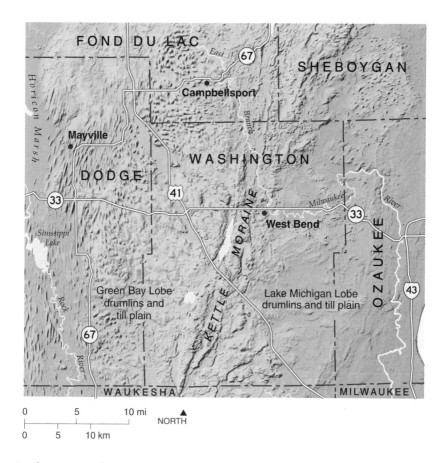

0   5   10 mi   ▲
                NORTH
0   5   10 km

Landscape image showing the northern Kettle Moraine and the orientation of drumlins.

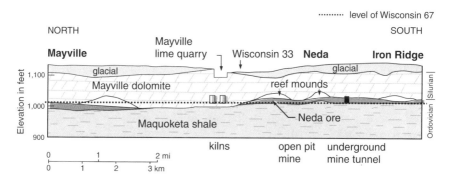

Section along the face of the Niagara Escarpment parallel to Wisconsin 67 showing the position of the Neda iron ore. The Maquoketa shale and lower part of the Mayville dolomite also are present along the escarpment at High Cliff State Park 50 miles north.

the industry. Today, it provides crushed rock for roads and other purposes. A historical marker at the north edge of Mayville discusses the old blast furnace, and a small museum in an old stone schoolhouse at the center of town tells more about the past iron industry.

A labyrinth of 4 miles of mine tunnels dug into the base of the Niagara Escarpment at Neda is now the winter home of at least 200,000 bats, who migrate from as far as 1,000 miles away to hibernate here. Abandoned mines have become increasingly important bat refuges. The Neda mine is one of North America's three most important wintering sites; an abandoned sandstone mine in western Wisconsin on the Mississippi River is another. To protect the bats' habitat and for safety reasons, the mine entrance has been capped with a grate that allows access for bats, but not people.

Kettle Moraine State Forest: Northern Unit

At Lomira take Wisconsin 67 east about 6 miles beyond Campbellsport to the Henry S. Ruess Interpretive Center of the Ice Age National Scientific Reserve on the south side of the road just west of the intersection with County G. The headquarters for the Northern Unit of the Kettle Moraine State Forest is about 3 miles south on County G. The interpretive center, which is on a high point in the Kettle Moraine, provides excellent views with explanatory signs, access points to the Ice Age National Scenic Trail and other trails, interpretive displays, and events. Distinctive conical hills, called *kames*, formed where holes in the glacier filled with a variety of sediment including outwash, lake sediment, and till. When the surrounding ice melted, a hill of sediment was left behind. Dundee Mountain is a kame that you can see from the observation deck at the interpretive center.

McMullen Hill, a kame in the northern part of the Kettle Moraine, is about 3 miles northeast of the Henry S. Ruess Interpretive Center. —Nelson R. Ham photo

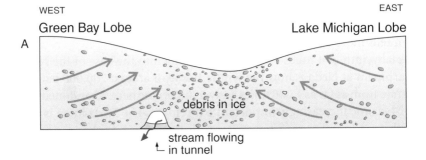

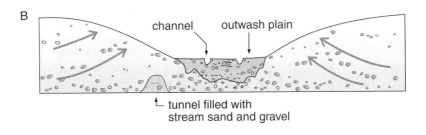

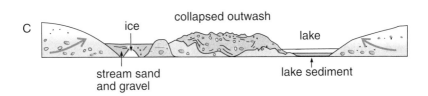

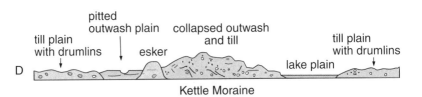

Sequence showing the formation of the northern Kettle Moraine. A. Debris collects in the ice where the two lobes flow together. B. Meltwater deposits outwash on top of the ice. C. The outwash collapses into hummocky topography as the ice beneath the outwash melts. D. With the final recession of the glacier, the moraine forms a high point in the landscape.

The consistently even thickness of layers of this Fond du lac–type Silurian dolomite make it popular for building purposes. The fine lamination was formed on tidal flats covered by mats of algae, which helped to bind the fine sediment particles. The many pores formed where mat material decayed following burial. —R. H. Dott, Jr., photo

Green Bay–Fox River Lowland

Between Lomira and Fond du Lac, U.S. 41 descends from the Niagara Escarpment into the Lake Winnebago lowland, which was occupied by Glacial Lake Oshkosh. Five miles south of Fond du Lac around Hamilton, there are several active quarries in Silurian dolomite. Fond du Lac Stone is one of the state's most widely used building stones along with Lannon Stone from the Menomonee Falls area. For a discussion of the Fond du Lac quarries, see **U.S. 151: Madison—Manitowoc**.

The erosion of Ordovician shale, dolomites, and sandstone in preglacial times formed the Green Bay–Fox River lowland, but scouring glacial ice further enhanced it. In the early days of European settlement, Ordovician Maquoketa shale was quarried on the east side of Lake Winnebago for making bricks and Silurian dolomite was quarried for making lime. From Fond du Lac, U.S. 41 traverses most of the length of this lowland all the way to Green Bay. Along the route, bedrock is exposed only in quarries exploiting Ordovician dolomites in the Neenah-Appleton area and at Green Bay.

North of Fond du Lac, U.S. 41 rises onto a gently rolling till upland and crosses a subtle hummocky moraine formed along the west side of the Green Bay Lobe at the Fond du Lac–Winnebago County line, before descending back onto the floor of Glacial Lake Oshkosh just north of the intersection with Wisconsin 44 at Oshkosh. Three miles north of Lake Butte des Morts at the intersection of U.S. 41 and U.S. 45, a large mound on the east side of the highway is an old landfill known locally as "Mount Trashmore." U.S. 41 continues across the glacial lakebed through the Neenah-Menasha area. In Menasha, visit the Weis Earth Science Museum at the University of Wisconsin Fox Valley Center at 1478 Midway Road.

On the north side of Appleton, the highway turns east and rises onto a till upland with some hummocky topography, then descends back onto the nearly flat plain of Glacial Lake Oshkosh through De Pere and Green Bay. This section of road provides excellent views of the Niagara Escarpment to the east.

The aroma of paper mills, especially at Kaukauna east of Appleton, reminds us that the Fox River valley between Neenah and Green Bay has long been a major paper manufacturing area. After the decline of lumbering in the early 1900s, lumber mills in the Fox Valley, as well as in the Wisconsin River valley between Wausau and Wisconsin Rapids, converted to paper manufacture, making Wisconsin the center of that industry for the entire nation. While the state is still important for paper, the industry is now more dispersed. Federal legislation between 1965 and 1972 addressed industrial pollution, and the cleanup of the Fox River was a model program.

Between Oshkosh and Green Bay, arsenic detected in well water at many localities caused alarm and prompted research into the source of this poison. Was it natural or caused by manufacturing? Geologists determined that the arsenic is present in trace amounts in iron sulfide minerals, which occur as cements in the upper part of the Ordovician St. Peter sandstone, a major aquifer in this region. It does not cause a problem unless vigorous pumping of wells draws the water table down below the top of the sandstone, which allows the oxidation of the iron minerals and the release of arsenic into the groundwater. The obvious remedy is to avoid severe drawdown of the water table, but this is difficult because of a rapid expansion of suburbs in the area.

High Cliff State Park

High Cliff State Park, on the scenic, rural eastern shore of Lake Winnebago about 10 miles southeast of the Appleton area, is on the Niagara Escarpment. The Mayville dolomite of Silurian age is responsible for the escarpment here and is exposed in outcrops and old quarries. A kiln for making lime from crushed dolomite is also preserved.

High Cliff State Park on the Niagara Escarpment overlooking Lake Winnebago. View is to the south. —Photo courtesy of the Wisconsin Department of Natural Resources

Fossils in the dolomite include corals, stromatoporoids, and fragments of other animal skeletons. The Maquoketa shale of Ordovician age underlies the Silurian strata but is concealed by rock rubble and vegetation. Less resistant to erosion, the shale is largely responsible for the adjacent Lake Winnebago lowland, which was gouged out and broadened first by preglacial rivers and later by glacial ice moving southwestward from Green Bay parallel to the escarpment.

This area provided much of the materials needed for building the early towns around Lake Winnebago. Quarrying began in the 1850s for making lime and to provide crushed rock. At Stockbridge, 6 miles south of the park, clay was quarried from the Maquoketa shale for making bricks. Transport across the lake by boat in the summer and sleds in the winter was relatively cheap. Quarrying continued until 1956, when the state acquired the land for a state park.

Old lime kilns at High Cliff State Park. —R. H. Dott, Jr., photo

Green Bay to Marinette

At Green Bay, where French explorers and traders first landed in 1634, U.S. 41 passes near the famed Green Bay Packers football stadium. The Neville Museum in downtown Green Bay highlights the natural history of the area and includes a few geological displays, especially of glacial phenomena. The museum is on Dousman Street on the west bank of the Fox River.

On the northwest edge of the city at Duck Creek, just half a mile west of the junction with U.S. 141, is a very deep quarry in the Ordovician Platteville and Galena dolomites, which span the state from the southwestern lead mines to Green Bay. From Duck Creek northeast to Marinette at the Michigan border, bedrock is not exposed along the highway, although a few outcrops form rapids along the Menominee River, which defines the border inland from Marinette.

Between Green Bay and Marinette, U.S. 41 crosses a nearly flat, sandy lake plain. This plain is in part the floor of Glacial Lake Oshkosh but may also include the sandy floors of other lakes that formed along the west side of the Green Bay Lobe as it receded from the area. In places the sandy lake sediment is draped over older sand and gravel or till. You may see a few excavations that expose reddish brown till. The till uplands several miles to the west of this part of U.S. 41 have many northeast-southwest-trending drumlins formed beneath the southwestward-flowing ice of the Green Bay Lobe. Sand dunes, which dot the lake plain, are typically less than 10 feet high, but some are over 30 feet high. The dunes probably formed shortly after the lakes on the margin of the ice drained, exposing an unvegetated surface of uniform fine to medium sand that the wind easily moved.

At Oconto, Copper Culture State Park is on the site of a 4,500-year-old cemetery used by Indians who made many implements from copper obtained in northern Michigan. At Peshtigo a museum commemorates the disastrous forest fire of October 8, 1871, which burned parts of six counties, including half of the Door Peninsula across Green Bay. More than one thousand lives were lost, far more than in the famous Chicago Fire, which occurred the same night.

Paleozoic strata extend northeastward into Michigan. Silurian dolomites show along the lakeshore from Marinette to Escanaba, Michigan, and on the Garden Peninsula east of Escanaba. The interesting restored town of Fayette on the Garden Peninsula was a primitive iron smelting center in the late 1800s similar to Neda and Mayville in Wisconsin. Across Michigan's Upper Peninsula 50 miles to the north, Cambrian sandstones reappear in the spectacular Pictured Rocks National Seashore overlooking Lake Superior.

U.S. 141
Green Bay—Pembine
55 miles (88 km)

U.S. 141 and U.S. 41 are together for 16 miles between Green Bay and Abrams; refer to **U.S. 41: Milwaukee—Marinette** for that section. Between the intersection with U.S. 41 in Abrams and the area of the intersection with Wisconsin 22 (7 miles), U.S. 141 crosses a nearly flat, sandy lake plain. The lake sediment was deposited in lakes flanking the western margin of the Green Bay Lobe as it receded from the Green Bay lowland. Gullies along the Oconto River and numerous sand dunes break the nearly flat surface. The dunes are typically about 10 feet high. About 3 miles north of the intersection with Wisconsin 22, the highway rises onto a till upland with poorly formed northeast-southwest-trending drumlins formed beneath the Green Bay Lobe. One mile north of Lena, at the Lena Cemetery, the ridge you can see just east of the road is a small esker, a linear ridge of gravel deposited in the bed of a stream flowing in a tunnel beneath a glacier. The gravel pits on both sides of the highway at the intersection with Wisconsin 64 just north of Pound are in another esker. This esker trends almost east-west and can be traced for several miles.

Between the Wisconsin 64 intersection and Crivitz and Wausaukee, U.S. 141 crosses uplands of till and extensively pitted outwash, separated by low wetlands and outwash plains. Many long, well-developed eskers run through this area, but most do not cross the highway. The till, typical of the late advances of the Green Bay Lobe, is redder and contains more silt than the reddish brown tills deposited during earlier late Wisconsin advances.

North of Wausaukee, U.S. 141 crosses a very hilly landscape where outwash sand and gravel were deposited on top of ice. With the eventual melting of the ice, the sand and gravel collapsed to form the many hills and depressions. Just north of Amberg, the highway crosses an area of hummocky topography that is part of a north-south-trending moraine deposited along the west edge of the Green Bay Lobe when it stabilized here for awhile during its eastward recession. This is one of several generally north-south-trending moraines in this part of Wisconsin that mark places where the margin of the Green Bay Lobe stood still or readvanced during its general recession. At Papoose Lake about 3 miles north of Amberg, the highway descends the front of the moraine onto the outwash plain deposited while the ice stood at the moraine. This flat outwash plain extends to Pembine. There are nice views eastward across the outwash plain to the moraine for several miles south of Pembine.

Because bedrock in northeastern Wisconsin is so obscured by glacial deposits and wetlands, only drilling allows us to locate the boundary between Precambrian and Paleozoic bedrock; water wells indicate that Wausaukee is at that boundary. Seven miles north of Wausaukee, a long uphill roadcut exposes Precambrian metamorphosed volcanic rocks, which have been cut by a granite dike. Farther north 1.6 miles, a side road leads west a short distance to Dave's Falls, where the Pike River has created a fine exposure of glacially smoothed granite that intruded metamorphosed volcanics. For the next 3 miles north, there are scattered exposures of granites, some of which were quarried near Amberg. The Amberg granite is exceptional in this part of the state. At 1,750 million years old, it is younger than the Penokean granites so typical of north-central Wisconsin, so is related instead to the granites and rhyolites at Baraboo, Montello, and Redgranite in southern Wisconsin. We discuss the Precambrian bedrock of the Pembine area in the Northern Highlands chapter. See **U.S. 8/U.S. 141/U.S. 2: Pembine—Florence**.

U.S. 151

Madison—Manitowoc

125 miles (200 km)

U.S. 151 extends diagonally across Wisconsin from the Mississippi River at Dubuque, Iowa, through Madison to Lake Michigan at Manitowoc. Much of its route follows old Native American trails long used for trading. In the northeastern part of Madison, Cambrian and Ordovician strata are exposed at several places, chiefly in quarries and excavation sites for construction of buildings. An example is on the north side of the highway half a mile west of the intersection with I-90/I-94, where upper Cambrian strata are visible in front of a service station and behind the adjacent motel. Four miles northeast of Sun Prairie, Ordovician dolomite (Platteville formation) is exposed in a quarry on the south side of the highway. Beyond this point, bedrock is not exposed along U.S. 151 until east of Fond du Lac. Ordovician dolomite is quarried, however, a few miles north of Beaver Dam and on the west edge of Waupun. Scattered exposures north of U.S. 151 together with drill holes provide us with a good idea of the Cambrian and Ordovician rocks in spite of the pervasive cover of glacial materials in this part of Wisconsin. These buried strata are generally similar to those exposed at the surface in western Wisconsin.

Between Madison and Columbus, U.S. 151 crosses a till-covered bedrock upland. The brown, sandy till is typical of that deposited by the southern Green Bay Lobe. The southwestward-flowing lobe grooved and scratched the dolomite bedrock before depositing the till. Some of the hills here are drumlins—elongate, parallel hills—but they are difficult to recognize from the road. Between Columbus and Beaver Dam, U.S. 151 crosses through an area of spectacular drumlins formed beneath the southern part of the Green Bay Lobe.

Drumlins are common in many parts of Wisconsin that were covered by the late Wisconsin Laurentide Ice Sheet, but nowhere are they more spectacular than in the southern part of the area covered by the Green Bay Lobe. The flow of the ice etched the land, forming a fan-shaped pattern of drumlins that covers hundreds of square miles. Some of the drumlins are made up of till deposited at the base of the ice, others are erosional features composed of older till and outwash or bedrock. The best-formed drumlins are streamlined. Like the hull of a submarine, they are blunt on their northern ends that faced the flow of the ice, and taper to the south.

In this area, U.S. 151 generally parallels the northeast-southwest-trending drumlins, which are typically between 1 and 2 miles long, 30 to 50 feet high, and 1,000 to 1,500 feet wide. The ridges that you can see on either side of the road, many with farm buildings on top, are drumlins. Just north of Columbus, at the Columbia-Dodge County line, the highway cuts through a drumlin. In similar fashion, County S about 4 miles north of Columbus cuts through a drumlin immediately east of U.S. 151. The ridge to the west of the County S intersection is a classic drumlin. The drumlins tend to get longer and narrower near Beaver Dam.

At the intersection with Wisconsin 33 at Beaver Dam, U.S. 151 crosses an east-west-trending moraine formed along the margin of the Green Bay Lobe as it receded from the area. Notice the slightly hummocky nature of the moraine. Between Beaver Dam and Waupun, the highway crosses a low-relief till plain. Well-formed drumlins are less common in this area.

As you approach Waupun from the south, a long wooded ridge appears on the eastern horizon about 5 miles away. This is the base of the Niagara Escarpment, which rises about 200 feet abruptly from the Horicon Marsh lowland just east of U.S. 151. Resistant Silurian dolomite forms the escarpment, whereas the marsh rests on easily eroded Ordovician shale.

Between Waupun and Fond du Lac, U.S. 151 crosses a low-relief till plain that furnishes many good views eastward to the Niagara Escarpment. Several miles south of Fond du Lac, the highway descends onto a flat area of silt and clay-rich sediment deposited on the floor of Glacial Lake Oshkosh. In places this lake sediment is well over 100 feet thick. Layers of till within the sequence of lake sediment attest to readvances of the Green Bay Lobe. Glacial Lake Oshkosh filled and drained several times as the lobe advanced, receded, and readvanced across the area.

Horicon Marsh

Horicon Marsh is worth a side trip via Wisconsin 49 east from Waupun. Hundreds of thousands of Canada geese gather here during their annual migration south along a major flyway from Hudson Bay. The marsh is a broad, shallow wetland drained by the south-flowing Rock River. As the southern margin of the Green Bay Lobe receded across the area, a lake formed between the edge of the glacier and an east-west moraine near Horicon. The lake drained as the Rock River eroded an outlet in the moraine and the ice margin receded farther northward. Over time, vegetation filled the broad, shallow lake basin. At one time, humans attempted to drain the marsh and use the land for agriculture, but today, it is managed as a wildlife area with an extensive dike, ditch, and pool system. The northern part of the marsh is the Horicon National Wildlife Refuge, and the southern part is the Horicon Marsh State Wildlife Area.

About 1 mile east of Waupun, Wisconsin 49 begins to descend into the Horicon Marsh basin. You can see the marsh ahead with the Niagara Escarpment rising beyond. About 2 miles east of U.S. 151, watch on the right for the entrance to a Horicon National Wildlife Refuge trailhead, parking lot, and access to a driving tour with interpretive signs and hiking trails.

The Egret Trail is a floating boardwalk from which to view the marsh, the Niagara Escarpment to the east, and a great variety of birds and other wildlife. To the north of Wisconsin 49 is the Marsh Haven Nature Center, which has many displays about the natural history and geology of the marsh. Just to the east is a highway interpretive sign about the marsh.

Continue east on Wisconsin 49 for about 4 miles, crossing the north end of the marsh, to County Z and take it south 3.5 miles to the Horicon National Wildlife Refuge Visitor Center, which has more displays, interpretive materials, and an overlook. Be sure to look to the east where the Niagara Escarpment is very well expressed as a steep slope rising about 100 feet. About 8 miles farther south at the north side of the town of Horicon, the Wisconsin Department of Natural Resources Visitor Center also has an overlook, interpretive materials, and hiking trails.

Alternate Route over the Niagara Escarpment
Waupun—Fond du Lac

From the standpoint of bedrock geology, a more interesting route between Waupun and Fond du Lac crosses over the Niagara Escarpment. Turn east on Wisconsin 49 at the east edge of Waupun and cross the north end of the Horicon Marsh to County Z. Turn north on County Z for 2 miles and turn east on Breakneck Road, which climbs steeply east up the Niagara Escarpment. A roadcut on a hairpin curve shows Silurian dolomite. At the top of the grade beside a T junction is a small parking lot, from which

Quarry near Fond du Lac in Silurian dolomite of the Burnt Bluff formation. —R. H. Dott, Jr., photo

a trail leads north along the top of the Oakfield Ledges, which are cliffs in the Mayville dolomite of Silurian age. Continuing east, Breakneck Road passes several shallow dolomite quarries. Proceed east and north past Oakfield via County Y and B for 8 miles to Hamilton, where a group of deeper quarries are exploiting the Silurian rocks for what is known as Fond du Lac Stone, one of the state's most popular decorative building stones. The light gray, fine, homogeneous dolomite with even stratification was deposited in shallow tidal environments. The ease of splitting the stone along this stratification makes it valuable for various building purposes. From Hamilton, Wisconsin 175 leads north into Fond du Lac and back to U.S. 151.

Fond du Lac to Manitowoc

Fond du Lac, which is French for "bottom (or end) of the lake," claims to be the "Handcuff manufacturing capital of the U.S.A." U.S. 151 skirts the eastern shore of Lake Winnebago for 20 miles. This large but shallow lake and the large Horicon Marsh 15 miles southwest lie within the broad lowland that extends southwestward for more than 100 miles from Green Bay. Lake Winnebago is famous for a large population of sturgeon.

About 4 miles northeast of Fond du Lac, U.S. 151 rises onto the base of the Niagara Escarpment. This section of highway provides views westward across Lake Winnebago and the Green Bay–Fox River lowland, especially from waysides 6 miles and 20 miles from Fond du Lac. The Niagara Escarpment was named for the Silurian Niagara dolomite, which can be traced around the northern end of Lake Michigan and southeastward across Ontario to Niagara Falls, New York, where the rock was named in the early 1800s. Near Stockbridge, 5 miles north of U.S. 151 on Wisconsin 55, the Maquoketa shale was quarried for clay to make bricks during the 1800s. High Cliff State Park 10 miles farther north is on the Niagara Escarpment where dolomite was quarried and processed to make lime (for a discussion of High Cliff State Park, see **U.S. 41: Milwaukee—Marinette**). From the Wisconsin 55 intersection, U.S. 151 climbs up the escarpment and proceeds east across the upland to Chilton. No bedrock appears along this route, but at Valders, a large quarry extracts Silurian dolomite. Rock debris contained in the southward-flowing ice of the Green Bay Lobe and the westward-flowing ice of the Lake Michigan Lobe scratched the surface of the dolomite.

Between Chilton and Valders, U.S. 151 crosses a low-relief till plain with north-south-trending drumlins. Near Valders the drumlins have more of a northwest-southeast trend, but they are hard to see from the road. About 2 miles east of Valders the highway crosses an area of hummocky topography composed of reddish brown till overlying the Kettle Moraine. Throughout

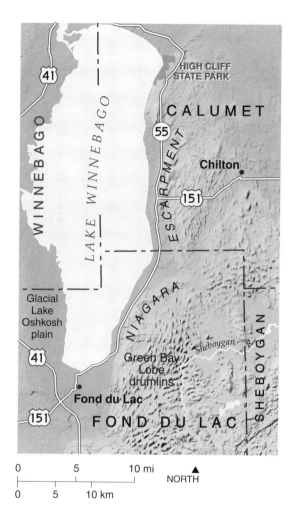

Landscape image of the Niagara Escarpment along the east side of Lake Winnebago.

this area the till is reddish brown and rich in silt and clay, typical of the late readvances of the Lake Michigan Lobe. Eastward to Manitowoc, the highway crosses low-relief till plains and pitted outwash plains.

U.S. 151 ends at the Lake Michigan shore in Manitowoc, where a car ferry provides transportation across the lake to Ludington, Michigan, during the summer. The mouth of the Manitowoc River, one of many short rivers that drain the east side of the Niagara Escarpment, provides a good harbor.

Glacially grooved and scratched dolomite. —J. W. Attig photo

Wisconsin 21
Coloma—Oshkosh
51 miles (82 km)

As in most other glaciated parts of Wisconsin, bedrock exposures are few along this stretch. About 3 miles west of Coloma, Wisconsin 21 passes out of the Central Plain and rises onto the outermost moraine of the Green Bay Lobe. Here, the broad, flat outwash and lakebed of the Central Plain give way to the hills and lakes of the area glaciated during the last part of the Wisconsin Glaciation. East of Coloma, Wisconsin 21 crosses an extensive pitted outwash plain and several north-south-trending moraines deposited along the margin of the Green Bay Lobe as it receded. Two miles east of Coloma take County GG north for about 1.5 miles to visit Mecan Springs, which feed several lakes at the head of the Mecan River, a widely known trout fishery. These are kettle lakes formed along the trend of a tunnel channel eroded by westward-flowing meltwater at the bed of the Green Bay Lobe. Between the intersection with County B near Richford and Wautoma, Wisconsin 21 crosses an area of broad sand flats deposited in lakes that formed between the receding ice margin and the higher moraine topography to the west. The surface sediment is typically sandy in this area, but finely layered lake silt and clay are present below the surface. The uplands throughout this area are typically sand and gravel or till-mantled sand and gravel. East of Wautoma many of the hills are poorly formed southeast-northwest-trending drumlins.

About 3 miles west of Redgranite, near the intersection with County Z, Wisconsin 21 descends onto the floor of Glacial Lake Oskhosh. The hill on the north side of the road here is a drumlin. In the center of Redgranite opposite the municipal building, a large, abandoned, water-filled granite quarry is now a park with hiking trails. You can see a 5-foot-wide vertical dike of black basaltic rock cutting though the granite. Debris-rich ice at the base of the Green Bay Lobe has scratched, grooved, and polished the surface of the bedrock. These features show that the ice was flowing almost due west here, the same as the trend of drumlins.

The first important bedrock is exposed at Lohrville and Redgranite about 23 miles east of Coloma. As the latter name implies, red granite has been quarried in this area for years. This granite is part of the 1,750-million-year-old igneous event that caused the widespread volcanic eruption of rhyolite across southern Wisconsin and the intrusion of small bodies of granite. A vast blanket of rhyolite extended from Baraboo on the west for at least 80 miles northeast to Berlin, where this rock was quarried.

Just south of Redgranite, at the south edge of Lohrville, County EE and N lead to a long ridge of red granite with many old quarries. The coarse granite is indistinguishable from the Wausau Red Granite, the state rock. Two miles southwest on County N is the abandoned Flynn's Quarry, which is largely filled with water. The granite here is finer and has fewer dark minerals than the previous one. All of these red granite quarries were active in the early 1900s. Their chief product was paving blocks, which were trimmed by hand. An average trimmer could produce as many as three hundred blocks per day, which earned him a few cents each. Trains carried the blocks south to the rapidly growing cities of Milwaukee, Chicago, and St. Louis. After 1915, quarrying declined as concrete became the dominant paving material. Other uses of the granite kept the quarries active at a modest level until 1931.

Ten miles southeast of Redgranite at Berlin and also at Utley 15 miles farther south, 1,750-million-year-old black rhyolite was quarried for paving blocks and for other building purposes. Utley provided stone

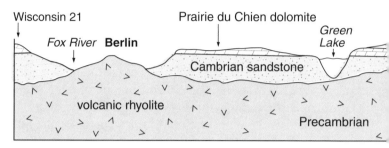

NORTHWEST

Section of the bedrock across the central Eastern Uplands from near Wautoma southeast to Horicon Marsh. Cambrian sandstone was deposited on the eroded, irregular Precambrian surface.

for Chicago streets. The base of Science Hall on the University of Wisconsin campus in Madison, which was completed in 1888, was constructed of large blocks of this unusually dark rhyolite. At Berlin, flat-lying Cambrian sandstone overlies the rhyolite, and at Utley Ordovician strata buried an ancient hill of rhyolite. Today in Utley, a very different kind of rock—the Ordovician St. Peter sandstone—is quarried right next to the abandoned rhyolite quarry. The sandstone is so poorly cemented that it is extracted by high-pressure water jets. The pure quartz sand from here has several uses, including sandblasting and foundry moldings.

Fifteen miles east of Redgranite, the early Ordovician Prairie du Chien dolomite is exposed in a roadcut and in a large quarry just south of the highway. In this part of the state, early Paleozoic strata are exposed at many small, scattered localities like this one, including those to the south at Berlin and Utley, a cliff on the south shore of Green Lake between Ripon and Utley, and some as far north as New London (25 miles). Exposures such as these help us to understand the nature of the Paleozoic strata in this otherwise glacially dominated region. The relationships of these strata to the rhyolite and granite indicate that here, as at Baraboo and elsewhere, many hills and islands of Precambrian rock littered the early Paleozoic landscapes of Wisconsin.

East of Redgranite, Wisconsin 21 continues to Oshkosh across the former floor of Glacial Lake Oshkosh. The area contains extensive wetlands that in places overlie more than 100 feet of finely laminated lake sediment. The uplands are till and till-mantled bedrock.

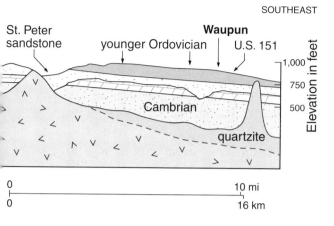

SOUTHEAST

Wisconsin 29

Ringle—Green Bay

70 miles (112 km)

At Ringle, which is in the Northern Highlands, Wisconsin 29 crosses a gently rolling landscape covered by a thin, discontinuous layer of clayey material derived from the weathering of the underlying bedrock. About 1.5 miles east of Ringle, the highway enters the Eastern Uplands where it crosses the outermost north-south-trending moraine of the Green Bay Lobe. The bedrock is all Precambrian between Ringle and Shawano. Thanks to a veneer of glacial materials, exposures are scant. The western margin of the Wolf River batholith is about 5 miles west of Ringle, but the first exposures of Wolf River rocks near the highway are at Wittenberg 17 miles east. The Wolf River igneous complex differs from the older Penokean granitic and volcanic rocks to the west and north both in composition and in tectonic setting, so must have had a very different cause. Most of the igneous complex is granite richer in sodium and potassium but poorer in calcium than the Penokean ones. There is no evidence either of subduction or structural compression associated with this granite, so it appears to be a type of granite that forms within continental interiors rather than mountain belts. Its ultimate cause is poorly understood.

The ice of the Green Bay Lobe flowed nearly straight west across the Wolf River batholith, gouging out the abundant boulders of red granite

that are now scattered throughout the landscape. The size of the boulders reflects the spacing between joints in the granite. Many of the boulders
appear rounded, probably because the granite had weathered along joints
to nearly spherical shapes prior to being carried in the glacier. In a few
places the granite beneath the glacial sediment is weathered into particles,
much like the so-called rotten granite in the area south of Rib Mountain in
the Northern Highlands.

Where Wisconsin 29 crosses the westernmost moraine of the Green Bay
Lobe, its route follows a tunnel channel cut by meltwater at the base of the
glacier. Sandy outwash now partly fills the tunnel. Where the highway crosses
the Plover River near Hatley, it is on a southwestward-sloping outwash plain.
As the margin of the Green Bay Lobe receded eastward, it deposited a series of moraines and outwash plains, which form a set of stair steps in the
landscape that get lower and lower eastward toward the center of the Green
Bay lowland. The tread of each stairstep is a westward-sloping outwash
plain. The riser of each step is the moraine at the eastern edge of that plain.
The meltwater that deposited the outwash plain flowed southward between
the ice margin and the next older moraine to the west. The modern rivers
crossed by Wisconsin 29 in the Eastern Uplands follow this north-south

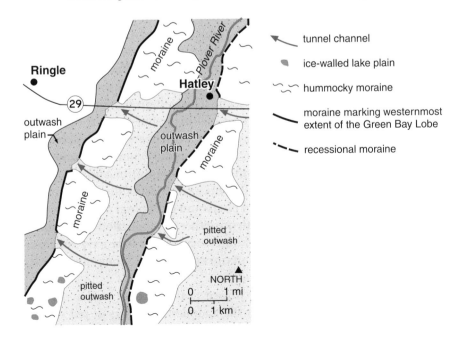

*The westernmost moraine of the Green Bay Lobe is just east of Ringle.
Meltwater spilled west through tunnel channels onto the outwash plains.*

meltwater drainage pattern. The outwash plain along the Plover River was deposited when the west edge of the Green Bay Lobe stood about one-half mile east of Hatley. Wisconsin 29 passes through a tunnel channel in this moraine just east of Hatley.

Pit in rotten granite. The rounded boulders of Wolf River granite in the foreground were probably farthest from fractures and are less weathered. —J. W. Attig photo

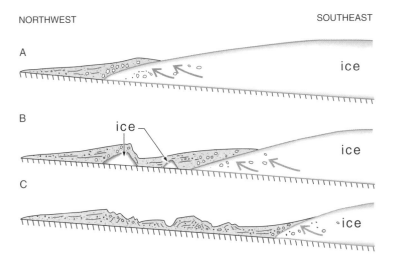

Stair stepped moraines and outwash plains formed along the west side of the Green Bay lowland as the Green Bay Lobe receded to the east.

Between Hatley and Wittenberg, Wisconsin 29 crosses a number of small moraines deposited by the eastward-receding margin of the Green Bay Lobe. Nearly flat, pitted outwash plains occur between the moraines, which are littered with large reddish boulders of Wolf River granite.

At Wittenberg and 7 miles east on County J just south and north of Wisconsin 29, a rare igneous rock called anorthosite is exposed. This unusual phase of the Wolf River complex is composed almost exclusively of plagioclase feldspar. Seven miles south of Wittenberg via U.S. 45 in Tigerton are some of the best accessible exposures of Wolf River granites. Between Wittenberg and Tigerton there are spectacular large, rounded granite boulders 2 to 3 feet in diameter in the fields, which are like those just east of Ringle. At the north end of the bridge over the Embarrass River in Tigerton, there is a large exposure of coarse-grained granite, a more common phase of the complex than anorthosite. This granite is a peculiar type in which the large feldspar crystals have two different compositions. Their central cores are potassium feldspar, but the outer rims are a sodium feldspar. The composition of the granitic magma from which the rock crystallized changed as it rose up through the crust, presumably due to decreasing water pressure, which caused a marked change in chemical equilibrium within the magma. Some very coarse veins cut through the granite here. Two miles east on County M at scenic Tigerton Dells are additional picturesque exposures of the same coarse granite.

Between Wittenberg and Shawano, there are virtually no outcrops along Wisconsin 29, but two additional short side trips can remedy this deficiency. At Bowler, 5 miles north (via either County J or D), anorthosite is exposed at the high school athletic field. And 10 miles farther east at Gresham (4 miles north of Wisconsin 29 via County U and A), granite is exposed on the Red River at the south end of the County G bridge over the dam between upper and lower Red Lakes.

The hills between Wittenberg and Thornton are east-west-trending drumlins formed beneath the westward-flowing Green Bay Lobe. A number of small, north-south-trending recessional moraines cross this section of highway, but they are difficult to recognize without the aid of topographic maps and air photographs. The broad sand flats near Shawano are part of the floor of the northern arm of Glacial Lake Oshkosh.

At Shawano, Wisconsin 29 crosses the Wolf River, namesake to the Wolf River igneous complex. The route also crosses the concealed boundary between Precambrian bedrock to the west and Paleozoic strata to the east; only drilling reveals the exact position of this boundary. Between Shawano and Green Bay, the route is entirely on glacial materials with very few exposures of bedrock. About 4 miles east of Shawano, Wisconsin 29 rises onto a till-mantled bedrock upland with some poorly formed northeast-southwest-trending drumlins formed beneath the Green Bay Lobe.

Ordovician Prairie du Chien dolomite is quarried on some hills, for example 4 miles east of Shawano.

Between the intersection with County F and Angelica, Wisconsin 29 descends onto a low-relief area of sandy and silty lake sediment deposited on the floors of lakes that formed along the western margin of the Green Bay Lobe as it receded northeastward. Sand dunes are common on this lake plain. You can see small exposures of reddish brown lake sediment in farm fields and excavations. The highway crosses this lake plain to Green Bay. Just west of Duck Creek, the highway crosses a till upland with well-formed drumlins before descending back onto the lake plain at the intersection with U.S. 41. Also at Duck Creek is a very deep quarry in Ordovician limestone and dolomite.

DOOR PENINSULA

The Door Peninsula rivals the Baraboo-Dells region as Wisconsin's most popular tourist district. Picturesque villages such as Egg Harbor, Fish Creek, Ephraim, and Sister Bay nestled in harbors between bold headlands have long been compared to New England coastal retreats. Like much of the state, the peninsula first attracted lumbering interests, then agriculture (especially cherry growing), fishing, and shipbuilding; Sturgeon Bay was for many years a major shipbuilding center but that industry is declining. Tourism, however, has become the largest industry, at least for the northern half of the peninsula, which boasts no less than five state parks and more than ten county parks with scenic appeal.

How did this peninsula acquire such an odd name? Perhaps even in English the notion of a doorway to the state from the Great Lakes is obvious, but the name actually derives from the French *Porte des Morts*, the passage between the end of the peninsula and four offshore islands. This "Death's

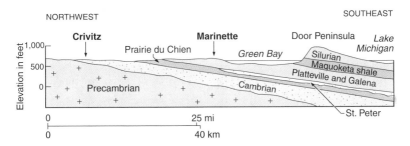

Section of the bedrock from U.S. 141 southeast across Green Bay and the Door Peninsula.

Typical fine lamination in Silurian dolomite on the Door Peninsula. Algal mats on tidal flats trapped thin layers of sediment. —R. H. Dott, Jr., photo

Door" was well named by the early French explorers, for its treacherous waters have claimed hundreds of vessels trying to enter or leave Green Bay.

The Peninsula reveals its bedrock heritage more clearly than does the main part of the Eastern Uplands to the south. It is an obvious segment of the great Niagara Escarpment, having for its backbone Silurian dolomite, which forms cliffs that loom almost 200 feet above water level on the west side of the peninsula. As to the south, the strata of the peninsula are tilted gently toward Lake Michigan. Precambrian rocks 2,000 feet beneath the peninsula are 16,000 feet deep beneath the center of Michigan.

The Ordovician Maquoketa shale underlies Green Bay; a lobe of the Wisconsin continental glacier was able to gouge out a long depression from this soft rock. The top of the Maquoketa is visible along the northwestern margin of the peninsula. The shale is inclined downward to the southeast beneath the more resistant Silurian strata that form the backbone of the peninsula. Because of the eastward-dipping strata, the western side of the peninsula is higher and has the most precipitous scenery. Cobbles of dolomite cover the beaches here, whereas sandy beaches line much of the topographically lower Lake Michigan side. The Silurian strata are similar to those all the way south into Illinois, but in the peninsula fossils are less common and reefs are rare. The dolomites of Door County and adjacent northern Michigan were deposited in very shallow, ocean-margin environments lying northwest of the reef belt of southeastern Wisconsin. There are scattered fossil-rich layers.

The upland of the Door Peninsula is the divide between the Green Bay–Fox River lowland to the west and the Lake Michigan basin to the east. Although the eastward-dipping strata underlying the Niagara Escarpment control the overall shape of the Door Peninsula, Quaternary glaciations molded the landscape we see today. Because the deposits of several early Wisconsin ice sheets exist far to the south, in the southwestern part of the Eastern Uplands of Wisconsin and in Illinois and Indiana, those glaciers must have covered the Door Peninsula and played a role in shaping the bedrock surface. However, no evidence for those early glaciations survives on the peninsula. Although the Door Peninsula lay near the junction of the late Wisconsin Green Bay and Lake Michigan Lobes, the orientation of drumlins, scratches on bedrock, and other indicators of ice-flow direction show that it was the Green Bay Lobe that shaped the glacial landscape here.

Although solution features are common in areas of dolomite in Wisconsin, they are especially well expressed on the Door Peninsula, where the cover of glacial materials is very thin. Dolomite, like its cousin limestone, can be slowly dissolved by slightly acidic water. Over time, such water moving through preexisting fractures in the dolomite widens the openings, forming caves. Sinkholes occur where the solution of dolomite undermines near-surface rock or glacial sediment. When the undermining gets too close to the surface, the thin cap over the void collapses. Solution features such as caves and sinkholes are collectively called *karst*. Geologists have mapped hundreds of karst features on the Door Peninsula north of Sturgeon Bay. For the most part these are quite small. The most pervasive impact of karst on the Door County landscape may be the pattern of the valleys. All the major ones on the peninsula have trends similar to the orientation of the dominant fractures in the dolomite. These valleys have been widened and deepened over a very long period of time by the dissolving of dolomite and by glacial and river erosion.

It is not uncommon for landowners to contact geologists to learn why a hole has suddenly appeared in a cornfield or backyard. The most serious impact karst has on humans on the Door Peninsula concerns the quality of water from wells. Solution-widened fractures in the dolomite allow groundwater to move very rapidly under some circumstances. A septic system, an area where farm animals are concentrated, or a parking lot, if placed over a solution-widened fracture, may contaminate water moving hundreds to thousands of feet through the ground in only a few days to a place where it is pumped from a well.

Wisconsin 42
Manitowoc—Sturgeon Bay
62 miles (100 km)

Although commercial fishing and shipbuilding in Manitowoc have declined from past greatness, it is still a significant Lake Michigan port. It is also the western terminus for ferry service across Lake Michigan to Ludington, Michigan.

Between Manitowoc and Two Rivers, Wisconsin 42 follows the lakeshore closely, but it is well above lake level. Several waysides provide excellent views. Just north of Manitowoc near the Little Manitowoc River crossing, the highway descends below 600 feet to the lake plain deposited near the shore of Lake Nipissing, a higher-level, postglacial ancestor of Lake Michigan. It existed about 5,000 years ago, and its highest shoreline is at about 600 feet in elevation, about 20 feet above modern Lake Michigan.

At Two Rivers the East Twin and West Twin Rivers flow into Lake Michigan. The East Twin River occupies a channel that formed along the margin of the ice. The West Twin River is in the eastern part of the Neshota–West Twin outlet of Glacial Lake Oshkosh. Water from that lake spilled eastward through this outlet, across the drainage divide formed by the Niagara Escarpment, and into the Lake Michigan basin.

North of Two Rivers, Wisconsin 42 is inland; a more scenic lakeshore route is via County O and V through Point Beach State Forest, which has interesting sandy shoreline features, a bathing beach, and a historic lighthouse. A series of about thirty parallel ridges several feet high and composed of dune and beach sand alternate with narrow swampy swales. These formed over a period of several thousand years as lake level dropped from the Nipissing position of about 600 feet (about 5,000 years ago) to the modern average level of Lake Michigan at 580 feet above sea level. As the level dropped, the shoreline in this area was pushed lakeward by sedimentation, but this process proceeded in fits and starts as indicated by the ridge-swale pairs. Two loop trails provide access to the ridges and swales. As you leave the state forest you will cross the ridges, then a broad wetland up to a half mile or more wide. The rise at the west side of this wetland is the beach formed during the highest level of Lake Nipissing.

North of Point Beach State Forest, Wisconsin 42 rises onto a gently rolling till upland. Just north of the Point Beach Nuclear Power Plant at the Manitowoc-Kewaunee County line, the highway intersects County BB to the west. Directly east of this intersection is a small gravel parking lot. A trail provides access to the bluffs above the lakeshore and, if you are lucky, an exposure of the Two Creeks Forest Bed, the buried remnants of a prehistoric spruce forest. Look for logs, in-place stumps, and the organic layer

Beach ridges at Point Beach State Forest were former shorelines of Lake Nipissing. —U.S. Department of Agriculture photo

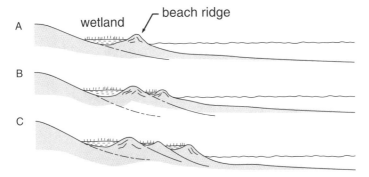

A series of beach ridges form as water level falls.

of the forest floor in the upper part of the bluff. The access to the bluff is not easy. In recent years, because Lake Michigan has been low, the bluffs are badly slumped and it is difficult to see the forest bed. Another, better access is Two Creeks County Park about one and a half miles to the south via Two Creeks Road. Here, a good parking area provides easy access to the beach and bluffs, but it is a longer walk to the site.

A spruce forest grew here as the ice receded from the area. It grew for about 250 years, beginning about 12,000 years ago. At that time, the Lake Michigan Lobe had receded far enough north to allow Lake Michigan to drain through the Straits of Mackinac into Lake Huron. The ice then readvanced, and by about 11,750 years ago, it blocked the northern outlet of the basin, causing the lake level to rise and submerge the forest. The forest was first covered with lake sediment and later with till when the advancing ice reached this area.

Wisconsin 42 continues across a gently rolling till upland to Kewaunee. The Kewaunee River flows in a large, steep-walled valley that was cut when it was an outlet for Glacial Lake Oshkosh. About 5 miles north of Kewaunee at the intersection with County D, the highway passes to the east of the Alaska Lakes, which are kettle lakes formed where ice buried in till-covered outwash melted.

Two Creeks Forest Bed (dark band) *is a layer of organic debris. Silty lake sediment encases the stump of a spruce tree still in place.* **Inset:** *Closeup of stump.* —J. W. Attig photo

The road continues across gently rolling till upland before descending to near the shoreline of the Nipissing phase of Lake Michigan near the wayside park 3 miles south of Algoma. The highway then rises back onto the till upland before descending into Algoma. Downtown Algoma is on a bar deposited across the mouth of a bay along the Nipissing shore. The Ahnapee River at Algoma was also an outlet for Glacial Lake Oshkosh. Here, Wisconsin 42 turns inland and follows along the scenic east side of the Ahnapee Valley for several miles before rising onto a till upland and entering Door County. The Ahnapee State Trail, a segment of the Ice Age National Scenic Trail, from Algoma to Potawatomi State Park, follows the floor of the valley for several miles north of Algoma.

From the Door County line northward to Sturgeon Bay, Wisconsin 42 continues across a dolomite upland with a thin mantle of till. Low north-south-trending drumlins are present in some parts of this area.

Sturgeon Bay

Sturgeon Bay is the largest commercial center on the Door Peninsula and is the gateway to Door County's resort country. It used to be a major commercial fishing and lumber shipping center, but today sportfishing and boating are most important; it was once a major shipbuilding center, but this industry is much reduced. There is a Door County Maritime Museum in the city center. The bay itself was a preglacial valley that was eroded along northwest-southeast-trending fractures in the dolomite bedrock. The southeastern end of the valley near present Lake Michigan later became choked with dune sand and beach ridges formed at the shore of Lake Nipissing and possibly earlier postglacial lakes. To provide a shorter and safer shipping route from Lake Michigan to Green Bay, people took advantage of the old natural channel and reopened it to form the Sturgeon Bay Canal in 1878. Canal Road, a 3.5-mile drive southeast, follows the canal to Lake Michigan.

Potawatomi State Park

Three miles northwest of Sturgeon Bay is one of the two larger parks on the peninsula. It is accessible either from the west end of the bay bridge over city streets or from the Wisconsin 42/57 route at a point 2 miles west of Sturgeon Bay using County PD (Park Drive). Potawatomi State Park was named for a tribe of Native Americans who inhabited the Green Bay region. In the park, hardwood forests obscure cliffs of Silurian dolomite. A network of roads and trails provides access to several viewpoints; an observation tower at the north end of the park gives spectacular views northward to Green Bay and the mouth of Sturgeon Bay. Cabot Point, a spit at the east end of the peninsula, was formed by wave-driven currents that carried sand along the southeast margin of Green Bay and deposited it at the mouth of Sturgeon Bay.

In the cliffs at the north and east sides of the park, you can see small caves well above the water. About 11,000 years ago waves cut caves on the shore of Lake Algonquin, a high pre-Nipissing phase of Lake Michigan. A series of Lake Algonquin shorelines, up to 60 feet above Lake Michigan, are present in the area. Beaches formed at the shore of Lake Nipissing occur up to 20 feet above the modern lake level. The Nipissing beaches are nearly horizontal, but the older Lake Algonquin beaches rise northward. The older the shoreline is, the more differential rebound of the earth's crust following deglaciation has raised it.

Across Sturgeon Bay to the northeast, a very large, abandoned quarry is visible from Potawatomi State Park. This quarry is now Olde Stone Quarry County Park accessible 5 miles north from downtown Sturgeon Bay via County B. Originally known as the Leathem and Smith Quarry, Silurian dolomite was quarried here beginning in 1893. At first it provided large blocks of stone for building harbor structures around Lake Michigan, but as the demand grew for crushed stone for roads and railroads, and for concrete, the emphasis changed. The quarry's location at lake level in a protected place made it ideal for loading the stone into barges. Today, the site is a favorite boat launch and fishing site and provides geologists a good place to study the Silurian bedrock.

Wisconsin 42
Sturgeon Bay—Porte des Morts
48 miles (76 km)

North of Sturgeon Bay, Wisconsin 42 passes over flat farmland for 17 miles to Egg Harbor. The uplands between Sturgeon Bay and Egg Harbor are dolomite with a thin, patchy cover of glacial till.

All the way to the tip of the peninsula, many roadcuts expose Silurian dolomite and the bays at the north end of the peninsula have impressive cliffs of the same rock. Egg Harbor is the first of several resort villages along the Green Bay shore. County G crosses an impressively large gravel bar, or beach ridge, at the head of Egg Harbor. This bar, which is composed of well-rounded pebbles and cobbles of dolomite up to 6 inches in diameter, was built on the shore of either Lake Nipissing or Lake Algonquin.

From Egg Harbor to Fish Creek, abundant outcrops of dolomite attest to the thinness of the Quaternary glacial sediment. The village of Fish Creek is on a wave-cut bench formed by Lake Nipissing and possibly earlier lake phases. The prominent Lake Nipissing shoreline is recognizable through-out this area about 20 feet above modern lake level.

Peninsula State Park

Peninsula State Park, one of the three oldest parks in Wisconsin, has 3,700 acres of forest with a mix of conifers and northern hardwood species, such as beech, maple, and birch. The main park entrance is just east of Fish Creek. A nature center, nature trails, and a restored 1868 lighthouse on Eagle Bluff are open to the public. A network of roads and trails provide access to the most interesting features and many good viewpoints of the Niagara Escarpment and Green Bay. Here, the escarpment rises about 150 feet above bay level. Imposing dolomite cliffs overlook the lake, especially on the northern and eastern sides. As at Potawatomi State Park, caves eroded by waves during past, higher lake levels are visible in the cliffs 20 to 30 feet above present water level. As is typical of the Green Bay side of Door Peninsula, the beaches are composed mostly of rounded dolomite cobbles rather than sand.

Waves of former Lake Michigan phases cut this cave in the Silurian dolomite of Eagle Bluff in Peninsula State Park. —Photo courtesy of the Wisconsin Department of Natural Resources

Clockwise around the park along Skyline Drive, Sven's Bluff Overlook provides excellent views toward the north and west. Notice the "steps" in the bedrock headland to the north, which are wave-cut benches formed by late glacial and postglacial lake levels. On a clear day, you can see the Upper Peninsula of Michigan to the northwest. An interpretive sign at a viewpoint about 1.5 miles farther east explains the modern movement of water in Lake Michigan. At this and some other overlooks, you can see fossils in stone walls and walkways. On the east side of the park, 75-foot-high Eagle Tower provides spectacular panoramic views to the north and east, especially of Eagle Harbor, one of the most protected harbors on the peninsula. You can see ripple marks and animal burrows in stone walls and walkways near the tower. Eagle Terrace just south of the tower is the site of an abandoned quarry in dolomite.

The east park entrance/exit road emerges through a golf course to connect again with Wisconsin 42 at the edge of Eagle Harbor. Inland from here, a large swamp occupies a preglacial valley, of which the harbor is a drowned extension. The village of Ephraim fronts on Eagle Harbor on a broad Nipissing-level terrace. From Ephraim, the highway rises back onto the

Typical beach of dolomite cobbles on the west shore of the Door Peninsula. —J. W. Attig photo

dolomite upland before descending to Sister Bay. There are several well-developed beach ridges in the area. Some were the site of classic studies during the 1930s of the geology of pebble beaches. The most pronounced is a beach ridge of the Nipissing level about 20 feet above the modern lake. Other higher, older beaches likely formed along the shore of Lake Algonquin.

Ellison Bay to Porte des Morts

North of Sister Bay, Wisconsin 42 rises back onto the dolomite upland to Ellison Bay. Ellison Bluff Scenic Overlook 2 miles west of Ellison Bay provides spectacular views of cliffs facing Green Bay. Access is well signed from 1 mile southwest of the town via Porcupine Bay Road. Between Ellison Bay and Gills Rock, the highway turns inland for about 5 miles, but a side trip to Door Bluff County Park on Deathdoor Bluff headland is worthwhile. Follow Garrett Bay Road 2.5 miles north from Ellison Bay. Deathdoor Bluff is the western end of the navigational passage through Death's Door or Porte des Morts. Waves of the late glacial and postglacial lakes cut the steps in the bluffs and headlands that you can see from the park.

At Ellison Bay is the Clearing, a retreat built by the pioneer landscape architect and conservation visionary, Jens Jensen. Door County reminded Jensen of his native Denmark, and he worked to protect the Ridges Sanctuary and other sites. His innovative use of native plants in naturalistic gardens complemented the new "organic architecture" of Frank Lloyd Wright. In 1935 Jensen established a school here to promote conservation philosophy.

Wisconsin 42 leads to Gills Rock, the northernmost village on the peninsula. Tour boats provide trips to various offshore islands from here. The highway continues for 2 more miles to Northport, where a car ferry operates across the Porte des Morts to Washington Island, 5 miles northeast.

Newport State Park

East of Ellison Bay 2.5 miles, County NP (Newport Road) leads 3 miles to Newport State Park on the tip of the Door Peninsula. This wilderness park has great variety—rocky headlands, coves, sandy beaches, second-growth forests, wetlands, and a network of trails. Just west of the entrance, grass covers old sand dunes.

Native Americans first lived here and the French traders undoubtedly passed by in the late 1600s. It was not until the 1880s, however, that Europeans settled and built a thriving sawmill with a pier for loading lumber. As in most of northern Wisconsin, by 1915, the forests had been cut. A Chicagoan named Ferdinand Hotz bought this property in 1919 for a retreat for family and friends. He built a handsome log house and other supporting facilities, and for half a century, the Hotz family nursed the property back to health from the lumbering disaster. The state purchased the land for a park in 1966.

The geology of Newport State Park is dramatically different from the west shore of the peninsula. Here, the beaches are sandy rather than cobbled, and outcrops of dolomite are few. Gone also are the high bluffs. Europe Lake at the northern end of the park must have been part of a larger bay before sand dunes and beach ridges formed along the shore of Lake Nipissing and cut the bay in two.

THE ISLANDS

Washington, the largest of the offshore islands, has a substantial population, especially in the summer. It is served by passenger and car ferries from Northport and a passenger ferry from Gills Rock. Much of the perimeter of the island is composed of low cliffs of Silurian dolomite, but most of the land is privately owned so access to these is limited. Percy Johnson County Park on the east shore has some richly fossiliferous ledges at the south end of a sand beach. There is also public access to sand dunes and a beach on the southeast shore as well as access to Schoolhouse Beach, composed of rounded cobbles of dolomite, on the north shore.

Aerial view of Rock Island looking northeast. Islands in the distance are in Michigan. —Photo courtesy of the Wisconsin Department of Natural Resources

During the summer, passenger ferry service is available from Washington Island to Rock Island. This outermost of Wisconsin's islands is now a wilderness state park, and it lives up to its name, being encircled with dolomite cliffs except for sand dunes and a beach on the eastern side. Potawatomi Light on the north end is the state's oldest lighthouse (1836). From 1910 to 1945, Rock Island was owned by Icelandic immigrant Chester Thordarson, who was a Chicago inventor and manufacturing genius. He bought Rock Island because it reminded him of his native Iceland. He then built Viking House of local stone in an Icelandic style, which took twenty masons three years to complete. It is now the park visitor center. The island served as a vacation retreat for his family, his company's employees, and many friends. Thordarson, who had only a seventh-grade formal education, began collecting books as a young man and accumulated a library of eleven thousand volumes of valuable, rare pieces, which he kept in his Rock Island mansion. When he died in 1945, the University of Wisconsin purchased the library and in 1964 the entire island became Rock Island State Park.

Thin till covers the dolomite bedrock in the higher portions of both islands, but there are also extensive areas of sandy beach and nearshore lake sediments deposited during higher late glacial and postglacial lake levels.

Wisconsin 57
Green Bay—Sister Bay
76 miles (122 km)

From the northeast edge of Green Bay, Wisconsin 57 ascends the Niagara Escarpment, but the highway was built through an embayment so the slope is gentle. Atop the dolomite escarpment, the landscape is gently rolling with a thin cover of reddish brown, silty till. The first point of geologic interest is at Wequiock Falls Wayside, 6 miles from I-43 on the west side of Wisconsin 57, where you can view the oldest strata exposed on the Door Peninsula, the Maquoketa shale. A 20-foot-high waterfall exposes the contact between a few feet of resistant Silurian Mayville dolomite and the underlying Ordovician shale. Steps and a path lead from the west side of the wayside to the falls. The Silurian strata here are the same early Silurian age as those at High Cliffs State Park and Neda in the Eastern Uplands to the south.

Six miles farther north is a wayside with a historical marker on top of a precipice of lower Silurian dolomite 20 to 30 feet high, which overlooks Green Bay. There is a statue of the French explorer, Jean Nicolet, who was the first European to set foot in Wisconsin. He did so in 1634, one mile west of this point at Red Cliffs. The base for the statue as well as the sur-rounding low walls are made of slabs of local Silurian dolomite.

Three miles farther northeast is Bayshore County Park, which exposes about 50 feet of lower Silurian dolomite along a steep road down to a boat landing and a stony beach. The Maquoketa shale at the base of the cliff is obscured by rock talus and vegetation.

North of Bayshore County Park for several miles, there are many good views of Green Bay. Two miles north of Dyckesville is Red River County Park a short distance west of the highway. A ridge in the field just north of this park is an excellent example of a beach ridge formed at the shore of Lake Nipissing, a higher phase of Lake Michigan. A few miles farther on, the highway turns inland and passes through the village of Brussels, an old Belgian settlement as the name implies. Two miles east of the village, the wooded Brussels Hill rises nearly 100 feet above otherwise flat farmland where cherry orchards once were plentiful. The southward-flowing Green Bay Lobe sculpted this and other bedrock hills in this area. The Silurian dolomite is exposed in the roadside.

Near the junction with County K, where there is a wayside, Wisconsin 57 crosses the Ahnapee River. The valley this river flows in today was a late outlet for Glacial Lake Oshkosh; water spilled across the peninsula into the Lake Michigan basin. The till covering the dolomite in this area is only a few feet thick.

About 3 miles farther northeast is a junction with Wisconsin 42 from the south. Sturgeon Bay and Potawatomi State Park are described in **Wisconsin 42: Manitowoc—Sturgeon Bay**.

Three miles northeast of Sturgeon Bay, Wisconsin 57 departs from Wisconsin 42 for the southeast side of the Door Peninsula. Though not so high and rocky as the Green Bay side, there are several areas of scenic and geologic interest. The 14 miles to Jacksonport on Lake Michigan are over flat, agricultural land with thin till on dolomite. The valleys trend northwest-southeast, paralleling a prominent fracture pattern in the dolomite. A wayside rest area near Jacksonport has a spectacular outcrop of coral-rich dolomite in a cliff about 6 feet high.

Whitefish Dunes State Park and Cave Point County Park

You can reach Whitefish Dunes State Park by either of two side routes from Wisconsin 57. The more scenic alternative is County T directly east from Sturgeon Bay, and then northeast along the Lake Michigan shore to Whitefish Bay, where you turn north on Nelson Road to Clark Lake Road. The faster alternative is to continue on Wisconsin 57 for 1 mile northeast of Valmy, and then turn east on Clark Lake Road, which leads 2 miles to the park. As the name implies, this state park features coastal dunes fronted by

Silurian dolomite at Cave Point County Park. —J. W. Attig photo

a long, sandy bathing beach. A rocky headland 10 to 20 feet high of Silurian dolomite forms the northern edge of the park and the adjacent Cave Point County Park. A few fossils are visible in the dolomite, which is a bit younger than that on the opposite side of the peninsula. It is equivalent to the strata around Milwaukee and Racine. You can see coral colonies resembling saucers about 1 foot in diameter near lake level on the shore just north of Cave Point.

A visitor center has a small museum that tells of the area's earliest inhabitants from around 100 B.C., about the wildlife of the park, and a little about its geology. A trail network includes the Brachiopod Nature Trail, which begins in front of one of the picnic shelters at a small monument built of specimens of different Silurian fossils from the peninsula, including a large and distinctive brachiopod named *Pentamerus*. Clark Lake, inland from Whitefish Dunes, is a former large bay that was cut off from Lake Michigan by beach and dune deposits of the Nipissing postglacial lake level.

Jacksonport to Sister Bay

Where Wisconsin 57 comes to the lakeshore about one-half mile south of Jacksonport, near the intersection with Cave Point Drive, the highway drops below 600 feet onto the lake plain deposited in Lake Nipissing. There is a well-developed Nipissing beach ridge and dune complex to the west of the highway. Jacksonport was originally a major lumber shipping point. A few miles to the north, the highway passes Kangaroo Lake. Like Clark Lake, this originated as a valley deepened and widened by glaciation, then became a long bay as the ice retreated, and finally was isolated by beach ridges and sand dunes probably formed at the Nipissing lake level. North of Heins Creek, the outlet from Kangaroo Lake, the highway rises onto an area with thin till on dolomite, which continues to Baileys Harbor.

Baileys Harbor is the most important tourist center on the southeast side of the Door Peninsula. In the town center, a fine building made of Silurian dolomite serves as town hall, library, and information center. The harbor here, together with Moonlight (or Mud) Bay, North Bay, and Rowley Bay farther north, were valleys enlarged by glaciation. Extensions of them can be traced offshore on the lake bottom. At the head of Baileys Harbor,

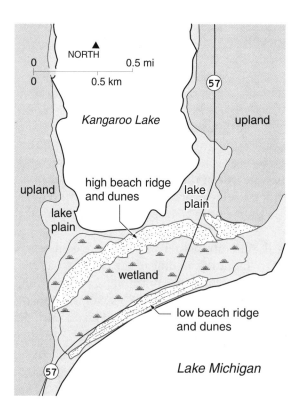

Water collects in a low area behind a beach ridge and dunes of the Nipissing lake level, forming Kangaroo Lake.

Cliffs of Silurian dolomite on the Lake Michigan shore near Cave Point on the Door Peninsula. —Photo courtesy of the Wisconsin Department of Natural Resources.

the Ridges Sanctuary encompasses about two dozen alternating, parallel, low sand ridges and swampy swales like those at Point Beach 60 miles to the south (and at Zion, Illinois, just south of the Wisconsin border). These ridges were beaches formed as Lake Michigan dropped from the Nipissing lake level at about 600 feet to the modern elevation of about 580 feet. A walk through the Ridges allows you to see vegetation that is more characteristic of the Canadian boreal forest than of Wisconsin. At the nature center, many Silurian fossils occur in stones rimming a small garden.

Half a mile east of the town center along the shore is a county parking lot and sandy beach. An old navigation light stands by the road near this park at one of the trail entrances into the Ridges. A side trip on County Q to the northeast takes you past the main entrance to the Ridges Sanctuary and its nature center. The route continues around Moonlight Bay, with an option to turn off to see Cana Lighthouse on a low island of dolomite.

North of Baileys Harbor, Wisconsin 57 crosses extensive wetlands with higher areas of old beach ridges and sand dunes. For the 4 miles south of Sister Bay, the road crosses an upland of till-mantled dolomite. This highway ends at Sister Bay.

GLOSSARY

amphibolite. A metamorphic rock composed almost entirely of black amphibole minerals. Commonly formed by metamorphism of an igneous rock like basalt, which is rich in iron, magnesium, calcium, and silica.

anticline. A fold in which layered rocks have been bowed upward, producing an archlike profile.

arthropod. The largest phylum of animals, which includes crabs, lobsters, and fossil trilobites. Arthropods have a segmented external skeleton and jointed legs.

banded iron formation. A Precambrian rock with alternating iron-rich and iron-poor bands averaging about one-quarter inch thick. The world's principal iron ore.

basalt. A dark, fine-grained volcanic igneous rock composed of calcium-rich feldspar and pyroxene minerals .

basin. A low area in the landscape where water may accumulate as a lake until it rises to the level of the lowest outlet. Also, a large-scale downwarping of the earth's crust in which relatively thick sequences of strata are deposited, such as the Michigan basin.

batholith. A large mass of granitic igneous rock with a surface area of several tens of square miles.

beach ridge. A ridge of sediment, usually sandy, that accumulates along the margin of a lake or ocean as a result of wave and wind action.

bed, bedding. Old quarrying terms for the stratification in sedimentary rocks.

bedrock. The hard rock at or near the surface of any region. Uncemented modern river, lake, glacial, or wind deposits and soil commonly conceal the bedrock.

boulder. A rock larger than 10 inches in diameter. Typically moved only by such vigorous agents as glaciers, flooding rivers, and gravity on steep slopes.

brachiopod. An invertebrate animal with two unequal shells, each of which is bilaterally symmetrical (unlike clam shells). Abundant and diverse until Cenozoic time with only a few living today.

braided river. A river whose floodplain is composed of many interconnected, shifting channels separated by coarse sand or gravel bars. Typical of rivers draining water from glaciers.

breccia. A rock made up of coarse, very angular fragments (unlike a conglomerate with rounded coarse fragments). May be sedimentary or due to crushing by faulting.

bryozoans. A group of invertebrate marine colonial animals that secrete calcareous skeletons with varied forms. Some colonies are branching, so resemble plants, with which bryozoans have often been confused.

cephalopod. A group of marine invertebrate animals with a head surrounded by tentacles and a well-developed eye. Modern examples include octopus and squid without shells, but fossil examples had either straight or coiled external shells.

chert or flint. A very fine-grained rock composed entirely of silica. It is a chemical deposit found primarily as nodules precipitated from pore waters percolating through limey sediments after deposition, but it can also be precipitated directly on the seafloor where unusual amounts of silica are dissolved in seawater, as near volcanic vents.

clay. A group of very fine-grained minerals composed chiefly of aluminum and silica. The term *clay* is also used to describe very fine particles of other minerals. Clay is so fine that it does not feel gritty when rubbed between the fingers.

claystone. A fine-grained sedimentary rock composed mostly of clay minerals but lacking the fine layering typical of shale.

cleavage. The tendency of either a mineral or a rock to split along closely spaced planes. Mineral cleavage is related to crystal structure, but rock cleavage is the result of stress during deformation of rocks.

cobble. A coarse fragment of rock between 2.5 and 10 inches in diameter. Cobbles are commonly, but not necessarily, somewhat rounded by abrasion.

collapsed outwash. Outwash deposited on top of glacial ice. When the ice beneath eventually melts, the outwash collapses to form an irregular surface.

conglomerate. A coarse sedimentary rock made up of pebbles, cobbles, and/or boulders eroded from some older rock or rocks. The large size implies a vigorous process of deposition, such as a mountain stream or outwash stream from a melting glacier.

conodont. Microscopic marine fossils thought to be mouth parts of extinct, swimming wormlike animals; these evolved rapidly, so conodonts are useful for correlating ancient strata.

coral. Marine, bottom-dwelling, mostly colonial animals that secrete an external skeleton composed of calcium carbonate. Their skeletons form major components of modern and ancient reefs.

crinoid. A marine invertebrate animal resembling a plant because its skeleton consists of a cup containing the vital organs mounted on a stem with roots attached to the sea bottom. Arms radiating from the top of the cup gather food from the water. These skeletal parts are composed of calcareous plates encased within the animal's body.

crossbedding. Laminations in sand or sandstone that are inclined about 30 degrees to the main bedding, or stratification. These inclined laminae represent fossil lee faces of dunes or ripples, and they are inclined in the direction of flow of wind or water currents.

crust (of the earth). The outer shell of the solid earth, which is 20 to 30 miles thick beneath continents and only about 3 miles under oceans. Continental crust has an average composition close to granite, whereas oceanic crust consists of basalt.

dike. A tabular body of igneous rock that cuts across the structure of the older, adjacent rock into which it was intruded as fluid magma.

dolomite. A sedimentary rock closely akin to limestone but with magnesium as well as calcium carbonate ($CaMg (CO_3)_2$). Typically forms by the alteration of limestone through the addition of some magnesium from pore fluids migrating through the limestone after burial.

dome. A broad, roughly circular upfold with strata dipping in all directions. The term is generally applied to large features that may underlie much of a state, as with the Wisconsin dome.

Driftless Area. The area of southwestern Wisconsin and adjacent parts of Illinois, Iowa, and Minnesota that was not covered by the Quaternary glaciers.

drumlin. An elongate, streamlined hill shaped by erosion and deposition beneath a glacier. The long dimension of a drumlin is parallel to the direction of ice flow.

dune. A mound or ridge of sand deposited by either flowing wind or water. Dunes vary from a foot or so to many tens of feet high. Dunes migrate downcurrent.

erosion. A general term for several processes that loosen, dissolve, or wear and then transport earth materials and thus wear away landscapes.

erratic. A glacially transported rock of a type that originated from an area different from where it is now.

escarpment. The steep face of a ridge or plateau from which the land drops abruptly to a lower level.

esker. A ridge, commonly sinuous in pattern, composed of sand and gravel that was deposited by a stream that flowed in an ice-walled channel beneath a glacier.

fault. A fracture along which there has been displacement of the rocks on either side. The movement might be measured in inches or miles.

feldspar. A group comprising the most abundant rock-forming minerals. They are divided between potassium-bearing feldspars and calcium- and sodium-bearing plagioclase feldspars. They are especially characteristic of igneous rocks.

flagstone. Any rock that splits readily into even, tabular slabs suitable for walkways, patios, and the like.

flint. See **chert**.

fossil. Any remains or traces of animals or plants preserved in sediments or sedimentary rocks. Besides actual skeletons, shells, or petrified wood, impressions, tracks, and burrows are also fossils.

gabbro. A dark, coarse-grained igneous rock composed mostly of calcium plagioclase feldspar and pyroxene.

galena. A mineral composed of lead and sulfur. It is the principal ore of lead. It occurs typically in cube-shaped crystals with a shiny metallic gray color. It is the state mineral of Wisconsin because of its importance to early mining in the state.

glacial flour. A common term for the silt-size particles commonly produced by glacial erosion. The abundance of glacial flour gives outwash rivers their characteristic milky appearance.

glacial sediment. A general term for unsorted sediment deposited beneath a flowing glacier or from melting, debris-rich ice.

glacier. A mass of ice that persists from year to year and shows evidence of flowing away from its center of accumulation under the influence of gravity.

glauconite. A green, iron and potassium silicate mineral related to the micas. It forms by alteration of clay or mica minerals in areas of the seafloor where sediment deposition is very slow.

gneiss. A coarse-grained metamorphic rock with a banded texture due to slight concentrations of darker minerals in bands alternating with lighter bands. It forms by the metamorphism of igneous rocks such as granite.

granite. Coarse-grained, light-colored igneous rock composed chiefly of quartz and potassium feldspar. **Granitic** refers to a broader range of composition such that the mineral plagioclase feldspar may also be present.

gravel. Loose, coarse fragments larger than about $1/12$ inch that have been at least somewhat abraded. Gravel includes pebbles, cobbles, and boulders. A rock composed of such material is a **conglomerate** (if the fragments were angular, the rock would be called a **breccia**).

graywacke. An impure, poorly sorted, usually dark-colored sandstone composed of grains of mixed composition (as opposed to a pure quartz sandstone).

greensand. A fine-grained sandstone containing an abundance of the green mineral glauconite.

gypsum. A mineral or rock composed of calcium sulfate ($CaSO_4$) that is formed by the evaporation of water (thus an evaporite rock). It is the ingredient of plaster and of school chalk.

horst. An elongated mass of rock that was uplifted along faults on either side.

hummocky lamination. Fine laminations with a broad wavy or undulatory pattern. It occurs in some fine sandstone strata and probably formed by deposition from storm waves.

hummocky topography. Hilly, irregular glacial topography with many lakes and wetlands. See pages 53, 54, and 282 for diagrams of its formation.

ice age. A time of extensive continental-scale glacial activity.

ice lobe. An elongate, rounded projection of the edge of a glacier. The shape of an ice lobe is controlled by the shape of the land surface over which it flows.

ice margin. The area near the margin of a glacier.

ice sheet. A large, thick glacier that spreads outward from a central area.

ice wedge. Silt or sand occupying the space formerly filled by a wedge-shaped mass of ice that froze in ground cracks under permafrost conditions.

igneous. Rocks that crystallized from molten magma.

intrusive. Rocks that have penetrated through other rocks. Most examples are igneous intrusions into older igneous or sedimentary rocks.

iron range. An area of banded iron formation within a region of Precambrian rocks.

kettle. A pot-shaped depression formed where buried ice melted, causing the overlying sediment to collapse.

kimberlite. A variety of peridotite, a dark igneous rock, rich in minerals such as olivine and pyroxene, that has been intruded from the mantle up into the crust. Kimberlite is the source of diamond, the high-pressure form of carbon, which is stable at the high pressures in the mantle.

lake plain. A nearly flat surface formed by sedimentation and wave action in a former lake.

Laurentide Ice Sheet. The most recent ice sheet to cover northeastern and north-central North America. Named for the Laurentian Highlands of northeastern Canada.

lava. Melted rock or magma that has erupted at the earth's surface.

limestone. A sedimentary rock composed of calcium carbonate ($CaCO_3$); commonly composed largely of calcareous skeletons of invertebrate fossils.

lithosphere plates. Large, rigid units of the outer zone of the earth (60 to 150 miles thick) that are capped by continental and/or oceanic crust. These plates are defined by the earth's major earthquake zones at their margins and are moving slowly over the pliable mantle beneath.

loess. Windblown, silt-size dust derived mostly from the glacial flour carried by outwash rivers. It typically forms a cover over the landscape that thins with distance downwind from braided outwash rivers.

magma. Molten rock; termed **lava** where it erupts to the surface of the earth.

mammoth. Large, elephant-like, tusked mammal with a high, foreshortened skull. Tusks were long and strongly curved. Now extinct, but widely distributed during the Quaternary Ice Age. Its flat-crowned teeth were adapted for grazing, so its preferred habitat was tundra grasslands.

mantle. The largest division of the earth's interior (80 percent), which lies between the lithosphere and the very dense core. It is rich in iron, magnesium, and calcium.

mastodon. Large, elephant-like, tusked mammal. Now extinct but widely distributed during the Quaternary Ice Age. Preferred habitat was open spruce woodlands. Mastodon means "nipple tooth," describing the pattern of tooth cusps, which were adapted for browsing in forest and brush lands.

metamorphic. Minerals and rocks that have been changed by heat and/or pressure so that their mineral compositions and/or textures have been modified. Examples are the metamorphism of shale to slate and sandstone to quartzite.

moraine. A ridge of sediment that accumulated along the margin of a glacier. Moraines mark places where the margin of a glacier stood for some period of time.

mound. A term used widely in Wisconsin since European settlement for any prominent hill that stands high above its surroundings.

Niagara Escarpment. A prominent ridge of Silurian dolomite extending from southeastern Wisconsin northward through the Door Peninsula, northeast across northern Michigan, then southeast across Ontario to Niagara Falls, New York.

oolite. Sedimentary rock of limestone composition consisting of spheres approximately 1 millimeter in diameter, which are composed of microscopic, onionlike layers. Grains agitated in very shallow, supersaturated water act as nuclei for precipitation of calcium carbonate.

ostracods. Microscopic arthropods with tiny protective shells of varying shapes and ornamentation.

outlet. The lowest point on the rim of a lake basin where water from the lake can drain across a drainage divide.

outwash. The stratified sand and gravel deposited by a stream draining from a glacier.

outwash plain. The broad, nearly flat floodplains of braided rivers carrying water and sediment from a glacier.

outwash river. A river, typically braided, that carries water and sediment from a glacier.

pebble. A particle of rock between the size of sand and a cobble; that is, between about $1/12$ and 2.5 inches in diameter.

peridotite. A dark green or black igneous rock rich in olivine and pyroxene but lacking quartz and feldspar. It forms in the earth's mantle.

permafrost. A condition in which the temperature of rock, soil, or water beneath an area stays below the freezing point for many years.

pillow basalt. Ellipsoidal masses about 6 to 12 inches in diameter within a solidified lava rock; groups of them resemble a pile of pillows. This structure forms where lavas flow into water and are rapidly chilled.

pitted outwash plain. An outwash plain with a pockmarked appearance as a result of the melting of masses of buried glacial ice. The collapsed depressions are commonly called pits or kettles.

plate tectonics. A theory that most large-scale structures of the outer earth are formed by the relative movements of lithosphere plates. For example, mountains form where two plates collide; rifts form where two plates pull apart.

pothole. A cylindrical hole drilled by particles whirled in the bottom of a permanent eddy or whirlpool in a river.

pyroxene. A group of rock-forming minerals rich in iron, calcium, magnesium, and silica that occur in igneous and metamorphic rocks. Many, but not all pyroxene minerals are dark.

quartz. One of the most common minerals in the earth's crust, quartz is composed of silicon and oxygen (SiO_2). The most common variety is colorless and clear like glass.

quartzite. A sandstone metamorphosed by heat and/or pressure so that the rock breaks across the individual sand grains.

readvance. An expansion of a glacier following a period during which the glacier diminished in size.

rebound. Removal of the weight of a large ice sheet hundreds or thousands of feet thick allows the crust to rise or rebound after being depressed by that weight.

reef. Densely populated areas of the seafloor in which the calcareous skeletons of animals form mounds. Today, reefs develop in warm, shallow, well-lighted tropical waters that are unusually rich in nutrients and oxygen.

rhyolite. A light-colored, fine-grained volcanic rock containing quartz and potassium feldspar in the same proportions as a granite.

rift. Long, narrow zone of downfaulting due to stretching or pulling apart of the earth's crust.

ripple marks. Undulatory surface on loose, granular sand or fine gravel sculptured by either wind or water currents or water waves.

sand. Loose particles larger than silt and finer than gravel (a fraction of a millimeter to about $\frac{1}{12}$ inch in diameter).

schist. A medium to coarse metamorphic rock rich in platy minerals like mica that are oriented so as to produce a conspicuous leaflike layering in the rock.

serpentine. A soft, slippery rock composed of two or more magnesium-rich green minerals (including asbestos). Commonly formed from igneous rocks characteristic of the upper mantle and lower oceanic crust.

shale. An abundant, fine-grained sedimentary rock composed of soft clay minerals. Originally deposited as mud, compaction generally produces a characteristic flaky texture.

shatter cones. Clusters of nested, conically shaped broken zones in rocks formed by very high velocity impacts as by large meteorites striking the earth's surface.

shock metamorphism. Alteration of minerals by very high velocity impacts such as by large meteorites. Typically the atomic structure of a mineral is distorted in a distinctive manner by the intense pressure.

silt. Small particles of rock larger than clay but finer than sand. When rubbed between your fingers or teeth, silt feels slightly gritty. Glacial erosion produces much silt.

slate. A fine-grained metamorphosed shale with a well-developed cleavage; that is, smooth, parallel splitting surfaces, which formed in response to intense shear of the rock.

stratification. Layered structure formed during deposition of sedimentary and some volcanic rocks. The result is **strata**, or layers, of differing texture, composition, or color. Also called **bedding**.

stromatolite. Convex-up mound or columnar-shaped structures, primarily in limestones, formed by complex photosynthetic microbial communities whose mucous covering trapped very find sediment particles to produce a distinctive very fine lamination.

suture zone. Zone of collision between two lithosphere plates. Intensely compressed and sheared oceanic- and mantle-derived rocks such as serpentine characterize the zone.

syenite. A coarse-grained igneous rock resembling granite, but lacking quartz because its magma was deficient in silica.

syncline. A downbending of layered rocks such that the strata dip inward from each side (the opposite of an anticline).

talus. Angular rock fragments that accumulate at the base of a steep cliff.

terminal moraine. The outermost moraine deposited by the advance of a glacier.

tidal flats. Broad flat areas along coastlines across which seawater floods and ebbs with the rising and falling tide. Some are sandy while others are muddy according to the intensity of the tidal currents.

till. An unsorted mixture of rock fragments from clay to boulder size deposited at the base of a flowing glacier.

till plain. A gently undulating surface underlain by till. Drumlins are commonly present on till plains.

tonalite. A coarse igneous rock similar to granite but poorer in quartz and possessing calcium feldspar rather than potassium feldspar. (Also known as quartz diorite.)

trilobite. An extinct arthropod with an external calcareous skeleton and many appendages for swimming and walking. A distant ancestor of living arthropods such as the horseshoe crab.

tundra polygon. Surface expression of thermal cracking of the ground in areas of permafrost. Typically polygonal in shape.

unconformity. A break or gap in any sequence of strata that implies an interval either of no deposition or of erosion of strata before deposition began again.

weathering. General term for the physical and chemical processes that break down earth materials.

Wisconsin Glaciation. The most recent episode of continental glaciation in North America. It began about 90,000 years ago and ended in Wisconsin about 10,000 years ago. **Late Wisconsin** refers to the last part of the Wisconsin Glaciation, from about 26,000 to 10,000 years ago in Wisconsin.

ADDITIONAL READING

Attig, J. W., L. Clayton, K. I. Lange, and L. J. Maher. 1990. *The Ice Age Geology of Devils Lake State Park.* Madison: Wisconsin Geological and Natural History Survey Educational Series No. 35.

Clayton, L., and J. W. Attig. 1989. *Glacial Lake Wisconsin.* Boulder, Colo.: Geological Society of America Memoir No. 173.

Dalziel, I. W. D., and R. H. Dott, Jr. 1970. *Geology of the Baraboo District, Wisconsin.* Madison: Wisconsin Geological and Natural History Survey Information Circular No. 14.

LaBerge, G. L. 1994. *Geology of the Lake Superior Region.* Phoenix, Arizona: Geoscience Press.

Lange, K. I. 1989. *Ancient Rocks and Vanished Glaciers: A Natural History of Devil's Lake State Park, Wisconsin.* Madison: Wisconsin Department of Natural Resources.

Martin, L. 1965. *Physical Geography of Wisconsin.* Madison: University of Wisconsin Press. Reprinted in 2004 by the University of Wisconsin Press.

Mudrey, M. G., Jr., B. A. Brown, and J. K. Greenburg. 1982. *Bedrock Geologic Map of Wisconsin* (scale 1:1,000,000). Madison: Wisconsin Geological and Natural History Survey.

Nehm, R. H., and B. E. Bemis. 2002. *Common Paleozoic Fossils from Wisconsin.* Madison: Wisconsin Geological and Natural History Survey Educational Series No. 45.

Njaa, B. B., and F. M. Langlois. 1995. *When Door County, Wisconsin Was a Tropical Sea—Fossils of the Niagara Escarpment.* Newport State Park: Newport Wilderness Society.

Palmquist, J. C. 1989. *Wisconsin's Door Peninsula.* Appleton, Wisconsin: Perin Press.

Paull, R. K., and R. A. Paull. 1977. *Geology of Wisconsin and Upper Michigan.* Dubuque, Iowa: Kendall-Hunt.

Paull, R. K., and R. A. Paull. 1980. *Field Guide—Wisconsin and Upper Michigan.* Dubuque, Iowa: Kendall-Hunt.

Schultz, G. M. 1986. *Wisconsin's Foundations.* Dubuque, Iowa: Kendall-Hunt. Reprinted in 2004 by the University of Wisconsin Press.

Wisconsin Geological and Natural History Survey. 1976. *Glacial Deposits of Wisconsin* Map No. 10 (scale 1:500,000).

Wisconsin Geological and Natural History Survey. 2001. *Landscapes of Wisconsin* (scale 1:500,000).

For further information, the reader may consult the Wisconsin Geological and Natural History Survey at 3817 Mineral Point Road, Madison, Wisconsin 53705-5100, or its Web site at *www.uwex.edu/wgnhs/*. Also of possible interest are Web sites for the following agencies:

Wisconsin Department of Natural Resources, Bureau of Parks and Recreation (*www.dnr.state.wi.us/org/land/parks/*)

Wisconsin Department of Tourism (*www.travelwisconsin.com*)

Milwaukee Public Museum (*www.mpm.edu*)

Kenosha Public Museum (*www.kenoshapublicmuseum.org*)

Neville Museum in Green Bay (*www.nevillepublicmuseum.org*)

University of Wisconsin Geology Museum in Madison (*www.geology.wisc.edu/~museum*)

Wisconsin Ice Age Park and Trail Foundation (*www.iceagetrail.org*)

REFERENCES CITED

Ager, D. V. 1980. *The Nature of the Stratigraphical Record.* Second Edition. New York: John Wiley & Sons.

Attig, J. W., L. Clayton, K. I. Lange, and L. J. Maher. 1990. *The Ice Age Geology of Devils Lake State Park.* Madison: Wisconsin Geological and Natural History Survey Educational Series No. 35.

Attig, J. W., D. M. Mickelson, and L. Clayton. 1989. Late Wisconsin landform distribution and glacier-bed conditions in Wisconsin. *Sedimentary Geology* 62:399–405.

Brooks, W. B. 1880. *The Geology of Wisconsin.* Vol. 3.

Brown, B. A., L. Clayton, F. W. Madison, and T. J. Evans. 1983. *Three Billion Years of Geology: A Field Trip through the Archean, Proterozoic, Paleozoic and Pleistocene Geology of the Black River Falls Area of Wisconsin.* Madison: Wisconsin Geological and Natural History Survey Field Trip Guide Book No. 9.

Chamberlin, T. C. 1883. *Geology of Wisconsin—Survey of 1873–1879.* Vol. 1. Milwaukee: Commissioners of Public Printing.

Clayton, L. 2001. *Pleistocene Geology of Waukesha County, Wisconsin.* Madison: Wisconsin Geological and Natural History Survey Bulletin 99.

Clayton, L., and J. W. Attig. 1989. *Glacial Lake Wisconsin.* Boulder, Colo.: Geological Society of America Memoir 173.

Cordua, W. S. 1987. The Rock Elm Disturbance, Pierce County, Wisconsin. In *Field Trip Guidebook for the Upper Mississippi Valley, Minnesota, Iowa and Wisconsin.* Edited by N. Balaban. St. Paul: Minnesota Geological Survey Guidebook Series No. 15.

Cordua, W. S. 1989. Bedrock geology of the Dresser–St. Croix Falls area, Polk County, Wisconsin and Chisago County, Minnesota. *53rd Annual Tri-State Geological Field Conference Guidebook.*

Dalziel, I. W. D., and R. H. Dott, Jr. 1970. *Geology of the Baraboo District, Wisconsin.* Madison: Wisconsin Geological and Natural History Survey Information Circular No. 14.

Dott, R. H., Jr., and R. L. Batten. 1988. *Evolution of the Earth*. New York: McGraw-Hill.

Hansel, A. K., D. M. Mickelson, A. F. Schneider, and C. E. Larsen. 1985. Late Wisconsinan and Holocene history of the Lake Michigan basin. In *Quaternary Evolution of the Great Lakes* Edited by P. F. Karrow and P. E. Calkin, 39–54. Geological Association of Canada Special Paper 30.

Maas, R. S., L. J. Medaris, Jr., and W. R. Van Schmus. 1980. Penokean deformation in Central Wisconsin. In *Selected Studies of Archean Gneisses and Lower Proterozoic Rocks, Southern Canadian Shield* Edited by G. B. Morey and G. H. Hanson. Boulder, Colo.: Geological Society of America Special Paper 182.

Moore, R. C., C. G. Lalicker, and A. G. Fischer. 1952. *Invertebrate Fossils*. New York: McGraw-Hill.

Muir, J. 1965. *The Story of My Boyhood and Youth*. Madison: University of Wisconsin Press.

Ostergren, R. C., and T. R. Vale. 1997. *Wisconsin Land and Life*. Madison: University of Wisconsin Press.

Owen, D. D. 1840. *Report of a Geological Exploration of Part of Iowa, Wisconsin, and Illinois*. Washington, D.C.: U.S. Government Printing Office.

Priestly, T. M., and W. E. Smith. 1924. Excerpt from *The Outcrop*. Madison: University of Wisconsin Geology Club.

Sartz, R. S. 1977. Soil erosion in the Lake States Driftless Area—A historical perspective. *Transactions of the Wisconsin Academy of Sciences, Arts and Letters* 65:5–15.

Whittlesey, C. 1862–63. The Penokie Mineral Range. *Proceedings of Boston Society of Natural History* IX:235–44.

Yochelson, E. L., and M. A. Fedonkin. 1993. Paleobiology of *Climactichnites*, an enigmatic Late Cambrian fossil. *Smithsonian Contributions to Paleobiology* 74:69.

INDEX

Page numbers in *italics* refer to photographs, maps, or illustrations.

ROBERT H. DOTT, JR.   JOHN W. ATTIG

ABOUT THE AUTHORS

Robert H. Dott, Jr., a native of Oklahoma, fell in love with the mountains of the western United States at an early age. He studied geology at the Universities of Oklahoma and Michigan and earned a Ph.D. at Columbia University in New York. He spent two years on active duty in the U.S. Air Force and three years in the petroleum industry, and then joined the faculty of the University of Wisconsin in 1958. Though he has conducted research on sedimentary rocks and mountain building in the western states, southern South America, and Antarctica, he's found equally interesting rocks in his own backyard; he and his wife, Nancy, raised five children in a house built in an abandoned sandstone quarry in Madison. Among his many publications is *Evolution of the Earth*, a pioneering undergraduate textbook now in its seventh edition.

John W. Attig is a transplanted New Englander who misses the ocean and mountains. He pursued his interest in glacial and Quaternary geology while a graduate student at the University of Maine at Orono (MS, 1974) and the University of Wisconsin (Ph.D., 1984). Since 1981 he has been affiliated with the Wisconsin Geological and Natural History Survey. He enjoys public education and is a Professor in the University of Wisconsin Extension Department of Environmental Sciences. He has conducted research in the Midwest and New England as well as in Antarctica, Alaska, and Scandinavia. He and his wife, Cathy, live on a till plain of the Green Bay Lobe in Waunakee, Wisconsin.